TABLE OF CONTENTS

W9-BPJ-746

TABLE OF CONTENTS

Dedication

*To Parker Turner, who lost his life diving
on November 17, 1991*

*To Sheck Exley, diving pioneer and
visionary explorer, who was lost in
Zacaton cave April 6, 1994*

*and to the many others who went before
and led the way...*

we dedicate this book

ACKNOWLEDGMENTS

The preparation and research necessary to produce this book would have been impossible without the cooperation of numerous individuals who generously gave of their time and expertise to assist with the manuscript.

For interviews in the historical section thanks to Sheck Exley, Jim Lockwood, Parker Turner, Dustin Clesi, Hal Watts, Bob Halstead, Tom Mount, Dr. Ann Kristovich, Jim Bowden, Evie Dudas, and Dr. Dan Manion. Our appreciation goes to Dick Rutkowski for input on NITROX and chamber therapy; Ed Betts for detailed material on oxygen cleaning and NITROX blending systems; and Dr. Bill Hamilton, who graciously consented to interview and supplied important information on custom tables and oxygen physiology.

For bravely consenting to be our photographic models, thanks to Lynn Hendrickson, Lina Hitchcock, Bill Walker, Cathy Castle, Lamar English, Dustin Clesi, Rick Nicolini, Tanya Burnett, Mitch Skaggs, David Sipperly, Rick Thomas, Jim Mims, Tom Mount, Rob Palmer, Rich Bull and Mark Leonard. Thanks to contributing photographers Rock Palermo, Wes Skiles, Ned DeLoach, Ken Loyst, Ann Kristovich, Rob Palmer and Steve Barsky.

For assistance in editing and preparing the manuscript, many thanks to Theresa Slusher, Blake Hendrickson and Greg Kalian.

And a closing thanks to our courageous publisher, Ken Loyst.

Bret Gilliam • Robert von Maier • John Crea

FOREWORD

Photo: Lynn Hendrickson

Bret Gilliam at controls of deep diving submersible 1994.

Controversy over deep diving has been around for as long as I can remember. It's an "in" topic again since the so-called diving underground came out of the closet a few years back and began openly discussing various aspects of what has come to be known as "technical diving". New books, articles, magazines and even manufacturers have evolved to meet the demands of that diving market.

As a preamble, consider the following points:

1. Control infrastructure on divers is only present in the instructional phase.
2. Once certified, a diver cannot be realistically "controlled".
3. Is scuba diving, and in particular diving activities deeper than 130 fsw, experiencing a safety problem in actuality? Arguably,

no. Accident and mortality rates are roughly comparable to that of bowling!

4. Artificial and unrealistic limits tend to drive divers into a continuing pattern of denial and subterfuge in order to avoid criticism. This leads to inaccurate reporting of actual dive practices and contributes to reluctance in reporting decompression sickness (DCS).
5. Current programs (some dating back over two decades) that offer professional training in air and mixed gas diving below 130 fsw do so with an unblemished safety record. Liability insurance is available and affordable to such instructors.

Recent surveys have shown that divers are admitting to far more aggressive practices than many "experts" would have us believe. Some of these experienced divers have learned by trial and error with years of practical diving and their own efforts to ferret out the technical information to perform dives with relative safety. In fact, they conduct their deep diving activities with far better safety records than that of the general sport diving community.

I believe that is our role to provide technically accurate information on a variety of subject matter that will educate divers. We should not pass judgment on how people dive. It should be our goal to provide responsible information so that divers can make an informed choice. We should recognize the reality of how divers dive. It's no secret that divers are doing decompression diving, that underwater photographers disdain the buddy system, that divers explore wrecks and tropical drop-offs beyond 130 feet. Active divers need a forum for information to educate and, hopefully, make advanced diving activities safer by giving real divers answers to real questions about how they are actually diving.

The deliberate sensationalism and breast beating of some "experts" who call for all divers to adhere to their supposed "limits" is not only preposterous but reaches new heights of hypocrisy since many critics on these newly platformed soapboxes have been active deep divers for years and continue to be.

Deep diving is only one small element of underwater exploration. The cave diving community had to endure similar criticism 20 years ago until they finally made their point: Education and training are the key to safety, not absurd and unenforceable regulation and restrictions. Divers are an independent lot and they will make their own decisions. A policy of "Just Say No" to deep diving is just as ineffective as it was in the war on drugs!

Oxygen administration training was criticized back in the 1970's by ultraconservatives as being beyond the capability of sport divers, or even instructors, to handle. Now virtually everyone agrees that field oxygen first aid is a basic component of diver training and a vital cog in accident management. Only a few brief years ago the use of dive computers was considered to be unsafe by vocal opponents whom I suspect never completely understood that the concept of multi-level diving had been around for at least two decades. Now it seems the majority of divers use computers, and tables may well be a thing of the past by the year 2000. (Probably many of you can remember the inane arguments against buoyancy compensators, alternate second stages, and submersible pressure gauges). The use of Enriched Air Nitrox by sport divers was initially branded as inappropriate by the same watchdogs of diver security until the actual facts were delineated by qualified experts from NOAA, NASA, hyperbaric technicians and operations specialists. Now the growth of Nitrox in the sport diving community is one of the most rapidly expanding markets.

Captain Bob Halstead, owner/operator of the legendary liveaboard vessel *TELITA* in New Guinea, recently conducted a survey of diving practices by his guests and offered some perspectives on actual dive habits and on those who would pontificate on restriction. "One thing I have learned is that the way that successful experienced divers really dive differs from the way that fundamentalists and safety nuts say they should. I define a 'safety nut' as anyone who believes that rules are more important than thinking.

"Unfortunately, in this life, there are many ignorant people who just love to tell you what you *should* be doing. Anyone would suppose that the rules for safe diving were inscribed in some Dead Sea scrolls, true to eternity, instead of being a code of practice constantly evolving in the light of research and experience.

"Much research is now taking place trying to discover what causes diving accidents. On reading these reports, I realized, with some shock, that they were being analyzed with reference to what the authors *imagined* was the way the divers *should* be diving and not the way experienced divers actually *are* diving."

Halstead's survey sampled the data obtained from 234,631 dives. It revealed that only 11% of those divers never ventured below 130 feet. 64% admitted to diving to as deep as 200 feet with another 23% owning up to dives deeper than 200 feet. 78% made decompression dives. Interestingly, 81% of those divers used computers as opposed to dive tables. That represents some pretty aggressive diving, but Halstead (and most others with practical experience in liveaboard operations) agree that the responses are typical for that segment of the diving population.

Based upon the recent "go below 130 and you will die" theory as promulgated by less realistic "experts". Perhaps we should believe that these divers were dropping like flies from decompression sickness or dying in alarming numbers due to their diving habits. But: surprise, surprise! There were no fatalities and less than .01% incidence of bends, a far better safety record than that of the general sport diving population. The results of a similar blind survey (data base of nearly 80,000 dives) conducted for Ocean Quest International yielded almost identical demographics and diving styles with a DCS incidence rate of .02% in the total diver population *and zero percent DCS in computers users and dives conducted below 130 feet.*

It's very important to realize that in any discussions of statistics with regard to diving safety, most data centers such as DAN or URI are only aware of the reported accident numbers, not the total number of scuba dives that are actually conducted annually. To put it another way, mathematically we know the numerator in the fraction but we have no idea of the denominator. At least in the above mentioned surveys the totals on both ends were known so some perspective of actual risk and incidence rate can be determined. This yields a measurable percentage of DCS or mortality rates across a given diver population's exposure. Hopefully, future surveys will greatly contribute to our broader understanding of how many dives are being made, to what depths, how many per day, training levels, tables or computers employed, etc.

A 60 foot dive in cold water with limited visibility and current is certainly more physiologically stressful than a 150 foot dive in warm, clear, calm water on a Caribbean wall. Quite obviously, the real elements in the diving risk equation are swayed heavily by the diver's experience, frequency of diving, training, and discipline in incorporating proper ascent rates, safety and/or decompression stops, hydration, gas management, dive planning, and recognizing personal limits and comfort zones. Depth, per se, has no quantifiable role in diving accidents. In fact, some bona fide experts suggest that long shallow dives may place the individual at higher risk than short deep ones. This has also seen a major shift to more conservative tables and computer algorithms by members of the technical community.

The problem is not so much with the experienced divers who generally do not get into much trouble. It's with divers who *think* that they can attempt deeper diving when their training is insufficient. The fact is that current training programs offered through the traditional recreational agencies tend to lead divers to the false conclusion that they are qualified as "deep divers" or "master divers" when their actual level of experience still has them in "learner's permit" mode.

It is these incompletely trained neophytes with a few superficial "specialty" ratings and some patches sewn on their wet suits that scare the hell out most professionals. These people *will* get hurt because they are truly "rebels without a clue" lulled into thinking that they can attempt deeper diving because they did a couple of dives to 100 feet and got a neat certificate. These are precisely the participants that most need an avenue for supervised training because they are already in over their heads. No amount of colorful patches and specialty cards will produce a qualified diver in more advanced disciplines unless the curriculum and training match the demands of the environment and challenge of his intended diving.

We should remember that how you choose to dive is up to you. It's a personal decision. We need to continue to believe that our role as diving professionals is to objectively provide technically accurate information and up to date breaking news in equipment and diving technique. Education and training are the key to safety in any potentially dangerous active sport, be it skiing, kayaking, mountaineering or darts (if played with the British after a couple of beers). Let's give divers the straight facts with no hysterical "holier than thou" sermonizing and, most importantly, with no hidden agenda fueled by editorial policies that blow with the wind (and whims of advertisers). A safe diver is an informed diver and one who dives within his own limitations. Experienced divers are mature enough to make those decisions for themselves. We only continue to lose credibility with the diving public (not to mention the liability box we create legally) by perpetuating unrealistic "limits" that are ignored as often as the 55 mph speed limit was on the freeways.

The dive training industry has done an excellent job of educating entry level divers and providing them with a safe introduction to the joys of scuba. But just as grade school led to high school and on to college or further advanced degrees, it would be appropriate to explore the options for meaningful advanced diver training beyond traditional open water instruction. Diving doesn't stop for sport divers in the confines of unrealistic "limits". More importantly, some have postulated "limits" that are not only unenforceable but disdained by a significant portion of active experienced divers.

Wouldn't it be better to provide responsible training and information as diving educators and operators than to omnipotently condemn widespread diving practices because they may not be appropriate for *beginners*? By this reasoning, one would also have to believe that if you don't educate kids about birth control then there will be no teenage pregnancies. Neither philosophy works very well in the real world.

We have a duty to provide the best underwater education to divers of all levels and experience. Deep diving and decompression diving are not going to go away simply because certain factions refuse to recognize those activities. Likewise, those elements of diving will not be for everyone. But let's meet the true challenge of education and help provide the best and most complete training we can. There is a large segment of sport divers in need of more "in depth" programs who will benefit. The alternative is continued ignorance and misapplied theory that *will* lead to accidents.

In closing, two quotes from opposite spectrums seem appropriate:

"Let's not ground the albatross simply because the penguin can't fly",

Gary Gentile, deep wreck explorer, at the 1992 International Conference on Underwater Education's Deep Diving panel.

"Those who say it cannot be done... should get out of the way of those who are already doing it." Attributed to an early Air Force test pilot.

If some people don't wish to dive below 130 feet, smoke cigarettes, or wear day-glow lime green wet suits, no one is going to force them to. Likewise, they shouldn't presume to tell other experienced divers how they choose to dive. This attitude is reminiscent of a philosophy that goes like this: *"I'm* cold, so *everyone* put on a sweater."

BRET GILLIAM, December 1994

INTRODUCTION

The reader has probably selected this text precisely because he desires more information about deep diving than is addressed in conventional sport diving texts. It should be recognized from the outset that much of the discussion material in the following chapters is geared toward a diver who has made a clear and conscious decision to pursue a type of diving that is beyond what is considered "normal" sport diving limits. This personal decision also burdens the participant with some heavy baggage (mentally and physically). Responsibility for one's actions has to be foremost in the deep diver's mind as he contemplates deeper excursions. In fact, a high degree of self-sufficiency in physical conditioning, equipment systems, and gas volume control is desirable. Most experienced deep divers will not be looking for a "buddy" to solve problems for them. Indeed, the "dependent" diver as typically found in much of the actual practice of the "buddy system" is largely absent in deep diver communities.

The emergence of the deep diving sports enthusiast has provoked much controversy. Many have misappropriated the position of the national certification agencies that 130 fsw (39.4 m) is the absolute depth limit for sport divers while in training. Recently, limitations as shallow as 100 fsw (30.3 m) have been suggested. Many land-based resort operations in tropical sites have instituted enforced depth limits; the Cayman Islands Association of Dive Operators has advocated the 100 fsw limit. Meanwhile, such restrictions are blissfully ignored by the resort divemaster staffs on their day's off and most live aboard vessels pay only lip service to a depth limit (primarily as a reaction to a potential negligence litigation) .

Sport divers of all experience levels seem to have a universal disregard for current recommended depth levels and anyone who has observed everyday diving routines recently has to admit the reality of deep diving in an ever-expanding segment of the traditional diver population.

Like evolution and all changes in the sport diving industry, sharply polarized perspectives have surfaced and the debate still rages as to even what these more aggressive divers should be called. Egstrom and Bachrach (1990) note, "the problem has been compounded to some degree by a blurring of the distinctions that once differentiated commercial and military divers from the sport diving community. In recent years, increasing numbers of sport (or recreational) divers have entered diving activities that involve decompression... wreck diving necessitated divers staying longer at depths to perform tasks. In addition, some cave divers have developed dive profiles that go as deep as 700 fsw and require the use of helium/oxygen mixtures... It is our position that once a diver enters a decompression schedule dive or uses a mix that is not a standard compressed air mix, the dive should no longer be considered recreational. Even if the purpose of the dive is adventure and recreation, the character of the dive has changed and the diver is now a working diver, subject to all the subsequent demands of needing to know more about operations and equipment than the shallow, "no-decompression", warm water diver has ever considered."

Egstrom and Bachrach, long time researchers into human performance underwater, have hit the nail precisely on the head. Venturing into the realm of decompression, mixed gas and dives on air much below 130 fsw does require far more training and equipment/operational disciplines than most typical sport divers have or are willing to acquire.

Current recognized national training courses in "deep diving" are largely considered inadequate; lacking sufficient time in technical skills and a limited amount of actual dives. Admittedly their stated objectives are to train divers to 130 fsw but many professional instructors question if even that goal is realistically attained. More importantly, the mind set of a graduating "deep diver" may not fully understand how limited his training really is and attempt dives deeper and far beyond his experience. (The authors recommend that anyone interested in pursuing deep diving activities contact one of the specialized training facilities listed in Reference Materials.) Although such observations will possibly be misinterpreted as a slap at the training agencies, this is unintended by the authors. Those groups are consistently improving diver education and training in general, but the "sacred cow" of restricted deep diving "standards" needs review in light of known widespread disregard of current depth limits.

How then do we classify these "non-recreational" divers? Egstrom and Bachrach call them "working" divers but recently a new term has come into almost generic use: "technical" or "high-tech" diving. This seems to get a better grip on the activities of cave divers, wreck divers and tropical drop-off wall divers. All are usually operating beyond traditional sport depths, most are conducting decompression dives regularly and all are producing and using equipment that you will not find on your typical Grand Cayman flat-top tour boat. But it's important to remember that their activities are still recreational since they are not actual "working" divers and they spend recreational dollars in pursuit of their niche in the sport.

Michael Menduno, editor of *AquaCorps* journal, is generally credited with introducing the term "technical diver" to our lexicon and his publication has been responsible for providing a responsible public forum for emerging technologies and field practices. Along with the birth of *AquaCorps*, a new era of specialized "high tech" training centers for advanced divers has been born.

From *AquaCorps'* winter 1991 issue on deep diving: "The question today is not whether 130 fsw should be exceeded. It clearly is already by those willing to accept the risks. Rather the issue is how these dives should be responsibly conducted given the methods and technology at our disposal, particularly at the outside of our envelope. The sport diving community is at... a crossroad. As explained by Dr. R. W. Hamilton, a pioneer who has made significant contributions to commercial diving and now is working with the fledgling technical community, 'In many ways we are reinventing the wheel. But it's a different wheel.' He wasn't referring to PADI's".

OK, at least we have now defined the playing field and the participants. But, as we'll see, they are not all wearing the same uniforms.

ABOUT THIS BOOK

"I've always felt at peace with the sea. Even the endless crashing of the waves and the relentless fury of oceanic swells instill in me an inner feeling of calm and determined harmony. And if upon the surface I find such solace, how intensely marvelous the depths must be. I often dream of diving deep with the great leviathans and experiencing their world of sound and liquid darkness."

John David Roberts

When this book was originally conceived back in 1991, there was really nothing out there like it that presumed to address the issues of practical deeper diving methods and more "in depth" information about physiological considerations and the real world of first hand accounts from those who had ventured beyond the pale... and back. That first edition sparked some controversy from neo-conservative purists but became a runaway best-seller. This second edition updates a lot of material, adds some new topics, and tries to keep you current. We dropped the chapter on scientific diving to allow space to further develop topics on which you had requested more information. Please keep your input coming for the next edition.

The text was conceived and written with advanced divers in mind. That's all well and good, but what exactly does advanced mean?

It's very difficult for many industry professionals to even agree on the boundaries and terminology of the elusive subject of "advanced diving." It's a diving niche that is constantly evolving and is strongly influenced by regional practices. Any such discussion will usually include an attempt to define so-called "recreational" or "sport diving" limits and therein lies another major source of controversy.

Within the current structures of the national dive training agencies, a diver can aspire to become certified as an "advanced diver" after proceeding through his introductory training, commonly referred to as "open water" certification. This certification can be obtained with as few as four scuba dives, none of which are required to be in the ocean (requirements vary with each agency). Our stalwart entry level participant is now under no obligation to ever seek any more training. To draw an analogy, he has achieved his "divers license" and theoretically can now choose to dive anywhere he desires much the same as a licensed driver can freely travel the interstate highway systems. It should be reflected upon, however, that this "open water" certification is really a "learner's permit" to gain more practical experience, hopefully under the supervision of more qualified divers such as local instructors, resort guides or simply others with the benefit of more water time.

Ideally, this allows our diver the opportunity to build on his experience and to make mistakes while still under the influence of responsible care and supervision. This affords that potentially dangerous or unsafe errors can be observed and corrected before escalating into crisis. In this type of system, the diver can make his inevitable blunders a positive learning experience, not a life-threatening survival exercise.

The goals of the national training agencies are to influence divers to remain within the umbrella of a progressive system whereby they build on skills and actual diving experience through a series of continuing educational programs including a variety of specialty courses such as wreck, rescue, night and deep diving. These are admirable intentions and the training agencies do a remarkable job of producing a reasonably competent diver if he remains in the system. Sadly though, most divers do not. And it must be realized that in order to provide incentives for divers to stay in the "system", we have to provide a perceived benefit for their cooperation in shelling out the money and time to complete a pyramid of extra training.

In 1971, the rating of "advanced diver" was really the only stepping stone between a basic class (that sometimes only had one actual scuba dive) and the rating of "instructor" representing the top of the heap. If you managed to make it through an advanced diver certification of that era you were usually one hell of a diver. In fact, the advanced divers twenty years ago met a far higher standard of curriculum and watermanship than we require for many instructors today.

Somewhere along the way, we lost focus on what our training ratings actually meant. It is now possible, in some certification systems, for a newly certified diver to obtain a certification card that proclaims him an "advanced diver" or, God help us!, a "deep diver" with less than 15 dives total experience in open water. With just a little more effort you can become a "master diver", a term once reserved for a handful of the U.S. Navy's elite and most experienced diving supervisors. Oh well... progress.

In our opinion, an advanced diver will not be readily identified by some colorful patches or chevrons sewed onto his jacket. A solid background of practical diving obtained in a variety of open water conditions over the course of approximately 100 to 125 dives will generally produce a diver with competent skills, good watermanship, and a basis to formulate judgments based on real experience. By no means is 100 dives a magic number, many divers may acquire the requisite skills and knowledge base in less time while others may never really be worthy of consideration as a true "advanced diver". But over the years, this definition seems to fit the majority.

Controversy abounds as to what are appropriate "limits" for sport or recreational divers. The national training agencies have standards and procedures for training divers. They do not, nor could they attempt to, set "limits" for divers once they have left their training programs. Within those training programs, we set limits that include a depth limit of 130 feet and a prohibition against planned decompression etc. This is entirely appropriate within these agencies existing programs. However, once free from the supervision of training, you must make personal decisions as to what limits you will set for yourself.

To undertake more demanding diving activities, deeper depths, decompression diving, or the use of alternative breathing media requires training and experience that will not be found within the existing programs of NAUI, PADI, SSI, YMCA, et al. It is incumbent upon the individual diver to seek out this type of training in order to participate safely. One of our greatest concerns is divers who undertake activities beyond the scope of their training, education and experience.

Likewise, by definition "advanced diving" is not necessarily "technical" or "high-tech" diving. The latter terms apply to far more sophisticated commitments to operational and equipment systems with an attendant emphasis on more knowledge in physiology, rigging, gases etc.

"Advanced diving" is sufficiently broad a term to allow us several years of exciting exploration. "Technical diving" frequently defies agreement on definition, but most advanced divers are primarily interested in the pursuit of diving activities that are within their reach financially without sacrificing a mega-bucks budget to get a foot in the door. Definitions and semantics will always be subject to refinement. But in our rush sometimes to place labels on levels of achievement in diving, we may obscure the real perspective on what "experience" is all about.

Is a pilot considered "advanced" with 15-20 flights? Is a boat operator considered "advanced" with 15-20 outings? Has a skier attained "advanced" skill status after 15-20 runs down the mountain? Finally, is an automobile driver considered "advanced" after 15-20 hours or so of highway experience? Most divers would answer "no" to these questions. If you've ever been on a dive boat and observed "advanced divers" with this same level of experience, some reservations about the ratings terminology have to have arisen.

Yes, diving has evolved and is now offered and marketed as a recreational activity for the masses. A significant portion of entry level participants only intend to dive on tropical vacations and many only purchase snorkeling equipment as personal items preferring to rent scuba gear during their once a year outings. The same trend is prevalent in other active sports markets such as skiing, rafting, cycling etc. These types of participants do not benefit from experience gained "at home" in more challenging conditions. They are not as actively involved in the sport of diving as most divers were only a decade or so ago. Is this inherently bad? No, but let's recognize that these more casual enthusiasts can be easily misled as to their true capabilities if we continue to perpetuate the "quick and easy" path to advanced ratings. There is still a disparity between national agencies as to the equivalencies of various achievement levels and this only fuels further confusion by the consumer.

We would like to see the agencies attempt a consensus on ratings in the future and give serious thought to revising requirements to more accurately reflect training, experience and watermanship. That which is truly earned is always more respected and satisfying.

As you work your way through this volume note that the chapters are arranged in a particular order. This arrangement covers one facet (per chapter) of deep diving at a time and is structured so that the proceeding chapter will take-up (in an informational fashion) where the other chapter left off. The book has also been written so that if the reader should desire information about a particular subject, oxygen toxicity for example, they can turn to the respective chapter and procure the necessary information.

Keep in mind that this is a book about deep air diving and not mixed gas per se. However, a chapter on NITROX and a chapter on mixed gas have been included for informational purposes.

At the risk of being redundant, the authors would like to reiterate the fact that this work is not to be used as a training manual in lieu of experience and training for deep divers. Anyone who desires to become involved in deep diving should first honestly evaluate their skills, experience and level of training and education. With this in mind, we sincerely hope that **DEEP DIVING: An Advanced Guide to Physiology, Procedures and Systems** *will serve as an educated reference to the diving community. And we welcome your input for improvements, additions, deletions etc. for future editions.*

Bret Gilliam, Robert von Maier
December 1994

CHAPTER 1

History of Deep Diving

*"Naturally, like any explorer, I have been asked
what I intended to find, and whether it made any sense to
take unavoidable risks... I did not expect to find pirate's gold
in brass bound boxes. It's more the feeling of adventure,
the great feeling of putting your foot where no other
has been before."*

Dr. George Benjamin

*"Once a man has been bitten by the diving bug, he's done for.
For there's nothing that can be done against this mania,
either by fair means or foul. No nook or cranny seems safe from
manfish, no cleft, no cave too deep or too dark. He seems to have
a close affinity with the members of the mountaineering
fraternity. The latter also risk their lives for an experience of a
special kind... For them too, it is not really the rock face or the
mountain that has to be overcome, but their own selves."*

Hans Hass

THE RECORD HOLDERS

It's April 5th, 1988 in Tamaulipas, Mexico and even though it's a
bright, hot, sunny day Sheck Exley is cold and alone in the dark. Oh
yeah, he's also nearly 760 feet deep in Nacimiento del Rio Mante cave
system in pursuit of the deepest dive ever accomplished by an indepen-

dent, untethered, surface to surface diver. Right now he's got a little problem: over 100 feet deeper than a free-swimming diver has ever been and almost 450 feet deeper than his nearest alternate gas source (cylinders staged at 320 fsw), he has paused to check his pressure gauge that monitors the TRIMIX (He / N_2 / O_2) tanks on his back.

Even on mixed gas, there are traces of narcosis at this depth. The small percentage of nitrogen in his mixture has produced a partial pressure this deep equivalent to approximately 260 fsw on compressed air. He has been fighting an upflowing current for over twenty minutes on his descent and time has become a factor. "As I entered the unexplored cave zone, I was concerned about the slower than expected rate of descent. I forced myself not to pick up the pace. Instead of continuing its vertical drop, the crevice began to narrow and run at a 60-degree angle. Flashes of narcosis were becoming more prominent. I glanced at my pressure gauge; the reading hadn't changed since my last check. I banged the unit on the tank. The needle jumped a few hundred pounds lower. Pressure had forced the lens against the needle, but had it stuck again? I had no way of knowing. A projection to tie off on was just below. I passed it and dropped deeper. The tunnel began to flatten out, falling at a 45-degree angle. I looked at the pressure gauge; it showed a third of the gas was gone. Was the reading correct? I had been down just over 22 minutes. It was time to get out."

"My light beam fell on an excellent tie-off 20 or 30 feet down. I took a breath and moved toward the projection, when suddenly a jolting concussion nearly knocked me unconscious. I tried to look behind me for a ruptured valve or hose. There was no leak. Something had imploded from the pressure, but what? I drew another breath and kicked the last eight feet to the tie-off. Quickly I threw two half hitches around the rock, reeled in the loose line and made the cut. My down time was 24 minutes, 10 seconds."

Suspended at 780 feet, Exley has shattered the old mixed gas depth record (set by Germany's Jochen Hasenmayer) by 124 feet. But the surface was still a long way up and the implosion shock was numbing.

"I wanted to move fast from the deep water, 120 feet a minute if possible. The current that I had battled during my descent helped to lift me up the incline. I drew a breath and felt a slight hesitation from the regulator. The next breath came harder. Was I out of air? Again, I hit the gauge on my tank but this time the reading didn't change. If I was forced to use the gas in my belly tank, I would miss all the decompression to 330 feet where my first stage bottle was tied off. I switched over to my backup regulator and with relief drew a full breath."

Proceeding steadily upward in the chasm, he reaches 520 feet and retrieves his conventional depth gauges where he has tied them off. Beyond this depth he has had to calculate depth by means of a knotted line since no gauges had yet been made to handle such pressure.

> *"At 520 feet, it was strange to be decompressing at such a depth. I knew that only one person had ever gone deeper. I remained a minute and then began to ascend at the rate of ten feet a minute until I reached 340 feet. When I saw my first stage bottle and knew that I had spare gas around me, I finally began to relax. My stress was gone, but the long decompression stops were only beginning."*

For 22 minutes bottom time, he would pay a decompression obligation of nearly ten and half hours followed by thirty minutes breathing pure oxygen at the surface.

> *"Now with the extra time, I began to search for the cause of the deafening implosion. The source was the large Plexiglass battery housing for my primary light. The pressure had been so great that the three-quarter inch lid was forced into the casing crushing the battery pack. Amazingly, the light still functioned."*

Sheck completed his decompression uneventfully and surfaced at 9:30 PM wrinkled and exhausted. Hours later, support diver Ned DeLoach broached the inevitable question:

> *"Will you ever do it again?"*
>
> *Exley paused and considered his answer, "I don't know."*

Photo by Ned DeLoach

Sheck Exley returns from his record dive in Mante to resume a lengthy decompression and to retrieve stage cylinders.

Only days before his 40th birthday and almost exactly a year later on March 28, 1989, Sheck Exley eclipses his own world record in the same cave reaching 881 feet!

There is good reason that he is considered to be one of the finest scuba divers of all time. But what makes his accomplishments all the more compelling is that he has devoted virtually his entire career to the most challenging diving environment of all: deep caves. A veteran of over 3000 cave dives, Exley is the undisputed king of the hill. But he remains an almost reluctant hero, virtually unknown until recently outside of the cave and "high tech" communities. In addition to the mixed gas record of 881 feet, he holds the record for longest swimming penetration into a cave: a 10,444 foot push into Chip's Hole, a sinkhole in Tallahassee, Florida. He also set the record for longest scooter/DPV penetration at Cathedral Canyon at 10,939 feet, a distance of over two miles!

Sheck is also a prolific writer with over 100 articles and six books to his credit. He has been honored as a Fellow of the National Speleological Society and was a recipient of the prestigious Lew Bicking Award as America's top cave explorer. Even so, "experts" gave him only 50/50 odds at best to survive the 780 foot dive. His custom TRIMIX tables were totally experimental having been developed by decompression physiology pioneer R.W. "Bill" Hamilton. The computerized

Photo by Mary Ellen Eckhoff

Sheck Exley donning thermal underwear and dry suit before record dive in Mante cave in Mexico, 1988.

tables called for Exley to stage sixteen bottles and then carry four tanks with him for the final drop. Eleven different blends of TRIMIX were used with 52 decompression stops. The following year on the 881 attempt, the skeptics were less vocal. That required 34 stage bottles and thirteen and half hours of decompression. It's strictly limited participation at this level of diving, Sheck essentially can compete only with himself.

Although the mixed gas record changed hands almost annually for a while until Exley made it a one-man-show, the depth record on compressed air set by Neil Watson and John Gruener in 1968 seemed destined to hold up forever.

Both men trained intensely for a year prior to their record dive to 437 feet in the Bahamas. With the benefit of an almost 25 year perspective, their accomplishment is nothing short of phenomenal. Lacking the equipment advantages of high performance regulators and modern buoyancy compensators with power inflators, Watson and Gruener operated against incredible performance deficits. And the attempts of other record seekers offered a hodgepodge of success and tragedy.

Frederic Dumas, a colleague of Jacques Cousteau, established one of the earliest credible compressed air diving records in 1947 by reaching 307 feet but reported severe narcosis. Four years later, Miami lawyer Hope Root set out to attain 400 feet in the clear blue water of the Gulf Stream. At 52 years of age and with little practical experience in working up to such a great depth, his attempt seems particularly ill-advised.

Hans Hass speaks of Root's quest, "Many menfish, like men on land, have, so to speak, a screw loose. They are dare deviltry personified. But even so, they cannot be described as brave, since courage is the conscious mastery of a fear, quite naturally correlated with danger. Into this category must be placed Hope Root."

The dive plan was for him to enter the water wearing doubles and descend beneath a boat drifting in the current. No descent line was used, so the boat would track his progress and record his depth with an echo sounder (similar to sonar). A band of local press and representatives from *LIFE* magazine were all present to witness the record. Several underwater photographers joined Root in the water including veteran Jerry Greenberg. Around 70 feet Root paused in the water column and looked back up to the surface perhaps considering his fate. He then began swimming down into the bottomless Gulf Stream canyon. Greenberg followed him below 100 feet and continued snapping photos including a haunting portrait of Root drifting away in clouds of bubbles from his double hose regulator. As he passed the 300 foot level, Greenberg lost sight of him forever.

Meanwhile on the boat, the depth finder etched Root's progress and wild applause broke out as he passed the old record at 330 feet. Continuing his dive to destiny, he paused for almost two minutes at 430 feet (recorded on the echo sounder as a horizontal line at that depth). Then to the amazement of the onlookers, Root dropped another ten fathoms to 490 feet. Hesitating only briefly now, he dived to 500 and on to 650 feet before the echo sounder went out of range. Silence settled on the boat as the horrified witnesses realized that Hope Root would not be coming back. His body was never found.

In 1959, Ennio Falco of Italy reportedly reached an approximate depth of 435 feet but had no means to record it. In a subsequent dive to a lesser depth he drowned during decompression.

In the early 1960's, Jean Clarke Samazen declared, "All sports must have a champion. I want to be the champion of scuba diving." Wearing the ultimate in a cylinder package for his day, he utilized doubles on his back and his chest to reach 350 fsw. The rig was awkward, at best, but provided incredible air volume! An early *Skin Diver* Magazine account described him as "looking like a large sandwich." Hal Watts, who is still teaching advanced deep diving today, beat Samazen's record to 355 fsw.

Tom Mount and Frank Martz, two of the United States' cave diving pioneers, experimented with several 325 feet plus dives in the early sixties eventually setting a new compressed air mark for depth at 360 fsw in 1965. Hal Watts and A. J Muns posted a new official record in 1967 attaining 390 feet. One year later Watson and Gruener were poised on their historical threshold. They knew that narcosis and oxygen toxicity had claimed many of their forerunners. Both men were students of Watts and by 1968, they had discovered the value of "adaptive" dives to reduce these effects. They would descend together down a weighted cable and attach clips to it to certify the depth. Although they reached 437 feet, a new world record, both were so affected by narcosis that they could not recall even clipping on to the cable. When asked what it was like on air at 437 feet, Neil Watson replied, "I don't remember".

One of the last serious assaults to the Watson/Gruener record was planned in 1971 by the well experienced team of Archie Forfar, Anne Gunderson and Jim Lockwood. Sheck Exley, then 22 years old, was

Hal Watts and A.J. Muns after their record dive to 390 feet in 1967.

brought in as a support diver. Lockwood set up a regimen of progressively deeper dives for training purposes near the Andros drop-off walls. Although, the youngest member of the dive team at 21 (Forfar was 38 and Gunderson was 23), Lockwood had the most deep diving experience with numerous dives to 400 fsw and deeper. (In 1991, barring the sudden emergence of a credible challenger, he still remains the record holder for most dives below 400 fsw with almost 150 totaled in his career.)

Lockwood was visiting Tom Mount in pursuit of exploring the virgin "Blue Holes" in that area of the Bahamas when he was introduced to Archie and Ann. They had been making dives in the 380-400 fsw range and a discussion was initiated into the possibility of breaking the Watson/Gruener record. It was decided that they would work together and attempt 480 fsw. During the work-up dives, they made 40 dives below 400 fsw including 25 approaching 450 fsw (as measured by SCUBAPRO's helium depth gauge). They experienced no significant difficulties of impairment during the practice dives and on December 11, 1971 considered themselves ready for the official record attempt.

Forfar had decided to use a weighted cable similar to Watson and Gruener for descent and a "traveler" clip system that would slide down with the divers to record their maximum depth. In 1990, Exley provided this retrospective:

> *"For this attempt, Archie had designed an ingenious but simple system of drop-way weights to insure their survival. When losing consciousness from narcosis most divers will retain their regulator and continue breathing. All the dive team members had to do was to make sure that their BC's were fully inflated during the descent and hook*

some weights behind their knees. These would automatically drop away when the legs were straightened if a blackout happened and the diver would float up where I could recover him."

However, on the day of the record attempt things went awry. It was discovered that the clips for the cable would not slide freely. Lockwood discussed the events of that day nearly 20 years later:

"We had an engine block attached as the deadweight on the end of the 480 ft. cable but we had never unspooled the cable prior to the dive. When we did at the dive site we found it had a tendency to bend and sort of 'hockle' and wouldn't hang straight and true. The dive plan had to be changed." Forfar and Gunderson elected to abandon the fall-away weight system and make the drop with empty BC's. Lockwood stayed with the original system and would descend with his BC inflated.

Lockwood relates, *"I still wanted to use the positive buoyancy safety factor in conjunction with the weighted bar but Archie and Ann had their own ideas and decided not to. Almost immediately into the descent I realized that I was in trouble. The cable was oily and greasy and I got the stuff on my hands. This made it almost impossible for me to get any grip on the inflator valve for the pony bottle that fed air into my BC. I was dropping like crazy because of the weight behind my legs and I could not get anything into my vest to counteract this excessive negative buoyancy. My descent rate was probably in excess of 200 feet per minute. I remember thinking that Archie and Ann were not keeping up with me and I was frantically trying to wipe off my oily hands on my wet suit. This was requiring considerable energy and a lot of stress and eventually at some point I passed out."*

Exley, in his role as safety diver hovering at 300 feet, became witness to the ultimate deep diving nightmare. Somewhere in the depths, Forfar and Gunderson lost control. Lockwood lost consciousness below 400 feet and floated up to Exley who verified that he was okay and then made a heroic attempt to locate the two deeper divers. He descended well below 400 feet in his desperate attempt to save his friends but was unable to rescue them. They were not recovered.

The safety divers had agreed not to go beyond 300 fsw but when it became apparent that Archie and Ann could not come back on their own, each made a personal decision to attempt the rescue. Bill Wiggins and Randy Hylton made a simultaneous effort but were severely impaired by narcosis at 360 fsw and nearly 400 fsw respectively. Exley was left alone and remembers:

"The horror was even worse. From 400 feet on down, I could see Archie and Ann still breathing on the steeply sloping wall. Archie had his head down against the engine block and was still slowly kicking as if he were going down the cable, and Ann was lying on her back about 10 feet off to one side. I started to get severe tunnel vision and it was all I could do just to be able to survive at that depth. The last distance to Archie might as well have been a mile."

Lockwood speculates, *"I know I never got that inflator valve open and I think it's possible that I ran into the engine block when I bottomed out the cable. Archie probably was OK at that point but expended so much energy trying to inflate my BC that he succumbed to narcosis himself. Ann would never have left Archie so that would account for their double accident. I was out of it so I don't know what happened, but I have no recollection of anything after about the 400 ft. level and I doubt if I ever got any air in my vest. Archie probably saved my life. I don't even remember floating up to Sheck although he says I gave him the OK sign at that point. I really didn't come around until about the 50-foot decompression stop."*

Two decades later, professional diver Bret Gilliam is preparing to break Watson and Gruener's record which remains intact. All challengers to that record have died trying except Lockwood. Gilliam is unperturbed. He has devoted almost a year of adaptive diving and extensive research in physiological effects of depth on humans and other mammals. His work has included over 600 dives in the previous 11 months with 103 dives below 300 feet. He also has made use of recompression

Photo by Lynn Hendrickson

Bret Gilliam prior to February 1990 record dive to 452 feet off Roatan.

chamber dives to experiment with varying high partial pressures of oxygen to simulate conditions below 400 feet.

Like Exley, Gilliam has been professionally involved with deep diving projects for over twenty years. Since 1958, he has logged in excess of 12,000 dives around the world. Over 2000 of those have been below 300 feet. For 15 years he owned one of the Caribbean's most successful dive operations before selling out in 1985 to spend three years cruising and diving on his 68 foot motor yacht while doing diving and marine engineering consulting projects through his company Ocean Tech. Now (in 1989-90) he is under contract to Ocean Quest International as a corporate executive and Director of Diving Operations for their 487 foot dive/cruise ship. It's the largest sport diving program in the world.

From the outset, he set that ship up to support his "high tech" diving interests and launched a carefully conceived one year project to see if the compressed air record could be targeted with an acceptable assumption of risk.

> *"In the beginning, I wasn't even concerned with a record dive. I did not even remember what the record was. Later as I got nearer to it, I went back and looked it up and found that I was getting very close and that kind of jogged my interest. But I was really just getting sick and tired of listening to supposed experts make sweeping statements about deep diving that were so totally inaccurate that I finally just decided to see what I could do; more to disprove the misinformation that was postulated than to prove anything. Hell, at this point, NOAA had Gary Gentile tied up in Federal Court fighting an injunction prohibiting his access and right to dive the Monitor wreck. They had omnipotently informed him that 230 feet was too deep to be dived safely. Here they are telling one of America's best deep divers that he can't make what for him was a routine dive. What a crock!"*

At the time, Gilliam was sponsoring an Ocean Tech study of dive computers and testing several of the models to their limits with frequent 300 foot plus dives weekly. The ship's on board recompression chamber facility provided an ideal lab for several experimental dives. By January 1990, he decided that his adaptive level and physical training was sufficient for a major attempt at depth. A chance meeting with custom table producer Randy Bohrer provided the basis for air tables to 500 feet.

> *"The tables process was involved and required extensive field work. Randy would cut a table with his recommendations and send it off to me on the ship. It might take three weeks for me to get it and try it out. He leaned to a more conservative model and I kept modifying it*

based upon some work I had done with the Navy on exceptional expo-
sure proprietary tables under development back in the early seven-
ties in the Virgin Islands for an ASW (antisubmarine warfare) project.
Most of our work was conducted observing hydrophones and subma-
rines in the deep canyons between St. Croix and St. Thomas. This re-
quired pushing the 400 ft. plus barrier on several occasions We had
a lot of problems with sharks during decompression in the open ocean
and experimented with all kinds of theoretical models to shorten our
hang times."

After five months of fiddling with Bohrer's successive offerings,
Gilliam had dramatically altered the decompression schedules to minimal times with a margin for safety:

"But we were completely breaking new ground; no one had ever
field-validated air tables to these depths. I felt confident that we were
on the right track and I was having no problems with the extreme pro-
files I was running. But it was nice to know that I had the chamber
right on-site. Without that security, I doubt if I would ever have done
diving this deep so aggressively."

In addition to various instructor affiliations, Gilliam is a licensed
USCG Merchant Marine Master and recompression chamber supervisor. He directs all treatment protocols and therapy for ship divers and
occasional locals who get DCS hits. He has no intention of requiring his
own services.

"This type of diving is a mental exercise. You have to understand
the physiology and mechanisms of narcosis and oxygen toxicity to sur-
vive. Many academicians dismiss deep diving as suicidal with very
little real-dive experience to justify their arguments. I have an over-
whelming respect for the risks involved and seek to provide every edge
I can get through education and planning. Prolonged facial immer-
sion breathing to invoke the diving reflex and other little tricks are all
vital pieces of the equation to minimize CO_2 in the narcosis and O_2 tox
responses."

He will make his descent at 100 feet per minute only slightly over-
weighted. Ten minutes are spent on the surface prior to the dive with his
face in the water breathing through a snorkel and then five minutes more
with no mask breathing from a spare tank at 15 feet below the boat.
Surfacing only long enough to dry off his face, he begins the descent.
His heart rate and respiration will drop significantly on the dive. 12 to
15 beats a minute with deep slow ventilations of one to two per minute
are typical.

The dive site selected is known as Mary's Place in Roatan. He has picked this spot due because of its near vertical wall configuration offering immediate access to abyssal drop-off depths. The day is Wednesday, February 14,1990; eleven days after Gilliam's 39th birthday. Visibility is 100 feet at the surface depths and over 200 feet in the deep zone, water temperature is 81 degrees and no current. Conditions are ideal.

Only a handful of staff are aware of the upcoming dive. Just before he enters the water, one safety diver asks if he can borrow Gilliam's gold Rolex watch until he comes back. Another asks for his TV and stereo; a third wants his spacious senior officer's stateroom on the ship. The local Roatan deckhand wants his girlfriend. Gilliam keeps the watch.

His gear is kept to a minimum. A single cylinder pressurized to approximately 100 cubic feet with a high performance regulator attached with DIN fittings. A backup second stage and two pressure gauge consoles with helium depth gauges calibrated to 500 feet are plumbed into the regulator first stage. Three dive computers with a Casio watch are attached to one console. He discovered by accident that the Beuchat computer will accurately read depth digitally to at least 500 feet. He finds digital gauges far easier to read under the influence of narcosis. The computers will not provide any valid decompression information but their depth gauges and timing instruments will hopefully survive the pressure.

Slipping over the wall, he reaches 300 feet in just under three minutes. His descent picks up slightly now and one computer "locks up" in error mode at 320 feet. A large remora fish that has followed him since the 150 foot level is becoming distracting:

> "Here I am at 300 plus feet dropping like a stone with every nerve and impulse in my body going through a self-check a million times a minute for any warning sign of severe narcosis impairment or O_2 tox, and now I've got some damn friendly fish wanting to play with me! It kept swimming in and out of vision and my eyes didn't want to focus on my instruments and the fish simultaneously. I almost had to abort but it finally moved down towards my thigh and out of my vision path so I decided to ignore it."

Approaching 425 feet he begins to inflate his BC while timing his inhalations so the regulator would only have one volume demand on it at a time. He drops an eight pound weight belt and it disappears. Because his computers are calibrated in feet of fresh water he has prepared a 3% conversion table so he knows exactly where to stop; in large bold instructions on a slate is written: 464 FT.: STOP! He hangs motionless perfectly suspended about five feet from the wall; four minutes and 41 seconds have elapsed since leaving the surface.

There is plenty of ambient light even this deep. He retrieves a slate with ten problems involving math, simple word problems, daily event questions etc. (i.e.: what day is it? What time is it? 3 X 10 X 22 = ? ...) It takes one minute and 40 seconds to work the problems; he has not seen them before and it takes longer to finish than he expected. He slips slightly deeper by two feet and the computer will record 466 feet as the maximum depth. Later, all agree that 452 feet of sea water is a reasonable conversion; a new world record on compressed air by 25 feet.

Six minutes and 20 seconds have ticked off, time's up. Ascent commences at just over 100 feet per minute and he slows to 60 ft./min. at a depth of 100 fsw. The first decompression stop is at 50 feet. One hour and sixteen minutes later he surfaces and breathes pure oxygen at the surface for twenty minutes via demand mask. Although some handwriting flaws are apparent, all the test questions are answered correctly. "I've got lousy handwriting anyway," he replies defensively with a laugh.

"Narcosis is there but not to a level that I was uncomfortable with. Impairment is specific to individuals. O_2 tox is the real unknown; that scares me but I had no problems at all. I planned this dive to preclude virtually all exertions. Perhaps I'm an exception to nature but I suspect my conditioning through long term experience and adaptation due to diving constantly in deep situations plays a far greater role. Calculated risk is the operative phrase here. What is attainable for me is possible because of my commitment to detail and training and total discipline during the actual dive process. I also had a positive mental attitude; I knew I could do it."

Gilliam's plans called for an attempt to 500 feet later but he postponed that after leaving the Ocean Quest contract to pursue other business interests.

"I think that 500 feet would have been possible for me if I had followed closely on the heels of the 452 foot dive. But when I came off the ship, I was away from deep diving for a while and felt that I had lost the adaptive edge I had acquired. And I wanted a chamber overhead. In the right circumstances, I might try it if I had the time to work up to it again. If you could do the drop in five minutes I think you could handle the O_2 exposure. Who knows? No one believed that 450 feet was possible."

Exley and Gilliam conducted record setting dives that were vastly different in many ways but with one common denominator: Both elected to dive alone, regarding the presence of another diver as a potential liability. And both showed a single-minded intensity of preparation that was unprecedented.

Some critics will pontificate that such dives are reckless, crazy, without purpose... but man's competitive motivation is best exemplified in such individuals. Life is full of challenges: Chuck Yeager breaking the sound barrier to "push the outside of the envelope", Sir Edmund Hillary climbing Mt. Everest "because it's there", and now Sheck Exley and Bret Gilliam diving deliberately to bottomless depths "because it's not there!"

Gilliam's slate taken to 452 ft. to remind him that his depth gauge was calibrated in "feet of fresh water" and that he should stop when it read 464 ft. He added his thoughts when he reached that depth.

The point of any human performance record is individual and reduced to its simplest form: Doing what others cannot do. And that has to be a personal decision. Dangerous? Yes, extremely so. But the personal risk to these individuals was acceptable to them and their success a triumph. Neither Exley or Gilliam advocate such extreme diving for others. Will those records ever be beaten? Both men think so.

UPDATES SINCE 1991

In fact, Gilliam and Exley would both make attempts on their own records in 1993 and 1994. Gilliam reached a depth of 475 fsw in October of 1993 to best his existing record on compressed air. He had no reported narcosis or oxygen toxicity problems on the nine minute dive.

At least one diver attempting to better the compressed air record was killed in 1992 when he disappeared off the north shore drop-off wall on the island of St. Croix in the Virgin Islands. This individual swam from the beach (without surface support or safety divers) to the dive site, a distance of nearly a quarter mile. He had discussed his dive plans to reach 500 feet with friends and had made some earlier dives below 400 feet in the preceding months. On the day he had picked for his record attempt, he departed alone and was never seen again. His locked car was found parked by the beach entry.

Later that same year, a dive store instructor from Hollywood, Florida apparently reached a depth of 465 feet while diving in the Gulf Stream but was reportedly caught in a down draft current after attempting to abort the dive. He was only aware of his actual depth when he managed to fight his way up to shallower water. Several onlookers considered his attempt ill-planned and badly executed. Others regarded his survival as a miracle. No official reports or dive profiles were ever offered and it has been reported that this individual ceased deep diving shortly thereafter. None the less, his record was recognized at least as a *survival* record from an aborted dive until Gilliam went to 475 a year later.

The current compressed air record was set by Dr. Dan Manion on March 18, 1994 when he reached a depth of 509 fsw. Manion had successfully made several other deep dives that broke the 490 foot mark. Indeed, the day before his record he had reached 491 fsw at the same site, Clifton's Wall off Nassau in the Bahamas. Confident after that success, he planned to reach 500 fsw the following day. He had undertaken extensive correspondence with both Gilliam and Tom Mount in the previous year leading up to his record. He had also adhered to a rigorous personal training regime that dropped nearly 40 pounds from his frame and dramatically increased his overall fitness.

> *Everything started out fine that day: sunny skies and a light breeze across the calm ocean with a comfortable temperature in the mid-seventies. Manion recounts, "Gearing up went smoothly and after a short surface swim, my safety diver and I relaxed on the surface. We went through our check lists for gear and decompression and then descended." Two minutes and ten seconds into the dive Manion passed 330 fsw as his partner waited at 200 fsw. "Visibility was about a hundred feet, I felt in control. I remember having to fin away from the wall due to the mildly increasing slope. At 450 fsw, I added air to my BCD in short bursts. As the numbers slowed on the computer, I picked a touch down spot some 20 feet below me."*

That's apparently when the trouble started. Because he remembers absolutely nothing from that point in the dive until he found himself ascending in a cloud of foam and bubbles.

> *"The beep of the fast ascent alarm was actually reassuring to me as I came around. I had no memory of turning the dive or what depth I reached. My light and lift bag were gone along with my descent weights. I could see my safety diver at 150 feet easily and I began dumping air from the BCD. We exchanged OK signs as we linked up. It was not until I checked my computers that I realized how deep I'd been. Later as I exited the water, I felt sad that I had worked so hard to get to this point and then couldn't remember it. I'm positive I have reached my own physiological limits. I have no further plans to push this envelope."*

His two Monitor II dive computers recorded conflicting maximum depths (registered in feet of fresh water). One indicated 506 but the other notched 525. Corrected for sea water that would be 490 and 509 fsw respectively. Manion has no idea what depth he attained but suspects that 509 is correct since his other unit may still have been displaying the dive from the day before.

Dr. Dan Manion surfaces after his 491 foot dive in 1994 to beat Gilliam's record.

Exley and others discount a record in which the diver blacks out since they were not in control. But Gilliam points out, "Dan made it to 490 the day before in complete control and with no problems at all. That's deeper than anyone has made it to before. Maybe 500 feet is a psychological wall as well as a physical one. One thing's for sure, I'm probably getting too old to ever find out now."

Although Gilliam would break his own record at the age of 42, Exley's own attempt to reach 1000 fsw on mixed gas in April 1994 at the age of 45 would end in tragedy.

ZACATON

Zacaton is the deepest of five ceynotes located on a large ranch, El Rancho Asufrosa, in northeastern Mexico. It was "discovered" on a reconnaissance trip made at the end of two weeks of exploration and surveying in the Nacimiento Santa Clara, a cave system at the base of the El Abra near the Nacimiento Mante. The exploratory team lead by Jim Bowden and Ann Kristovich had laid more than 1400 ft. of line in the Santa Clara, but had ceased their efforts due to the depths encountered in the distant reaches of the cave. More than 1100 ft. back, depths exceeded 250 ft. At that time, 1989, the team was not routinely employing mixed gas techniques in their exploratory efforts in Mexico. The door to the Santa Clara was temporarily "closed". Jim had studied geological survey and topographical maps which revealed the possibility of inland "ceynotes" in the karst terrain found at the southern extreme of the Sierra de Tamaulipas.

On a ranch near the small town of Aldama, five ceynotes of variable size and character were located. Exclusive entry and permission to dive was granted by the owner and in late April, 1990, exploration began. The ceynotes proved to be extremely unusual. They are aligned generally east to west within a radius of approximately two miles. They are highly sulfurous in odor, in one named Poza Asufrosa, the sulfur precipitates and floats on the surface in raft-like formations. The waters discolor, and tarnish all metals, and seem to leech the surface of galvanized tanks. The systems are surprisingly warm, 93 degrees in Poza La Pilita, 87 degrees in Zacaton, 86 degrees in Poza Caracol, 87 in Poza Asufrosa, and a cooler 83 degrees in the huge oasis-like Poza Verde. Unlike the others, the waters in Poza Verde are layered in thermoclines and behave more as a lake in times of flood and drought and seem less responsive to the changes imposed by the water table.

The team began the systematic exploration of the ceynotes. Initial efforts were concentrated in Poza La Pilita. This 68 ft. by 120 ft. ceynote is the warmest of the five at 93 degrees F. The surrounding walls reveal tufa formations often associated with warm thermal springs. The side walls are coated with a dense algae which hangs like curious stalactites. Measurements made using the SCUBAPRO personal sonar device revealed a system that enlarges significantly with increasing depths. At 150 ft., La Pilita is 396 ft. from north to south and 239 ft. from east to west. The team initiated the search for a connection to the ceynotes located

The pristine beauty of Zacaton, Mexico, the world's deepest cave system.

Jim Bowden preparing his equipment prior to record attempt in April 1994.

immediately to the east or west, however, no ongoing passage was found in the early exploration. The depth of La Pilita was plumbed to 360 ft. and dives were made to 250 ft. On May 2, 1990, divers Jim Bowden and Gary Walten entered the Nacimiento at the western boundary of the ranch. The river is formed by the spring run emanating from Zacaton. A typical "boil" was noted on the water's surface near a limestone outcropping.

Pursuing this current, the divers located a small cave and followed a northeast azimuth until they had exhausted the line on their reel. With passage obviously continuing, they turned the dive, obtained an additional exploratory reel, returned to their tie-off and resumed laying line. Now in the lead, Gary soon noticed a bottle green glow ahead. He covered his light and confirmed a natural light source that could mean but one thing, they had made a connection to the surface. The exuberant divers emerged into Zacaton at a depth of 26' and surfaced in the beautiful ceynote which takes its name from the islands of tall grass, *zacate*, which float across it's surface.

The succeeding days were spent surveying the nearly 600' of passage (named El Pasaje de Tortuga Muerte for the frequently encountered turtle skeletons) connecting the Nacimiento and Zacaton and recording baseline information on this impressive system. The surface of Zacaton is approximately 70 ft. below the surrounding land. It is 380 ft. in diameter and roughly circular. It's lateral walls undulate and the system dimensions increase with increasing depth. A rough survey has been completed to 175 ft. of depth from the center of the ceynote using the SCUBAPRO personal sonar device. It is hoped that side scanning sonar techniques can be applied in the future to study the full extent of this ceynote which is now known to exceed 1080 ft. of depth. The depth recorded for Zacaton in 1990 was erroneously measured at 250 ft. when divers Walten and Ann Kristovich dropped the weighted plumb line onto a prominent ledge which projects markedly into the ceynote at 230-250 ft. Exploration continued on the ranch in August, 1990 with dives by Karen Hohle and Ann Kristovich in Poza Verde.

This tropical oasis is greater than 600 ft. across, somewhat cooler than the other ceynotes and surprisingly shallow, a mere 140 ft. by measurements in four quadrants. Bowden and Walten sought passage in Poza Asufrosa with side mount configurations, but the tight passage choked off after 30 ft. of penetration. Caracol, like her immediate neighbor, Zacaton, sits beneath a cliff face. To date only one dive has been made in this cave by Bowden, but he observed large going passage on an azimuth that would lead to Zacaton. The maximum depth in this system is not known as the passage travels beneath the cliff and could not be adequately measured by plumbed line. The maximum depth on Bowden's dive was 72 ft.

After this early exciting start, members of the Proyecto de Buceo Espeleologico Mexico y America Central spent the next two and a half years exploring cave systems associated with the inland Blue Hole of Belize. Solo efforts by Bowden from 1987 to 1988 had resulted in the connection of St. Hermann's Cave with Petroglyph Cave and the inland Blue Hole. The 1990-1991 efforts of the team added more than 1500 ft. of water filled passage to the survey, and discovered a previously unknown and spectacular pit in the jungle. Dives made in the downstream

Boiling Hole follow an azimuth which will likely result in a connection to the Actun Tah system. Work was halted in Belize in 1992.

The "Proyecto" resumed the exploration of the five ranch ceynotes in April, 1993, fully equipped with mixed gas capabilities to allow the safer exploration of the deeper systems. Sheck Exley joined the team for a week and with Bowden dived the previously unexplored depths. La Pilita revealed at greater than 358 ft. of depth, going passage to the southwest. Zacaton however revealed the greatest surprise. On air dives to 258 ft. by Bowden and 407 ft. by Exley, no bottom was in sight. The previously plumbed depth of 250 ft. was proven to be an error! The divers dived beyond the ledge which had captured the measured line in pursuit of the elusive bottom. The following day, Bowden, Exley, and Kristovich returned to Zacaton to attempt a more accurate plumb. The line spun off the reel, past 500' past 800', past 1000'! The weight finally stopped after some 1080' had been measured.

The line was secured to the north wall of the ceynote and the divers completed plans to make a deep mixed gas dive the following day. In April 1993, Bowden dived to 504 ffw. and Exley to 721 ffw. Tables for both dives were prepared using Dr. X. software. Neither diver experienced performance difficulties or physiological complications during or after the dives. These two would be the first of seven sub-500 ft. dives made in Zacaton in a twelve month period. As the week of diving came to an end, Exley and Bowden agreed to return together to Zacaton, and like Hillary and Norkay, pursue the exploration of the depths of this upside down Everest. The apparent perfect site for an open circuit dive to 1000' and beyond had at last been found. It was warm, there was no perceptible current, the natives were friendly, and access to the system was uncomplicated.

The goal was thus declared, that within the calendar year, a dive to obtain the bottom of Zacaton would be made by Bowden and Exley. Members of the Proyecto made six trips to Mexico during the ensuing twelve months. With each return, Bowden dived progressively deeper in order to prepare himself for the 1000' attempt. Exley meanwhile pursued the exploration of a huge underwater cave at Bushmansgat, South Africa, diving to 863' in this system. During this dive, Sheck experienced visual, somatic, and neurological symptoms of high pressure nervous syndrome (HPNS). The symptoms resolved during his ascent to his first deco stop at 400 ffw. and there were no persistent effects.

In September, Bowden dived to 744 feet. Team member Kristovich dived to 554 feet, setting a new women's depth record with this effort. On December 2, 1993, Bowden made a dive in excess of 800'. The exact depth of the dive could not be documented as all three of the digital depth gauges he was wearing ceased to function at various depths ranging from 684' to 756'. Bowden, however, had visually noted the 825' marker on the descent line before reversing the direction of his dive. Bowden experienced multiple joint DCS upon the completion of his decompression obligation. Symptoms resolved following aggressive hydration, oxygen therapy and in water recompression. There were no persistent symptoms.

The 1000' attempt had been slated for December 25, however, it was the consensus of the team in early December that the conditions imposed by the unusually wet rainy season were unfavorable for such an effort. The current in El Pasaje de Tortuga Muerte was fierce, and imposed a very undesirable heavy exertion dive prior to any deep attempt. It was necessary to traverse this nearly 600 ft. of linear cave passage prior to any dive in Zacaton, making all of the deep dives, in fact, repetitive dives. For the safety of the divers, the dive was rescheduled for April, 1994.

In April, 1994, the Proyecto, including Exley and Mary Ellen Eckhoff assembled on the Rancho Asufrosa. Two days were spent staging the required decompression bottles at their specified depths in Zacaton and El Nacimiento. The dive would be accomplished on independent descent lines, a condition both divers favored to avoid contact and potential interference during the very rapid descent. Each effort would be solo by necessity. Exley would use Heliair 6 as his bottom mix, Bowden, Heliair 6.4. Their tables were similar and were formulated utilizing Dr. X. software. Both divers carried an assortment of tables since the exact time of descent (bottom time) and maximum depth of the dive was unknown.

Both Bowden and Exley made multiple deep air acclimation dives to prepare themselves for the 1000' attempt. Early in the morning on Wednesday, April 6, 1994, all was felt to be in readiness and the divers and their support team assembled on the banks of El Nacimiento. Bowden and Exley geared up and swam together through "El Pasaje" and into Zacaton. The pre dive mood was positive and optimistic. The men began their descent at approximately 9:50 am central standard time. Bowden dived to 925' and would spend nine+ hours decompressing. Exley, for reasons we will probably never know, failed to return from his dive. He had reached a maximum depth of 906'.

Jim Bowden provides this account of that final day with Exley as they prepared for the 1000 foot dive.

"The time between December and April had passed rapidly with preparations and planning consuming every day and night. In addition to three sub-500 ft. dives, I made over 30 dives in excess of 300 ffw. Some were done on air to acclimate and build up my narcosis tolerance. Many of these dives included skills testing at depth, primarily problem solving questions or tasks posed by a colleague on mix while I was on air. It was essential that I be comfortable with an equivalent narcosis depth (END) of 330 feet. My bottom mix of heliair (69.5 He, 24.1 N_2, 6.4 O_2) called for an END of about 300 feet at 1000 feet. The bottom would demand that and more. I made one dive to 411 ffw on air, a record on air in a cave, but it was soon eclipsed by Sheck with his dive to 420 ffw on April 4th two days before our attempt for the bottom.

"Now was the time to fish or cut bait. The final preparations were made and the first support team left camp to put down decompression oxygen and my DiveComm full face mask that I planned to switch to at 20 feet. Shortly thereafter, we all left for the spring."

Present on the day of the dive was the team consisting of Exley, Bowden, Mary Ellen Eckhoff (Exley's ex-wife), Karen Hohle (Bowden's wife), Ann Kristovich, and Marcos Gary. Press representatives included a writer and photographer from *Sports Illustrated*, a photographer from *Destination Discovery*, and a television film crew from Channel 7 of Tampico. Also in attendance was the land owner and his family along with many of the local residents of the area.

Bowden continues, "Sheck and I geared up and swam through the 600 foot passage, El Pasaje de Tortuga Muerte. to access our dive site. Surfacing in Zacaton, we swam slowly over to our descent lines. We commented on the beautiful day and wished each other luck. We separated at that time and went to our respective down lines. Time passed in silence as we calmed our breathing and focused our minds on what was ahead.

"After a time, I felt all was right and glanced over at Sheck. He seemed to sense my glance and nodded affirmation. I submerged and hesitated at 10 feet for a minute or so and then went into a free fall. I had planned a descent rate of one hundred feet per minute to 300 feet on air, then the same rate to 600 feet on heliair (50 He, 39.5 N_2, 10.5 O_2) and then switching to my bottom mix. I planned to slow my descent around 750 to 800 feet where I had first noticed the HPNS symptoms on my previous dive. All went according to plan. As I passed the 800 foot mark, I was conscious of very little tremor. I could just see

Sheck Exley and Jim Bowden in Zacaton, April 6, 1994. Only Bowden would return.

Sheck's light in the distance. It was the last I saw of him."

However, at 900 feet Bowden was shocked to find that he had breathed far more gas volume than he had planned. His bottom mix cylinders contained barely more than 1000 psi. At that depth, his regulators could not deliver if the pressure dropped less than 500 psi. This was a big problem and Bowden had to deal with it quickly.

"I inflated my BCD wings and managed to stop my descent at 925 feet. I switched to the 80 cubic foot tank of bottom mix under my right arm and breathed that and then my travel mix back up to my first stop at 450 feet. By the time I got there they were both empty. To my horror, the regulator on my deep deco bottle free-flowed violently when I turned it on. It seemed to take a lifetime to shut it off again. I switched back to my back-mounted doubles to deal with the problem but I couldn't fix the regulator. The only solution was to open and close the valve with each breath. I had eight minutes of stops between 350 and 300 feet where my next bottle was hung."

Bowden could breathe easier when he made it to the fresh decom bottle with a properly functioning regulator. Now would come the really long decompression and the worry about oxygen toxicity and bends. Another switch to air at 260 feet would see him to 130 feet and a 30% oxygen nitrox mix. That's when he knew something was wrong with Exley.

"At 130 feet, I relaxed. Here I could clearly observe the line that Sheck used on descent. All of his stage bottles were still neatly packaged and unused. The sinking feeling in my heart was overcome by the confidence that he had gone deeper than I had and was probably still below me."

But on the surface, the support team already knew that Exley was in trouble. Ann Kristovich had watched the bubble paths of both men on the initial descent. Bowden's bubbles disappeared at two minutes and Exley's vanished a few seconds later as they both reached the deep ledge at 250 feet. Only one set of bubbles reappeared after about 15 minutes and she couldn't be sure if they were Bowden's or Exley's. Kristovich exchanged uneasy glances with Bowden's wife, Karen Hohle. As planned, she then dived to meet Bowden at the 47 minute mark of the dive profile. She was relieved to find him but chilled to see Sheck's stage equipment still hanging with no sign of him. The grim awareness of the situation gripped the pair.

Meanwhile, Mary Ellen Eckhoff (one of the world's premier cave divers and Exley's ex-wife) was watching from the cliffs with no knowledge of the problem. She joined Hohle at the surface and was appraised of the scenario. Concerned but not panicked by the situation, she grabbed an extra decom bottle to take to Exley and swam down to encounter Bowden and Kristovich. Now her worst fears were becoming reality. She hastily scrawled on a slate, "I'm going to 250 to look for bubbles". Dropping over the deep ledge, she could find no sign of Sheck or any bubbles coming from the depths.

Hohle had scrambled into her gear and caught up with Eckhoff. "I met Mary Ellen at about 100 feet on her way back up. She was crying and her mask was messed up. She wanted to go back to the surface but I grabbed her gauge and saw that it read 278 feet. I just held her. We stayed down for more than thirty minutes to get through the decompression. It was a very lonely time."

Bowden was finally told that Sheck was lost as he reached his 60 foot stop. He felt himself grow numb from the loss and describes the remainder of his decompression as a mechanical exercise with little conscious thought. After a total of nearly ten hours, he surfaced but suffered a left shoulder DCS hit that then was treated with in-water therapy on the site. Bowden was now the first diver to successfully break the 900 foot barrier on self-contained scuba. His record depth of 925 ffw eclipsed Exley's old 881 mark.

There was no consideration given to mounting a body recovery for Sheck since it was accepted that the only man capable of effecting such a recovery was the man who was already down there. Three days later while hoisting up the remainder of the equipment, Exley's body was found. He had apparently drifted up from the deep cave passage and become entangled in the line. One of his tanks still had gas and his computer read 904 feet, suggesting that whatever trouble he had did not occur until about nine minutes into the dive.

The best educated guess would point to an HPNS incident. Exley had experienced a bad one in Africa that resulted in uncontrollable muscular spasms and multiple vision. This may have manifested again with more violent tremors that could have triggered an oxygen convulsion or simply made it impossible to negotiate gas switches as necessary. His death will remain a mystery and a tragic loss to the cave community.

As Sheck's last dive partner, Bowden shares his thoughts, "I've been angered by unkindness and idle speculation by arm chair quarterbacks. And I have been touched by those who seem to understand and genuinely express sympathy without the need to pull something out of my soul. Much has been written in praise of Sheck and more will come. Ultimately, he will represent even more to us as history and recognized as the pioneer he truly was.

"I first met Sheck in Mexico in 1988 when he was making his then world record dive to 780 feet in Mante. I drive up to the spring while he was still underwater in the cave. He was alone in that great system. His support staff of only three, Ned DeLoach, Sergio Zambrino, and Angel Soto were awaiting his return. In this egomaniacal discipline of cave diving it was refreshing to see a man accomplishing the impossible without fanfare and entourage that we see so often with far lesser endeavors. Sheck sought my friendship as I did his for the same reason: we were loners. He was the only one of the north Florida group that respected my work. He did that with other explorers in all parts of the world. He was interested, humble and supportive of projects than many of "new age" cave divers didn't even know existed. We had a common bond, an obsession, a passion... our love of exploration.

"Exploration was a demanding mistress that got in the way of our relationships with others and I know could cause a lot of pain to those who loved us. We could spend most of day on a project without even talking to each other. Our personalities were direct opposites. He was the most disciplined man I have ever met with a brilliant calm intellect. On the other hand, I'm 52 years old, still get in fights, drink too

much at times and competitive to a fault. Yet, we got along great. Karen and Ann have both said that we looked like little boys who found the greatest treasure on earth when we found that Zacaton was the ultimate world class deep system. I do believe that we both were never more alive than in those moments of trial in virgin space.

"Mexico loved him. He truly respected their culture and ways. The rural poor of Mexico have a remarkable ability to judge courage, honesty, and sincerity. The only time I allowed myself to succumb to emotion during those days of our loss and the recovery was when I walked to the edge of Zacaton and saw the simple cross and flowers

Jim Bowden, the deepest scuba diver in history, attained 925 feet on mixed gas in Zacaton cave system, Mexico.

put there by the people of el Nacimiento and Higeron.

"Sheck met life head on, with few misconceptions. Only death deceived him, taking him by surprise. Project Zacaton will continue. There was never any question about it. I was quoted as saying it would be an insult to Sheck to shut it down. I found this system some five years ago and put it on hold to obtain the technical training and the support to make it possible. Sheck gave me that. I will miss him very much, but then we always dived alone anyway. Perhaps now he will be with me more than ever."

The Proyecto will continue it's efforts in Mexico after a brief pause for the rainy season. Bowden feels certain after reaching 925 ffw that a dive to 1000 ffw is possible and he will pursue his plans to see the bottom of Zacaton. With the use of Heliair, the survey of the distant passage of the Nacimiento Santa Clara will be resumed. The exploratory team also plans to aggressively explore the magnificent deep caves of the Sierra Madre Oriental, including the Rio Choy, Rio Frio, Rio Sabinos, Nacimiento Mante, Nacimiento Huichihuayan, and many others.

MILESTONES IN TRANSITION

The evolution of deep diving in practice has undergone several distinct generations of popular view and perception. Initial deep diving experimentation by naval divers and early explorers such as Cousteau were linked to a common enough interest: a certain fascination with the unknown. Navy divers needed access to deeper depths for tactical operative purposes and scientist/explorers sought entry to deep water zones for research and documentary applications. There was no stigma applied to deep diving per se; in fact, the element of danger and bravado summoned to challenge the unexplored abyss was greeted with a certain appreciative respect for these fledgling "aquanauts".

The initial penetrations to progressively deeper depths by free-swimming scuba divers quickly showed the severe limitations of these divers due to narcosis impairment. Early accounts by Cousteau and other team members relate romantic anecdotal accounts of narcosis so limiting as to preclude diving much below 150 feet. An examination of their methodology in deep diving sheds sufficient light to reveal serious flaws in dive planning that would never be tolerated by today's standards. But hindsight, of course, has the benefit of 20/20 vision in all circumstances. Dumas, Falco and Cousteau himself none-the-less continued with deep diving experiments in spite of several tragic deaths to associates.

It would be interesting to note at this point how the sport diving industry came to accept certain "axioms" about diving practice with little awareness of the true process of evolution that came to dictate some of our current "sacred cows." Most recreational diving instructors have all been schooled to accept the U.S. Navy recommendation of 60 foot per minute ascent rates and that the U.S. Navy tables were "holy wri.t" Only in recent years has closer examination shown the benefits of slower ascents that are now almost universally advocated. How then did the 60 ft./min. rate come into being? Like so many things that we would like to believe resulted from years of research by learned physiologists in nice white lab coats while surrounded by reams of theoretical and field testing data, the ascent rate was derived by a process a little less complex.

In a workshop meeting in the fifties, a group of various delegates from the U.S. Navy met to standardize certain practices for their divers. One item of heated discussion centered on ascent rates. The scuba diving faction wanted a 100 ft./min. rate; but the hard hat diver faction subscribed to a 25 ft./min. rate. Actually, to be more accurate the tenders for the hard hat divers wanted the slower rate and for good reason: they were responsible for winching these exceedingly heavy monsters on their stages back aboard ships or diving platforms. Many dive operations of this era still used manual winches to recover divers and the exertion required in such a hoist was considerable. Why do you think Popeye had such well developed forearms? At any rate, it was abundantly clear that the hard hat divers could not be winched aboard at anything close to 100 feet per minute, so a compromise was reached by all parties at 60 feet per minute and it was blindly adhered to by all who followed for over thirty years.

Then there is the supposed depth limit of 130 feet for scuba diving. At a recent international conference on diving safety held in 1991, representatives of the national scuba certification agencies were queried on the basis for the 130 foot rule. Although most admitted that they did not know its origin, all held true to the precept that it was a U.S. Navy recommendation and therefore it must be right.

Once again, the U.S. Navy reference was subjected to misinterpretation by well-meaning educators. In actual practice the Navy had found that it was not productive to assign a diver to a task deeper that 130 feet since he would have an allowable bottom time of only 10 minutes; scarcely enough time to evaluate an assignment and accomplish any useful work. If he was to do a job effectively this deep it was more efficient to equip him with a surface supplied gas source so he could complete the project and then manage his decompression. Somehow along the way, the sport diving industry misapplied the Navy's proprietary working diver recommendation into a sweeping condemnation of any diving below 130 feet. This has come back to haunt the certification agencies in two ways: 1) Since the depth "limit" is almost universally ignored by all but entry level divers, a significant segment of the sport diving population has been effectively forced into "outlaw" diving profiles and consistently deny deep diving thus distorting actual diving trends and statistics, 2) Increasingly more diving personal injury and wrongful death lawsuits are litigated on arguments of negligence based solely on the depth of the dive exceeding the "safe" limit of 130 feet.

THE *ANDREA DORIA* EXPEDITIONS

Deep diving has been practiced outside the traditional commercial and Navy communities for almost forty years. In 1956, Peter Gimble called a *LIFE* magazine editor to see if they would be interested in underwater photos of the ocean liner *Andrea Doria* which sunk off Nantucket Shoals following a collision with another ship only the day before. Assured that *LIFE* would purchase any such photos that Gimble could produce, he and Joseph Fox hired a plane and flew to Nantucket where, after considerable difficulty, they were able to charter a local boat to go out to the wreck site.

The wreck was a massive ship, 700 feet in length and displacing almost 30,000 tons. She settled on her starboard side in approximately 250 feet of water. This afforded access to her port side beginning in 160 feet. Gimble used the standard of equipment of his day: double tanks and a double hose regulator with no cylinder pressure gauges. Rubber suits over woolen underwear served as thermal protection in the cool northeast water. Less than 24 hours after her fatal plunge, the ship was still gleaming white as the two divers dropped onto her port rail. Gimble began working with a housed 35 mm Leica camera and had fired off only eight frames before Fox suffered dramatic incapacitation from carbon dioxide buildup. Reacting to his signal, Gimble abandoned his photography efforts and assisted his stricken buddy to the surface where he swiftly recovered. His dive had not been in vain however; the black and white Tri-X film pushed to 1000 ASA by the lab yielded usable shots and Gimble had his exclusive with *LIFE*. Thus was born a lifelong passion for him with the *Doria*.

Gimble would return to the site repeatedly over the years. At the age of 52 in 1981 he mounted an expedition to recover the Bank of Rome safe from the First Class foyer. With 33 days on site, and use of both scuba and saturation divers he successfully recovered the prize. After depositing the safe for dramatic effect in the shark tank of the New York Aquarium it remained for three years. On August 16, 1984 the safe was finally opened before an expectant international television audience. Much speculation had centered on the safe's contents. Would it contain the riches in personal valuables, jewelry and gold that had fueled rumors for twenty five years? Gimble's worst nightmare was that it might simply be empty. But as the door swung open finally, the safe revealed a mother lode of U.S. and Italian currency still neatly bundled in rubber

*The **Andrea Doria** lies fatally stricken and sinking following her collision with the Stockholm, July 25, 1956. The two vessels collided in the fog and 52 person were killed.*

bands. Although no gold bars were found, Gimble's monetary haul had considerable souvenir value. The thousands of bills, each etched by the sea's destructive influence, were marketed encased in plastic mounts with certificates of authenticity. The proceeds would not cover the 1.5 million dollar expedition cost but to Gimble the reward was adequate. He had accomplished what scores of others had attempted in vain. He died three years later.

The fascination with the *Doria* has tempted divers since her sinking. Numerous books and films have been devoted to the subject. In 1964, the team of George Merchant, John Grich, Paul Heckart and Dennis Morse accomplished what author Gentile describes as "one of the most incredible feats of underwater salvage ever accomplished on scuba. Their goal was to recover the life-sized bronze statue of Admiral Andrea Doria from his stance in the First Class Lounge." Dan Turner, captain of their salvage vessel *Top Cat*, carefully planned out the project while intensely studying the *Doria*'s blueprints. He wanted to enter the hull via the Promenade Deck to gain access from directly above the alcove encircling the statue. The divers made judicious use of explosives to blast away the glass weather shielding and metal framework to penetrate the interior. Careful to remove the blasted wreckage at each stage of the salvage so as to not damage the statue, they eventually established an entrance opening almost eight feet wide and five feet high.

At 210 feet, they found *Admiral Doria* still holding court to the silent ship. They rigged slings to prevent the statue from falling and then commenced on the laborious job of hack-sawing by hand through the legs of the old boy to free him from his pedestal. The four man dive team worked in shifts on compressed air for several days incurring then unheard of decompression by divers in the open ocean. At one point, the team exhausted their supply of hacksaw blades from the backbreaking work and operations had to be suspended while *Top Cat* steamed over to the Nantucket Lightship to beg replacements. Thus resupplied the cycle of diver rotation began anew and finally Admiral Doria was freed from his premature watery tomb. Only his feet remained behind.

Weather conditions had so deteriorated by this time that Turner elected to retrieve his dive team without in-water decompression and use the ship's chamber for surface decompression. In spite of the heaving seas, the statue was winched aboard unharmed and eventually found a home in the Sea Garden Hotel in Pompano Beach, Florida. One of the expedition investors, Glenn Garvin, had recently purchased the property and had a special platform built for the bronze relic to preside over a magnificent banquet room seating four hundred people. It was appropriately named the *Andrea Doria* Room. The Admiral seems happy in his current residence and his amputated feet still adorn the original pedestal 210 feet deep on the wreck.

Four years later, Italian film producer/director Bruno Vailati arrived

*The Stockholm lost her bow in the **Andrea Doria** collision but was able to limp back to port in New York.*

on the scene to shoot the classic *Fate of the Andrea Doria* with a crew including a young Al Giddings employed as a still photographer and backup movie cameraman. This was the last film team to observe the magnificent navigational bridge which collapsed into the sand shortly thereafter. Vailati's production featured panoramic footage of the entire wreck for the first time and chronicled the reclaiming of the ship by the ocean's inhabitants. Gentile quotes Giddings' relation of that experience in his book, "She is a city once again, more populated now by ten thousand times than during her brief life as a great ocean liner. Sea anemones grow from her rails by the scores, and huge schools of fish of every type swim down her teak decked passageways."

The first serious interest in the wreck by sport divers was organized by Michael de Camp during the summer of 1966. He and a group of other dedicated adventurers shared the cost of chartering the *Viking Starlight* for the inaugural assault on the *Doria*. One year later, northeast deep diving pioneer John Dudas entered the bridge station and recovered the binnacle cover and ship's magnetic compass. History was set the same trip when Evelyn Bartram became the first woman to dive the *Doria*. She would become Dudas' wife shortly in the future.

The *Doria* seemed to inspire creativity in would-be salvors and in 1968 the first saturation expedition was mounted by Alan Krasberg and Nick Zinkowski. Their motivation, as usual, was capture of the fabled chief purser's safe and its valued contents. By use of an underwater habitat, divers could go into saturation and continue working on the wreck virtually indefinitely with one large decompression schedule assumed when the job was completed. This was not a new concept but this application for "treasure salvage" was. The habitat itself was decidedly new; christened the *Early Bird*, it was constructed not of steel but wood! Its builders theorized that its building material would provide more insulation and make occupancy more comfortable. Obviously comfort, like beauty, must be in the eye of the beholder since the habitat was only ten feet long and four and a half feet square. This would be the first use of HELIOX as a saturation breathing gas for wreck salvage. Partially funded by MGM, the project would serve as a theme for a documentary film.

Krasber and Zinkowski were adept at securing an international all-star cast as crew. Giddings was brought in a chief cinematographer, significantly upgrading his status from that of Vailati's filming expedition three months earlier. He enlisted as assistants Chuck Nicklin, a California dive store owner, and Jack McKenney, then an editor with *Skin Diver* Magazine. All three men would go on to fame as celebrated film makers, McKenney with his Dive to Adventure series while Giddings and Nicklin would go big-time with such Hollywood features as *The Deep* and *The Abyss*. Now however, the compensation was not much over meal money. Elgin Ciampi was engaged by *LIFE* to operate an experimental multi-camera "sled" designed by Demitri Rebikoff that would function as a photomapping transect. Rounding out the distinguished ensemble was breath-hold diving champion Jacques Mayol of France.

Incredibly, with all this talent, virtually every thing that could go wrong did... in spades. Weather held them at the dock until October after construction delays on *Early Bird* forced them to miss the fair summer sea conditions. Following an abortive attempt to anchor and rough conditions that almost sank the habitat, their support vessel *Atlantic Twin* gave up and headed for the shelter of Martha's Vineyard. With more settled conditions the next day they steamed back to the site but gear failure in the rigging process so hopelessly fouled the support lines to the habitat that it was recovered on board just in time for yet another storm to blow in and force them to heave-to for three straight days.

The dive and camera crew utilized mixed gas which greatly improved efficiency when they were finally able to resume operations after the storm. Oxygen decompression was employed in one its earliest applications by nonmilitary and noncommercial divers. Following a productive day of filming, yet another setback showed up in the form of a double bends accident involving Ciampi and Mayol. Ciampi exhausted his gas supply while wrestling with a malfunctioning camera sled known as a Pegasus. He floated to the surface unconscious following an attempted free ascent and was rescued. Mayol, who was operating the other Pegasus unit, attempted to save both sleds by clipping them together but was unsuccessful and both sank. He arrived on the surface with skipped decompression and was loaded in the ship's chamber with the apparently lifeless Ciampi. Luckily, both responded to recompression therapy.

A combination of more bad weather and continued problems with rigging *Early Bird* to the wreck led to the expedition's backers finally throwing in the towel.

Not to be outdone, a new expedition was put together in 1973 by Don Rodocker and Chris DeLucchi, two ex-navy divers. They called their company Saturations Systems and intended to take up where the trouble-plagued *Early Bird* project left off. Equipped with a custom designed habitat called *Mother*, they joined the race for the *Doria*'s safe whose legend now had grown to be reputedly worth over five million dollars! Bob Hollis, founder and CEO of diving manufacturer Oceanic Products, came in as a financial partner with machinist Jack Clark. McKenney returned to direct photography along with Bernie Campoli and Tim Kelly.

Mother was far more sophisticated than *Early Bird* and substantially larger. She also could be handled in a less forgiving seaway and had the capability to operate independent of surface support for up to a week if the diving ship were to be blown off the site. Once again though, the *Doria* seemed to haunt these intrepid professionals in much the same manner as their predecessors.

Initially blown off the wreck, they successfully set up their mooring a day later only to realize they were made fast to the after section of the wreck and would have to start from scratch and re-rig further forward on the main bridge wing. After the time consuming and difficult task of relocating, the habitat severed a main power umbilical with Rodocker and DeLucchi already in saturation. The decision was made to hoist *Mother* aboard and return to port for repairs. Upon reaching the dock, the saturated divers were nearly killed when the crane unloading the habitat accidentally dropped them on the pier. Against all odds, *Mother*'s hatch seals held and the decompression continued without further mishap.

Finally on August 8th, a permanent mooring was established in the proper section of the wreck. But after eight days in saturation by Rodocker, DeLucchi and eventually Hollis they discovered that the sea's deterioration to the ship's interior had created an impassable mass of wreckage blocking any reasonable path to the safe. Once again, the *Doria* refused to yield her treasure.

Gimble's 1981 expedition would capitalize on the earlier work of *Mother's* team. Massive holes were cut into the hull and superstructure by Rodocker and DeLucchi; Gimble's team, armed with an even more refined habitat and support ship, leapfrogged on these penetrations to eventually reach the safe. But like a reluctant bride, the honeymoon was disappointing. Gimble spent almost two million dollars on this expedition and recovered only a fraction of his costs.

FIRST LADY ON THE *DORIA*: EVIE DUDAS

In 1964, Evelyn "Evie" Dudas took up scuba diving with less than an ideal motivation. She figured that it gave her the inside shot in winning the attention of a boyfriend away from a non-diving competitor. "I was nineteen then and he was an avid diver. He had another girlfriend who didn't dive, so I figured my ace in the hole was to learn all I could about the sport. My first dive was in Richland Quarry in Pennsylvania and I was so hooked I dived in another quarry the same day. I continued diving all over and even visited Canada to dive the shipwrecks up there. I broke up with the boyfriend, but had discovered a new calling: diving! I've been involved ever since."

Only three years after her first plunge into that dark quarry, she would become the first woman to ever dive the infamous wreck of the luxury liner *Andrea Doria* sunk in 1956 in a collision with another ship. Only a handful of men had ever visited the site by 1967 and she had to overcome superstition and other obstacles placed in her way to gain acceptance. "In working up to the *Doria,* I dived all the serious New Jersey wrecks. On most of the these dives I was the only girl aboard. In the beginning there was a strong male chauvinist reaction to my presence. But after I proved I could keep up with all of them and out dive some of them, I was heartily accepted. Especially by a guy named John Dudas."

John would be her partner on three historic dives to the *Doria.* A group of twelve divers and an all-male crew voted her a spot aboard the *Viking Starlite* for the expedition. "Captain Paul Forsberg headed the boat into three foot seas on a cold June morning that summer in 1967. We had plans to anchor over the wreck for three days and two nights. It's about 110 miles from Montauk Point, Long Island and 60 miles due south of Nantucket. Late that same day we zeroed in on the *Doria* and our first team of divers attached the anchor line to the stern wing railing of the wreck."

"As I toppled from the warm, safe confines of the dive boat into the dark, icy Atlantic, neither storms, sharks, currents nor the bends were going to prevent me from fulfilling my *Doria* dream. I followed John down the line that terminated on the most magnificent wreck I had ever set eyes on. In the fifty foot visibility the hull looked like an enormous freight train disappearing into the misty sea. Surprisingly, the whiteness of the upper decks gleamed brightly through the haze, sort of inviting us to explore them."

"My third dive on the last day was the most exciting. I was with John again and he was after the binnacle cover to the ship's compass, still

Evie Dudas, first woman to dive the **Andrea Doria**, *poses with some of the wreck's artifacts she recovered.*

intact in the wheelhouse. He had spotted it the day before and he rousted me out at six am to go after the darn thing. The visibility was good but the water seemed colder, forty degrees or less." After making their descent John occupied himself with the binnacle at 205 feet while Evie salvaged some brass door handles from the officer's duty lounge and chart room. The wreck site is plagued by changing currents, rapid weather switches and the hazards of ocean going ships passing over the area. Suddenly she was overcome by apprehension and cold. An unknown voice told her it was time to go. She made her way out of the wreck's interior to rendezvous with John.

"I needed John and I was ready to go. But he let his temper get the best of him and was trying to wrench the whole binnacle from its mooring. Somehow he regained his cool, gave the cover a twist and lifted it right off. There, beneath the cover, lay the compass that guided the 30,000 ton liner on a collision course with the *Stockholm* eleven years earlier. This was the most prized artifact and we thought other divers must have salvaged it long before us. I watched as John ripped it from its mounting."

"The cross currents fiercely swayed the unruly anchor line as we held on for dear life throughout the decompression stops. Fifteen minutes after we boarded the *Viking Starlite* the one and one half inch thick nylon line snapped! I guess my timing was perfect. We bade farewell to the *Andrea Doria* as storm warnings swept over her grave site. We had our souvenirs and I had fulfilled my dream."

John and Evie were married in 1970 and produced four children, all active divers. Widowed in 1982, Evie remains totally immersed in diving as a dive store owner in West Chester, Pennsylvania. Her business Dudas' Diving Duds is one of the premier pro facilities on the East Coast.

THE MIXED GAS PIONEERS

Paving the way for mixed gas users today, were early experimenters such as Arne Zetterstrom and Hannes Keller who conducted some of the most daring open water dives with then theoretical gases for divers. Zetterstrom, a Swedish engineer, was fascinated with diving and sought to extend the working depths of divers by manipulating the oxygen content of a gas mixture and replacing the narcotic nitrogen with a more "workable" inert gas. Alternatives such as helium and neon were in such short supply as to be virtually unattainable in Sweden in the early 1940's so Zetterstrom focused on hydrogen as a replacement. It had favorable properties with respect to density, viscosity and narcotic potency but had the major disadvantage of forming oxyhydrogen gas which is highly explosive if mixed with oxygen percentages in excess of 4%.

He was faced with several operational problems from the outset:

1. A 4% O_2 percentage would not support human life underwater until approaching the 100 fsw depth range.

2. Therefore a "travel" gas mix would need to be utilized to allow the diver to safely travel through the surface to 100 fsw range and back.

3. Now the curve ball... regular air as a travel mix could be used to 100 fsw and satisfy the oxygen requirements. However, if the oxygen-hydrogen mixture were to come into contact with a normoxic air mix, it would create oxyhydrogen gas and, at least theoretically, the diver would explode. So a third mix, a transition gas mixture, would be necessary to protect the diver.

Zetterstrom decided to use one of the earliest NITROX blends as his transition mix: a 4% oxygen and 96% nitrogen mixture. This would allow a safe bridge between the O_2/H_2 "bottom mix". The diver would switch to the NITROX cylinder at 100 fsw and breathe for a period sufficient to flush out the higher O_2 percentage and then switch again to the "bottom mix". This cycle would be repeated during ascent.

It should be noted that since Zetterstrom manufactured his own hydrogen aboard ship at sea by breaking down ammonia to yield 75% H_2 and 25% N_2, his final mix was actually a TRIMIX of 4% O_2, 24% N_2 and 72% H_2. This was one of the earliest uses of TRIMIX; nitrogen in such reduced percentages was not a narcotic factor. In his experimental dives to 130 fsw he encountered no difficulties but was unpleasantly surprised to discover the highly conductive thermal properties of hydrogen and became uncomfortably cold quickly. Also, the light density of hydrogen, like helium, produced "Donald Duck" speech making voice communications with his surface tenders virtually impossible.

His second attempt would be conducted much deeper. The 300 fsw barrier was largely regarded as the limit of practical diver performance, so deliberately he would test his mixture at 360 fsw. Lowered on a wooden stage by a winch from the stern of his support ship *Belos*, he negotiated his mixture switches flawlessly and reached his planned depth where he reported "slight breathing resistance and the narcotic effect practically nil". His dive was regarded as a huge success with implications for commercial applications and for submarine rescue operations.

On August 7th, 1945, Zetterstrom planned a monumental dive to 500 fsw for the first time, far in excess of any dives successfully attained at that point by any method. Tragically, a breakdown in communications within his surface support team led to disaster.

Once again, he employed the diving stage to control his descent and ascent with prearranged signals and time allotments for his mixture switches and bottom time. All went well on the descent and he reached 500 fsw without mishap. He signaled the surface that he was well and the ascent phase was initiated in accordance with his pre-planned schedule. He was winched up to 166 fsw to begin his decompression when all hell broke loose. He had rigged the stage platform not only with a lifting cable but with two lines on either side to counteract any effects of current or tide. Somehow the tender handling the line to the bow of the ship misunderstood his instructions and winched his end of the platform all the way to within thirty feet of the surface. The stern tenders held steady with the intention of leaving Zetterstrom at 166 fsw. An impossible angle of tilt resulted along with rapid decompression. This resulted in the diver's inability to negotiate gas mixture switches or to conduct normal decompression. The 4% O_2 mix was insufficient to maintain proper oxygenation and Zetterstrom died due to hypoxia and severe embolism.

Zetterstrom had dramatically demonstrated the practicality of his revolutionary gas mixes and shattered the depth record only to fall victim to the ineptitude of his surface support crew.

Hannes Keller began experimental dives in 1959 that would ultimately more than double the depths of Zetterstrom but again with fatal consequences to dive team members. Keller, a Swiss mathematician, joined forces with noted physiologist Albert Buhlmann to explore the highly controversial elements of accelerated decompression in conjunction with helium and oxygen mixtures (HELIOX). Both men could see the financial gain to be made by refining a system to place divers in working situations at incredible depths and bring them back to the surface without unreasonable delays due to decompression obligations. Much of their research was conducted cloaked in secrecy.

Working with a hyperbaric chamber capable of simulating 1500 fsw in November of 1960, Keller prepared for the first practical test of his new gas mixes and decompression schedules. This was to be a dual dive: Keller in the lower "wet" chamber and a team of French doctors in the upper "dry" chamber. Keller, equipped with a battery of diving equipment and varied cylinders for his mixes would dive alone to a simulated depth of 830 fsw! This was beyond conception even to theoreticians at this time. The French team would be exposed to a pressure equivalent to 200 fsw. Keller's rapid compression to twenty-five atmospheres was accomplished in only ten minutes and the consensus opinion of outside observers was that he could not survive such an exposure. However, Buhlmann was in voice contact with him and reported him well at the bottom depth.

An equally rapid decompression to the 200 fsw level of the French team was conducted and Keller opened the connecting hatch to join the doctors in the "dry" chamber. Removing his gear and drying off, he then entered the access lock six minutes later. Following only 30 minutes more decompression, he emerged at the surface! By contrast, the French team exposed to only a maximum of 200 fsw would require twice as much decompression time under their conventional tables. Keller had been over four times deeper.

He would not stop there. The second pivotal dive took place in actual open water conditions in Lago Maggiore and this time, incredibly, he took along a *LIFE* magazine reporter named Kenneth McLeish. They would reach 730 fsw while being lowered on a similar platform stage as utilized by Zetterstrom. This time the top-side commands were personally supervised by Buhlmann to avoid any possible problems in operational execution. The dive required four mixes to be employed and broke the in-water record of 600 fsw held then by British Royal Navy diver George Wookey. In startling contrast to Wookey's decompression time of twelve hours, Keller and McLeish completed their decompression in less than 45 minutes. Keller had proved the validity of his decompression theory and McLeish had forever set a new standard in "on scene" reporting. It's hard to imagine one of today's blow-dried news anchors donning a dive suit to report the story from the sea floor.

The Lago Maggiore dive finally prompted the major financial support Keller and Buhlmann so desperately needed. Funding was now supplied by a group of U.S. corporations including Shell Oil, General Motors and the Navy. Keller announced his goal to reach the average limit of the continental shelf and thus open up the exploration of mining raw mineral deposits and food resources previously unreachable. This 1000 fsw dive was scheduled off Catalina Island in southern California.

A custom built diving decompression chamber named *Atlantis* was constructed capable of carrying two occupants to the sea floor over 30 atmospheres down. It was fitted with two chambers and a connecting lock to allow Keller to exit *Atlantis* and then re-enter and conduct his decompression in the upper chamber. With an ever-mindful eye towards the international press, Keller once again chose a journalist to accompany him. Peter Small, a British newspaperman, was only an amateur diver but had obtained a commission assignment for a substantial fee on the stipulation that he personally write the article.

Hans Hass was a personal friend of Small's and writes of his misgivings about the upcoming dive in *Men Beneath The Sea* (1973):

> "*Peter Small had been married only shortly before this, and his wife, Mary, as attractive as she was energetic, was vital to his resolve, or so it seemed to us. From a long conversation with Peter I got the feeling that deep down in his heart he was undertaking more than he really wanted. I don't mean by this that he was afraid, but that he lacked the freedom from doubt, the confidence of Hannes Keller. Various circumstances soon deprived him of his freedom of choice {the newspaper commission among them, Ed.} Mary saw in him a hero, there was no escape... Somehow I felt uneasy. Peter was a true Englishman, and did not betray his feelings, but I knew him and all divers well enough to understand him.*"

Several practice dives were conducted working up to the 1000 fsw exposure and in the process two bends hits were sustained, one on Hermann Heberlein and one on Peter Small only two days prior to the planned primary dive. Keller and Small had taken *Atlantis* to a depth of 330 fsw and exited to spend over an hour outside on the bottom. Small had a minor hit in his elbow after surfacing and was recompressed. On

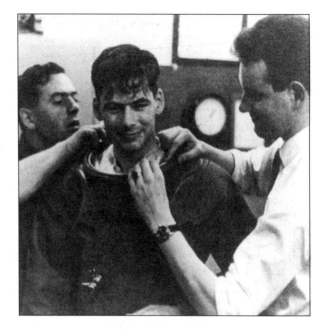

Hannes Keller before his remarkable dive to 1000 feet in 1962. Although Keller was successful in his application of mixed gas technology, his triumph was marred by two fatalities in less experienced support divers.

Monday, December 3, 1962 all was finally ready and the support ship *Eureka* was moved into position where the sea floor was exactly 1000 feet deep. An umbilical hose linked *Atlantis* with the ship down to 330 feet to supply gases and pressurization to the chamber. Beyond this depth the divers were on their own connected only via the steel lifting hawser. Keller had installed backup cylinders in *Atlantis* to provide extra breathing gas if needed. Each diver was equipped with a back mounted rig capable of providing 15 minutes time. It could be replenished by filling off the backup cylinders. Unfortunately, it was discovered that the backup units were leaking and Keller was forced into a difficult decision heavily influenced by the financial pressures of corporate endorsement and the desire to still maintain the secrecy of his mixes and decompression schedules.

> *Keller related to Hass, "Before the attempt, this was the situation: barely enough gas in the equipment carried on the back; on the other hand, the team in top form, weather perfect. Personally, a strong fear that it might be all called off. Knowing that one never has perfect conditions, an attempt under perfect starting conditions never happens. Never. There are only adequate starting conditions... Well then, I decided to make the attempt."*

His goal was to briefly swim out of the chamber and plant the Swiss and American flags on the bottom. He determined that his primary gas units would allow him a sufficient safety margin to exit the *Atlantis* and return. Upon reaching the planned depth, the divers opened the exit hatch and Keller dropped the short distance to the bottom. But the flags became tangled in his breathing apparatus and it took him over two minute to free himself and drop them. After he and Small successfully closed the hatch he was exhausted. At this point he should have refilled their breathing gear from the backup cylinders but felt himself passing out. He was just able to activate the compressed air vent to flush the knee-deep water from the tiny chamber before losing conciseness.

The remote television cameras linked the surface crew with the developments on the bottom and they immediately instructed Small to remove his mask and breathe the air atmosphere. This would probably result in his unconsciousness as well but with Keller unable to operate the inside gas selections during ascent, it was felt that Small was better handled in this manner. But Small froze in horror and continued to breathe the deep mix and collapsed shortly thereafter out of camera view.

The tenders quickly raised *Atlantis* to 330 feet where divers were sent down to reconnect the umbilical. But at the 200 fsw level, the chamber proved to be leaking and could not be raised without risking explosive decompression to the occupants. Dick Anderson, a professional California diver, and Chris Whittaker, an English friend of Small's, went down to ascertain the problem but could not locate the source of the leak. To Anderson it seemed that the chamber had solved its problems and the two returned to the surface. Whittaker was not nearly the experienced pro that Anderson was and had difficulty on the ascent with this safety vest. He arrived on the ship with a profuse amount of blood in his mask and thoroughly worn out. The surface crew informed them that the chamber was still leaking.

Since they were the only two safety divers, Anderson knew he would have to go back down but preferred to go alone.

> *"The boy was not very strong, and rather exhausted. He undid his weight belt and took it over his arm. I nodded to him. In an emergency, he could drop the belt and would then float to the surface. We swam down again. On top of the chamber I signaled to Chris to stay there and wait. I swam down again to the hatch. I had more than enough air and had a good look around... The cover was firmly attached but when I looked very closely I discovered a small crack in it.*

Something small was stuck there. I tried to get at it with my knife. Then I simply propped myself on the ladder and pressed myself upwards with my back as hard as I could. I did this for quite a while. Finally the hatch appeared to be sealed. When I swam up... Chris had disappeared. I thought he must have surfaced already since I couldn't see him anywhere. When I got to the top, they asked me where Chris Whittaker was..."

(excerpted from Hass' **Men In the Sea**)

Whittaker was never found. The *Atlantis* was hoisted aboard and Keller regained consciousness and hastened to cut Small from his dive suit and examine him. He reported to Buhlmann that he was alive. Later he came around and said he was thirsty. Keller got him something to drink while Small briefly spoke to Buhlmann on the phone. He then went to sleep seemingly OK. However, when Keller checked his pulse later he discovered that Small had died. He was stunned at Small's death. Keller was completely fine. The double fatality cast his remarkable achievement in shadow. Hillary Hauser, Dick Anderson's ex–wife, notes in her book *Call To Adventure*:

> *"The Keller dive was an awful paradox. It was a success because one man made a 1000 foot dive and lived, proving that the mysterious mixture of gases had worked. It also was a disaster because of the deaths involved. No one knew whether to cheer or boo. The effect was the same as if Neil Armstrong had landed on the moon and lived, while fellow astronaut Buzz Aldrin had not made it back to Earth. In that case, would the moon landing have been considered a success or failure?"*

Hass speculates that Keller's determination and confidence insured his survival while the less experienced and less motivated Small succumbed. Hass felt that had Dick Anderson been Keller's diving partner no lives would have been lost. With the benefit of hindsight, Keller would have been wise to ensure a more professional companion but Small had performed satisfactorily on the practice runs. Keller remained shaken but undaunted and continues today with consulting work in varying fields of diving and computer technologies. His vision of man's ability to work in extreme depths would provide the basis for commercial and naval systems that followed.

THE HABITAT EVOLUTIONS

That same year saw the introduction of the first significant advances in man's attempts to actually live in the ocean. Habitat and submersible pioneer Ed Link launched two short duration but important projects back to back in August and September of 1962. Using himself as a guinea pig in the first project nicknamed *Trial Link*, he spent a cramped eight hours at 60 fsw in a tiny 11'x3' cylinder in the Mediterranean. Robert Stenuit followed him the following month in the same cylinder now called *Man-in-the-Sea*; this time for two hours at 200 fsw breathing HELIOX. On the heels of Stenuit's dive, came the first of Jacques Cousteau's *Conshelf* missions with two divers spending a week at 35 fsw off Marseilles. Much as the "space race" was heating up, so it seemed the race for advances in underwater saturation habitats moved forward. In 1963, Cousteau followed up dramatically with *Conshelf II* in which seven "aquanauts" lived at 36 fsw on the ocean floor of the Red Sea for a month! During this same mission, Raymond Kientzy and Andre Portelatine spent a week in a specially staged mini-habitat called *Deep Cabin* at 90 fsw allowing them "excursion" dives with virtually

Conshelf II depicted on the edge of the Red Sea wall.

no decompression to as deep as 360 feet.

In 1964, Link sponsored his *Man-in-the-Sea II* mission off the Bahamas and the U.S. Navy deployed *Sea Lab I* near Bermuda. A plethora of progressively deeper and longer saturation projects followed including the two month mission of *Tektite* in the Virgin Islands in the late sixties. *Tektite* was utilized for multiple missions and in 1971 marked the first all female aquanaut team led by Dr. Sylvia Earle, now chief scientist for NOAA. Link also produced the venerable *Hydrolab* habitat that began operation in 1966 and into the mid-1980's before being retired to the Smithsonian Institution in Washington D.C. During its op-

The main living chamber, Starhouse, of **Conshelf II** where seven aquanauts would live and work for a month in 1963.

erational life it provided an underwater home to literally hundreds of scientists and researchers at its sites in Florida, the Bahamas and finally St. Croix in the Virgin Islands. Ultimately *Hydrolab* was replaced with the massive *Aquarius* habitat now in the process of relocating to a site in the Florida Keys. The saturation habitat fascination tapered off in the mid-1970's and now only a handful of projects remain in existence. Renewed interest is surfacing however as the possibilities of saturation exploration of deep wrecks and cave systems are discussed by the emerging high tech community.

Tragically, Ed Link, one of diving's true technical innovators, would suffer the loss of his son while a team member in *Sea-Link*, a deep diving submersible of his design. In the summer of 1973 during a project

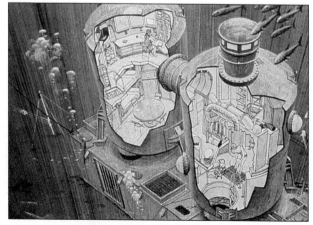

Tektite II, *one to the U.S.' most ambitious saturation projects, had missions as long as two months in their location off St. John in the Virgin Islands.*

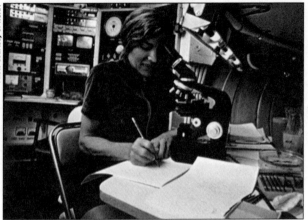

Dr. Sylvia Earle, headed the first all female saturation mission in **Tektite II**.

sponsored by the Smithsonian off Key West, Florida, the sub became entangled in a cable from a wreck they were exploring. The scuttled destroyer *Fred T. Berry* fouled the *Sea-Link* while she was attempting to pick up a fish trap at 351 fsw. All efforts by the sub's crew to extricate themselves proved to no avail. The submersible was configured with two chambers: A forward pilot's station for two crew and an after chamber capable of "locking-out" divers for exterior excursions. In the forward command station Bob Meek and Jock Menzies were surrounded by a large acrylic sphere and remarkably this would prove crucial to their survival. In the after compartment, Clay Link and Al Stover, an expert and highly experienced submariner, were encapsulated in highly thermally conductive aluminum.

Although the Navy dispatched its submarine rescue ship *Tringa* to the site, it was almost 12 hours before it finally was positioned over the trapped sub. A "roving diving bell" was airlifted from San Diego and delivered to the ship where it began its first descent the following morning at 9:20 am. At this point, the sub's occupants had been marooned for almost 24 hours. Swift currents in the area hampered the efforts to make contact with *Sea-Link* and time began to run out for the helpless four men. To conserve their precious on-board emergency air supply, the sub crew desperately spread baralyme in their compartments which would act to absorb CO_2 from the increasingly stale atmosphere. However, baralyme is ineffective below 70 degrees F. and in the aft compartment surrounded by the conductive aluminum the temperature rapidly plummeted. Stover and Link attempted to raise the baralymex temperature by spreading it over their exposed skin but this ceased to be effective after a time.

While the rescue crew furiously struggled to hook up with the sub, the trapped men finally turned to their emergency breathing system which supplied air to both compartments. The 36 hour ordeal held little hope that the rescue could be made before the air in the emergency cylinders was exhausted. Stover made a personal assessment of his situation with Link in the lockout compartment and decided that they held far less chance of survival than Menzies and Meek in the pilot sphere. In the ultimate heroic sacrifice to try to at least save his companions, Stover turned off the emergency air system for himself and Link. Both died before the sub was recovered but the other two men survived.

THE FREE DIVERS

Although this is a book primarily about deep scuba diving, the unique accomplishments of a small cadre of breath-hold divers bears mention in our historical narrative. Also known as free-diving, this esoteric diving form has almost become a lost art among American divers since the early seventies. In the infancy of scuba diving almost every new diver was also an accomplished free-diver. This was fueled by the popularity of competitive spearfishing almost exclusively conducted without scuba gear. This produced many divers capable of routinely diving to depths in excess of 100 feet to hunt fish on near equal terms. Many of the most proficient competitors would chalk up bottom times approaching two and half minutes and reach depths of up to 150 feet.

Bret Gilliam, a member of the Virgin Islands spearfishing team in 1974, recalls his introduction to the real world of free-diving,

> *"I was invited to got out with team captain Dave Coston originally back in '71. Dave was about 38 then, I was about 21, and I figured I would show these old guys a thing or two. Now the water in the Virgin Islands is clear but when we got to the dive site, I couldn't see the bottom. Not wanting to be un-cool since everyone else seemed unconcerned , I warmed up with a couple of dives to 50 or 60 feet but still couldn't see the bottom. Finally, after about a half hour or so of watching from afar as Coston and Carl Butler boated massive snapper and grouper, I swam over to inquire where in hell the sea mount was that they were diving on. I was reduced to the rank of rookie in a heartbeat when they informed me there was no secret; the bottom was right underneath me; only 140 feet. Was I having a problem or something?"*

Others like Jay Riffe, Terry Maas, and the Ernst brothers of California, Pepin Fernandez, Don Delmonico and the Pinder brothers had similar performances. And this was not simply diving down and coming up. A true free-diver could swim down, stalk a fish, then shoot it, and struggle his catch back to the surface from these depths... all in one breath.

The interest in competitive free-diving saw the introduction of a whole new form of diving emerge: extreme depth breath hold diving. This form of diving consists of three different categories. It was once under the auspices of CMAS, the World Federation of Underwater Activities but is now under the auspices of the Italian Federation of Underwater Professionals.

The Fixed Weight category is when diver descends to depth with a weight and then must swim back with the weight to the surface. The Changeable Weight category allows a diver to use weight up to one-third of their body weight for the descent and then swim back to the surface without the weight. The No-Limit Dive allows a diver to use as much weight as they want for their descent and then use a buoyancy device to carry them back to the surface once the dropped the weight.

Probably the earliest record holder would have to be the Greek sponge diver Stotti Georghios, who swam down to put a line on a lost anchor in 1913 with no fins in 200 feet of water.

During the Navy testing in 1968, diver Bob Croft set a modern day record by reaching 240 feet off Bimini. Al Giddings relates his account of the dive in the book **Exploring the last Frontier.**

"I went down using scuba to 250 feet to await Croft's arrival. At that depth the nitrogen in the compressed air I was breathing had a

Dave Coston, champion breath-hold spearfisherman, with world record silky shark taken in 1974 off St. Croix, Virgin Islands. During the 1970's, Coston held over a dozen world records for fish species all taken in depths up to 150 feet.

dizzying effect on me. It was incredible enough as it was, suspended in the open sea, an ethereal infinity of blue in all directions. Then Croft came racing down the guideline, skin loose, chest compressed from the pressure. After reaching 240 feet he let go of the weight and hand over hand, no fins, pulled himself back to the surface. It was remarkable to watch him go back to the surface under his own power." Croft's dive lasted just over two minutes.

Jacques Mayol studied marine mammals for 15 years and experimented with a variety of methods to extend his time underwater including yoga and meditational exercises. In 1976, he devised a unique weighted sled on a cable that he held onto with both hands during descents. A hand operated brake could allow him to stop at any depth. Mayol preferred not to use a mask at all since equalizing it would only deplete his breath reserve. Instead he wore specially adapted contact lenses that allowed him to see and allowed him to wear a nose clip. Incredibly, he attained 328 feet on his dive. His dive lasted almost three and half minutes.

He related, "When I am down there, I'm not a man anymore. I'm a sea creature... a diving mammal. I belong in the water." A movie based loosely on his amazing career called The Big Blue was released in 1988.

Like the compressed air diving record that held up for 22 years, Mayol's mark seemed untouchable until 1989 when a young Italian woman, Angela Bandino, dropped to 351 feet in breath hold competition. Today there are two new rivals on the circuit competing for the various breath-hold depth records. Umberto Pelizarri from Italy and Francisco Ferraras known as "Pipin" from Cuba are probably the best two free divers the world has yet seen. Pelizarri holds the Fixed weight record by swimming down to 230 feet off the coast of Elba, Italy, in 1991. In October, 1993, Pelizarri also set the No-Limit Dive record of 403 feet.

The changeable weight record of 315 feet was set in July, 1993, by Pipin, in Syracuse, Sicily. In December of 1993, Pipin captured the new No-Limit Dive record by descending to the remarkable depth of 410 feet. Well, the 400 foot barrier has been broken. Will the 500 foot barrier be broken? The answer is probably yes. Pipin believes that he can dive to 500 feet.

THE CAVE DIVERS

The earliest known use of scuba gear in United States caves was in

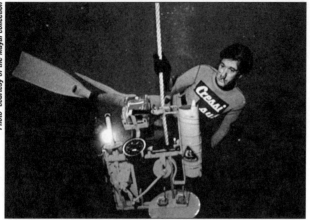

Jacques Mayol reaches 328 feet in 1976 while holding his breath and riding a unique weighted sled to take him to depth.

January of 1953 by Frank DenBlykker and Charles McNabb to explore the then unknown depths of Florida's Silver Springs. The pair discovered that the Springs were only the entrance to a large cave system and on that first dive they stumbled onto the petrified remains of the elephant's ancient ancestor, the Mastodon. Cave diving was a little practiced sport in these embryonic days of scuba diving and only a handful of participants could be found struggling through the underbrush and

RIGHT: Rossana Maiorca, holder of the women's free diving depth record, at 185 feet. She accomplished this dive by swimming down and up unassisted by extra weights or sleds. It required her to hold her breath two minutes and 3 seconds. Her father, Enzo, is one of the world's most accomplished breath hold divers and an ex-depth champion rival to Mayol. BELOW: Rossana Maiorca plucks the 56 meter (185 fsw) tag from her descent line to set a new women's record.

down slippery paths to access the mesmerizing call of the dazzling, clear inland cave systems. Jack "Gil" Favor discovered many other of the now popular caves and was active in cave diving from the early fifties until the mid-sixties.

Sheck Exley made his first cave dive in 1966 shortly after his initial scuba training and was "hooked". Looking back at that period of his life in 1984 he recalls:

> *"Now, for better or for worse, my life was set; I was a cave diver. Sports heroes such as Tarkenton and Gehrig, and military genius Lawrence of Arabia were now replaced with Watts, Mount and Harper on the list of people I most admired. Hall Watts was the best deep cave diver, Tom Mount had the most cave dives and was the best published, and John Harper was simply the best, period."*

Mount began cave diving in 1962 after discharge from a hitch as a Navy officer and UDT diver. His introduction was with Zuber Sink (later renamed Forty Fathom Sink) where he would make numerous dives to 240 ft. to bottom out the cave with Frank Martz, another early cave enthusiast. One of the most outstanding deep caves in Florida is Eagle's Nest. First discovered by Don Ledbetter in 1960, this cave is still unfolding as technology advances.

Ledbetter, along with others such as Lee Somers (now the head of the University of Michigan's diving program and a Ph.D.), explored the "Nest", then known as Lost Sink, to depths of 220 ffw. Later John Harper and Randy Hylton pushed on to 230 ffw with Mount and Martz laying permanent line in to a depth of 250 ffw in 1964. Hal Watts and members of his informal "diving club", the Forty Fathom Scubapro's, would reach 260 ffw while penetrating the upstream cave. In 1965, Mount and Martz set out to attempt to "wall out" (reach the end) of the Nest and with progressive pushes reached depths of 285 ffw. Joined by Jim Lockwood in 1969, they found a small passage that dropped to 300 fsw but did not appear to continue; Lockwood laid line in beyond that depth but ultimately encountered silt too thick to penetrate and that tunnel was abandoned.

The opening to the downstream cave was discovered by Mount and Martz in late 1968. This required the divers to negotiate a very tight restriction in the 280-290 ffw level before opening into a large and beautiful tunnel that is the major system of Eagle's Nest. In the years to follow, Lockwood and Jamie Stone would introduce the use of DPV's

Cave diving pioneer Tom Mount in 1966. Note equipment of that era included "jerry jug" to be used as a buoyancy compensator.

(Diver Propulsion Vehicles) and Exley would introduce the practice of multiple stage bottles to effect penetrations hundreds of feet beyond the early explorers. The lines laid by Lockwood and Exley would not be exceeded until the late 1980's when Jim King and Larry Green employed combinations of DPV's, staging and TRIMIX to reach 310 ffw for up to one hour and 18 minutes requiring seven hours of decompression. In Mount's opinion (1991), "The Nest has been explored to the limits of open circuit technology. The use of rebreathers for further exploration is being investigated by King and Green and other members of the Deep Breathing Systems Team. We don't know the ultimate possible penetration or depth."

Possibly one of the deepest caves is popular Morrison Spring in the Florida Panhandle. This is marked by one of the largest and prettiest headpools at its entrance. In the early 1960's, Atlanta dive instructor Jack Faver, made extensive dives into the system and reported depths attained of 270-350 ffw. Martz and Mount attained 285 ffw in 1965. In 1968, teams led by Hal Watts, John Harper and Randy Hylton made it past an extremely narrow restriction at the 100 ffw level by removing their doubles and squeezing through to discover a fourth room extending to the 240 ffw level. Here they were stopped as the passage narrowed to only a small slit.

Speculation that this later team missed a side passage taken by Faver and dive buddy George Krasle, stirs interest that the tunnels were not fully explored. Unfortunately, following the deaths of several divers, the local sheriff had enough and ordered the dynamiting of the passage leading to the third room thus sealing the passages forever.

Other deep cave penetrations included Jim Houtz's dive to 315 ffw into Nevada's Devil's Hole surrounded by Death Valley National Monument, and the Sheck Exley/Joe Prosser descent to 325 ffw in Mystery Sink in Orlando, Florida. Will Waters, Jamie Stone, Jim Lockwood andExley would be among the first to lead pushes into the infamous Die Polder II sinkhole near Weekie Wachee with Dale Sweet reaching 360 ffw in 1980 on HELIOX accompanied by Lockwood on air. At the time of the dive Lockwood did not know that Sweet was using mixed gas, he had kept it a secret. It would be over 12 years before any extensions to the Lockwood/Sweet line would be laid; this time by Lamar English and Bill Gavin who were followed by Dustin Clesi and Jim King on TRIMIX and DPV's to a depth of 380 ffw. The group intends to return in the future to continue with rebreathers.

The father of "Blue Hole" diving has to be Dr. George Benjamin of Canada. He became fascinated with the Bahamian blue holes in the late 1960's after trips to the western island of Andros. Local legend and superstition kept natives and divers alike away from this mysterious phenomena until Benjamin began diving in them. Due to the often violent whirlpool effects near the entrance of the holes, it was said that they were occupied by evil spirits or the dreaded "lusca", an octopus-like monster,

Photo by Tom Mount

Jim Lockwood in Picannie Ponds in Australia. Lockwood and Tom Mount completed what is still believed to be the deepest Australian cave dive on air to 320 ffw in 1973.

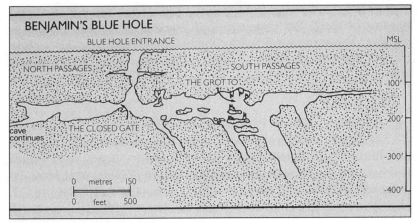

BENJAMIN'S BLUE HOLE

BLUE HOLE ENTRANCE

MSL

NORTH PASSAGES

SOUTH PASSAGES

THE GROTTO

-100'

-200'

cave
continues

THE CLOSED GATE

-300'

0 metres 150

0 feet 500

-400'

Line sketch of Benjamin's Blue Hole

that would drag fishermen and entire boats below the surface if they ventured too near. Benjamin quickly ascertained that the whirlpool effects were related to tidal cycles and was the first to develop dive plans designed around penetrations during the slack water period.

Since he took up blue hole cave diving at the not exactly youthful age of 50, he prudently decided that some younger assistants might be helpful in making the pushes into the labyrinth tunnels and an invitation was offered to veteran cave explorer Tom Mount to come over from Miami to help with the project. Mount proved an invaluable team member and led the way in Blue Hole #4 to discover the first stalactite formations in 1970.

Benjamin was something of an equipment inventor on his own, introducing the innovative "Benjamin Conversion" manifold that allowed the use of dual regulators on double tanks but provided the "isolation" capability in the event of a valve or regulator malfunction. The air from the "isolated" cylinder was channeled via his unique crossover bar so that the second regulator/valve system could still access it. (Although Benjamin has largely been credited with the design, Ike Ikehara was actually the brains behind the manifold system). But Mount arrived on the scene with other custom equipment like high intensity lights and specialized reels that he had not seen before. They were manufactured by Mount's close friend, Frank Martz, another veteran Florida cave diver.

After several months of joint work by Benjamin's team and other

American divers recruited by Mount including Ike Ikehara, Sharee Pepper, Dick Williams, Jim Lockwood, Zidi Goldstein and Martz, they had pushed well beyond the limits of Benjamin's earlier projections. In the summer of 1970, an offshoot of Benjamin Cave (#4) was discovered by Tom and Ikehara who squeezed through a major restriction at 240 fsw to enter a totally unexplored passage. Mount recalls:

> *"It was kind of a roller coaster tunnel that led down to a depth of 300 feet. Later Dick Williams and I placed permanent line in to 310 feet deep and ran into another restriction that we could just get through. At the end of this tunnel we reached a shaft that dropped out of sight. I leaned over at 330 fsw and shined my light straight down and we couldn't see the bottom. At this point, some thirty minutes had elapsed and narcosis was a complication coming back up the tunnel and through the restrictions. On the exit, I had to assist Dick from 290 feet up to 240 feet. He just sort of gave out; he could kick but there was nothing in his effort and he wasn't making any progress."*

In 1971, Mount and Martz discovered yet another deep tunnel with a major restriction beginning at 280 fsw but did not have the opportunity to explore it farther. In September, Martz arrived from Florida determined to push the new tunnel beyond the restriction. He enlisted Lockwood as his dive partner. From the beginning things didn't seem to go well. Martz seemed moody and out of sorts to his friends. Benjamin did not want the dive done since it conflicted with his work projects already scheduled and he considered it to be particularly hazardous. Mount was Martz's best friend and even found himself on the short end of an argument that day when he could never recall a strained word between them before.

Since Benjamin was paying the bills to support the mapping and survey of the Blue Holes, Mount explained that the work projects had to take priority. But Martz was insistent and Mount finally persuaded Benjamin to let the dive go forward. Lockwood and Martz set off together while Mount and Zidi Goldstein went into the north tunnel to extend the lines into that passage. Martz and Lockwood successfully negotiated the constricted passage and went on down to 300 fsw. While tying off a new reel, considerable silt was stirred up in the narrow area and Martz went through the restriction by himself. Lockwood waited, alone. In conversation with Gilliam in 1991, he reflects:

> *"Frank was a headstrong guy who was one of the country's top*

Frank Martz and Jim Lockwood just before entering the water to explore the south passage of Benjamin's Blue Hole in 1971. Martz would disappear in a speculated suicide and never be found.

expert cave divers. When you dived with him you had to accept certain things like the fact that he was going to do whatever he felt on the dive. I was 21 then and Frank was 35. Frank and Tom were the kings, I looked up to them and would never have thought to question either of them underwater. When Frank went through that restriction, I never saw him again. I thought that he must have come by me in the silt-out and headed to the surface. I finally went through and found only a cut safety line dangling into a blue bottomless void, with my light shining from 325 feet deep I couldn't see any end to that shaft."

Lockwood came back through and encountered Mount and Goldstein in the decompression area and briefly, by slate, conveyed that Martz had disappeared. Tom and Jim returned to the entrance of the south passage in the futile hope that Martz might appear but he was gone forever.

The loss of one of the U.S.'s top cave divers had a numbing effect on Mount and the rest of the Florida team. Two attempts were made by Mount and Lockwood to retrieve the body to no avail. In the notes from the police investigation report, Mount makes this statement:

> *"Frank Martz was probably one of the best cave divers in the world. He was a NAUI, PADI and NACD certified instructor. He was one of my best friends, and one of the people you think it is impossible for them to die diving. He had done more to develop safe cave diving equipment than anyone, and the cave diving world will miss him, his abilities, his excellent diving equipment and his devotion to the exploration of underwater caves."*

Tom may have been correct in his note that it was impossible to believe that Martz could die in a diving accident. All the team had noted his strange behavior in the time before the dive. Sheck Exley remembers that period:

> *"The summer of 1971 was especially noteworthy in Florida. A tiny amoeba had infested the water of many of the lakes and ponds in central Florida. It had been reported only a couple of miles south of Eagle's Nest and I think it's reasonable to assume that this amoeba was there as well. Why so much fuss over a microbe? If the amoeba infects a swimmer or diver, as it did in Florida that year, it was 100% fatal. It caused encephalitis, swelling the human brain so that severe headaches are felt in the early stages, then comes high fever and death a few short weeks after the initial infection. How does it get into the brain? Through the nasal passages. Frank had spent countless hours decompressing with his nose in the water (with no mask) at Eagle's Nest. At Andros, divers soon noticed Frank acting strangely. He seemed moody and depressed, and was intent on doing dives that were especially dangerous."*

Lockwood may have been an unwitting buddy to a diver focused on a

Phillipe Cousteau and Dr. George Benjamin rigging flares for use in the Cousteau television special on the Benjamin Blue Holes in 1971.

Photo by Bret Gilliam

Photo by Rob Palmer

An interior passage of the Andros Blue Holes shows the spectacular stalagtite and stalactite formations.

one-way dive. Mount has voiced the same speculation. Exley concludes:

> *"A terminally ill cave diver with no close family ties could scarcely pick a better way to commit suicide: in one of the world's most spectacular underwater caves, at a depth deep enough to insure that his passing would be rendered painless by narcosis and make it very unlikely that his body would ever be found."*

The Great Blue Hole of Lighthouse Reef Atoll located some 70 miles off Belize harbored similar superstitions as the Bahamian blue holes. In 1971, the Cousteaus traveled with *Calypso* to explore its uncharted depths for the first time. Widely rumored to be "bottomless", stalactite formations were discovered at a depth of only 140 fsw and with the use of their diving submersible the Blue Hole was bottomed out at just over 600 fsw. Following this expedition, they continued on to the Bahamas to visit Benjamin and Mount in Andros to film the local blue holes they were mapping. Ironically, Jacques Cousteau almost was killed in #4 when he got off the line on the way out of the cave.

The Lucayan blue hole, called Ben's Cave, located on Grand Bahama island ultimately proved to be one of the longest cave systems in the world. Shec Exley would explore another even larger system in Belize on Caye Cawlker. After diving the Great Blue Hole and Ben's Cave in the early 1970's, Bret Gilliam searched in vain for similar formations in the Virgin Islands. But he did discover tunnels cut into the face of the steep north shore drop-off of St. Croix. These began at extreme depths, usually 330 fsw or deeper and penetrated nearly horizontally back into the wall face. Some had entrances as narrow as three feet that extended in more than 200 feet before widening sometimes into rooms that were impossible to measure. They were initially discovered by accident on deep wall dives and were extremely difficult to locate. Due the depths and equipment available in this era, the explorations of these mysterious tunnels were largely discontinued after a DPV failure in one push that almost killed him.

Additional Andros Blue Hole expeditions were undertaken in 1981 and in 1987 by Rod Palmer, Bill Stone and their associates. They succeeded in discovering numerous additional inland blue holes and explored them to depths of 310 fsw with the use of mixed gas and rebreathers. Their discoveries were of dramatic proportions yet they still did not achieve depths beyond those of Mount, Martz, Lockwood, Ikehara and Williams almost two decades before on compressed air.

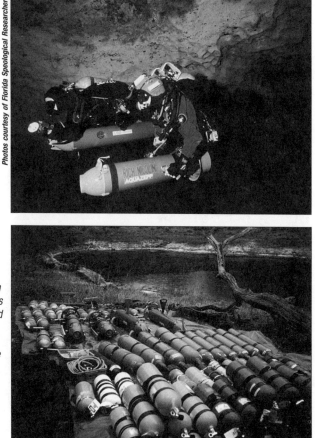

Photos courtesy of Florida Speological Researchers

Rick Nicolini and Dustin Clesi of Team Diepolder '91 made the farthest and deepest penetrations in that system to pass lines laid by Dale Sweet and Jim Lockwood almost eleven years earlier.

Almost $50,000 worth of high tech mixed gas equipment, DPV's, and surface supplied decompression gases were employed on the Diepolder push. Here multiple sets of doubles await "staging" into the cave system.

LEFT: Rob Palmer in updated MK VI rebreather during the Andros Blue Hole expeditions of 1987. BELOW: Bret Gilliam deep in one of the subterranean passages beneath St. Croix on a Farallon DPV in 1971.

Currently the fastest emerging technological advances in deep diving are coming from the cave diving fraternity. Individuals like Parker Turner (the Sullivan Connection), Wes Skiles and Bill Stone (the Wakulla project), Larry Green (recent Eagle's Nest penetrations) and Jim King with Dustin Clesi (Eagle's Nest and Die Polder II) are all on the leading edge of progress with mixed gas, DPV's and other developing equipment such as fully redundant rebreathers.

WOMEN DEEP DIVERS

In a diving niche that is already limited, there have been only a handful of women participants over the years. One of the earliest woman deep divers was Rosalia Zale Parry, who reached 209 fsw off Santa Monica, California in 1954. She enjoyed a long career in diving as an actress and stunt person in such series as Lloyd Bridges' popular hit *Sea Hunt.*

Well known scientists Dr. Eugenie Clarke and Dr. Sylvia Earle pursued research projects in depths far in excess of many men divers during the 1960's. During this same period, Zidi Goldstein and Dr. Sharee Pepper at the University of Miami were involved with open water and blue hole deep diving missions that regularly had them in 300 feet plus depths.

Zale Parry, women's depth record holder and queen of Hollywood's stunt women for diving, in 1954. She was a frequent actress on Sea Hunt and numerous movies with diving themes.

Evelyn Dudas was the first woman to dive the *Andrea Doria* wreck in 1966. Given the harsh conditions and depth of that site, her accomplishment is particularly significant.

Another trail blazer has been Mary Ellen Eckhoff, one of the top American cave divers, male or female, of the last twenty years. Since 1978, she has held all of the cave diving depth and penetration records for women in addition to sharing the record for overall penetration at Big Dismal in 1981. Her 5847 foot penetration with Sheck Exley and Clark Pitcairn was the world record that summer. She was also the fourth cave diver in the world to complete more than 1000 cave dives (Tom Mount Exley and Paul DeLoach were the first), and was the second diver in the world to dive to 400 fsw in a cave (on mixed gas). She was the first female diver to ever dive to 300 fsw in a cave and has "unofficially" equaled the women's open water record of 345 fsw on July 4, 1982 off Grand Turk Island while diving wit Exley.

Marty Dunwoody holds the officially recognized women's open water depth record of 345 fsw set December 21, 1988. She trained under Hal Watts methods and is now an active instructor with his Professional Scuba Association in Ocala, Florida. She continues a long line of Watts-trained record holders that dates back to the

Finally, the ultimate woman deep air diver has to be the late Ann Gunderson. During practice dives in working up to the 1971 record attempt in the Bahamas, she made over 40 dives below 400 fsw. Sheck Exley observed her on at least one successful drop to 440 fsw, and her dive buddy Jim Lockwood confirms that Ann made approximately 25 dives in this range. Although, Gunderson never attempted to claim the "shallower" dives in her pursuit of the world record at 480 fsw, there is no dispute to her rightful place in history. Sadly, she was lost on December 11, 1971 pursuing that record with her boyfriend, Archie Forfar. Her "unofficial record" may stand as a women's mark forever.

Dr. Ann Kristovich broke Eckhoff's cave record of 1989 and established the women's mixed gas depth record of 554 ffw on September 2, 1993 in a Mexican cave. Kristovich is part of the Zacaton project exploring one of the world's deepest cave systems. Her dive required over four hours of decompression beginning at 270 feet.

Mary Ellen Eckhoff, one of the world's premier cave explorers and co-holder of the depth record on air.

Dr. Ann Kristovich, the world's deepest woman scuba diver, reached 554 ffw in Zacaton, Mexico in 1993.

As we approach the twenty-first century, where will the historical reference be? If the past is a benchmark indicator, it will be deeper, longer and totally unexplored..

Progressive World Records for Underwater Depth

Open Water Dives

Year	Depth fsw	Gas	Location	Diver/s
1945	500	TRIMIX	Mediterranean	Arne Zetterstrom
1947	307	Air	Red Sea	Frederic Dumas
1961	350	Air	Florida	Jean Clarke Samazen
1961	730	HELIOX	Switzerland	Hannes Keller & Ken McLeish
1962	1000	HELIOX	California	Hannes Keller & Peter Small
1963	355	Air	Florida	Hal Watts
1965	360	Air	Florida	Tom Mount & Frank Martz
1967	390	Air	Florida	Hal Watts & A. J. Muns
1968	437	Air	Bahamas	Neil Watson & John Gruener
1971	440	Air	Bahamas	Ann Gunderson *
1988	345	Air	Florida	Marty Dunwoody **
1990	452	Air	Roatan	Bret Gilliam
1993	475	Air	San Salvador	Bret Gilliam
1994	490	Air	Nassau	Dan Manion ***

Cave Dives

Year	Depth ffw	Gas	Location	Diver/s
1955	210	Air	Vaucluse, France	Jacques Cousteau
1956	250	Air	Wakulla, Florida	Gary Salesman & Wally Jenkins
1965	315	Air	Devils Hole, Nevada	James Houtz
1969	335	Air	Sinoia Caves, Rhodesia	Frank Salt
1970	415	Air	Mystery Sink, Florida	Hal Watts †
1970	400	HELIOX	Mystery Sink, Florida	Hal Watts
1983	656	HELIOX	Vaucluse, France	Jochen Hasenmayer
1987	656	TRIMIX	Mante, Mexico	Sheck Exley
1988	780	TRIMIX	Mante, Mexico	Sheck Exley
1988	400	TRIMIX	Mante, Mexico	Mary Ellen Eckhoff
1993	554	TRIMIX	Zacatan, Mexico	Ann Kristovich ††
1989	881	TRIMIX	Mante, Mexico	Sheck Exley
1994	925	TRIMIX	Zacatan, Mexico	Jim Bowden †††

* Unofficial Women's Record	†	Current Men's Air Record
** Current Women's Record	††	Current Women's Record
*** Current Men's Record	†††	Current Men's Mixed Gas Record

CHAPTER 2

Physiological and Mental Preparation for Deep Diving

"How deep is DEEP?"

Michael Menduno

TYPES OF DIVING

Probably more deep diving is conducted in tropical settings on luxurious coral drop-offs than anywhere else. This is also the most "friendly" atmosphere in which to refine skills given the circumstances of clear, warm water usually blessed with excellent visibility. Typically, divers engage in multi-level excursions attaining the deepest depth for a brief time and then "stepping up" (ascending) to progressively shallower depths. It is a frequent practice for multi-day repetitive dives to be conducted in this manner, and many liveaboard divers will average 5-7 dives per day.

Diving styles vary widely and much discussion has centered on what constitutes "typical" sport diving. At land based resorts, most divers are limited to two dives per day with a possibility of a third. Liveaboards, as previously noted, tend to provide virtually unlimited diving within the constraints of either computers or tables. However, a myth of adherence to a 130 fsw limit has been perpetuated. Upon closer examination of actual logs and giving credence to the preponderance of anecdotal accounts, it becomes clear that considerable doubt must be placed upon statistics that reflect more than limited observation of recommended "limits".

Several surveys, including Gilliam's (1989-90) sampling of 77,680 sport dives, found that as many as 40% of those questioned admitted to routinely diving in excess of 130 fsw (39.4m) and as deep as 200 fsw (60.6m). In the opinion of many industry professional resort divemasters and photojournalists, the 200 fsw level is just as widely surpassed.

To examine the types of diving conducted by recreational divers, we must look at, in order of difficulty, the most common deep endeavors to the more difficult journeys.

WALL DIVING

In this type of diving, the easiest or most common, most participants use standard scuba equipment i.e. single cylinders, single BCD's, with some degree of backup/bailout system depending on depths. Rarely are multiple cylinder sets used or mixed gas systems employed. This is deep diving and equipment in its purest sense. One of the greatest lures to tropical wall diving is the relative ease of access and convenience to deep spectacular coral formations and marine life. The shallow water zones on top of the walls lend themselves perfectly to multi-level dives and provide optimal decompression "stages" (in many cases, the diver can use portions of the shallow reef for decompression stops without the discomfort of hanging on a line).

Photo by Bret Gilliam

Deep wreck divers are faced with additional considerations if penetrations are intended to the wrecks interior.

Cave divers are subjected to the most challenging deep environment including "overhead" conditions where the surface is not immediately accessible in an emergency.

Similar "excursion" type deep diving is practiced throughout the world, but most sites do not lend themselves to the easy access of vertical wall formations. Elsewhere, divers must also deal with less forgiving environments such as colder, darker water and restricted visibility.

WRECK DIVING

Next on the degree of difficulty index comes deep wreck diving. Most of this activity is regionally centered along the East coast of the United States and presents a wide variety of environmental considerations. Frequently, the Florida wreck diver enjoys warm water and good visibility, but may encounter stiff current conditions in areas washed by the Gulf Stream. At the other end of the spectrum, the Northeast wreck diver faces numerous obstacles to performance: cold water, bad visibility, swift currents and sites located as much as 100 miles (167km) from port. Additionally, all wreck divers can subject themselves to "overhead" conditions where no direct ascent to the surface is possible.

CAVE DIVING

Finally, we have the deep cave divers, long considered by many as the gatekeepers of the "lunatic fringe." In fact, cavers do face potentially hostile environmental concerns especially since their habitat of choice is almost totally an "overhead" situation. Currents and cold water can be a factor, although most sites enjoy clear water unless careless divers stir up silt rapidly reducing visibility to zero.

Deep divers are frequently exposed to cold water and prolonged decompression. Dry suits like this DUI CF-200 model and various thermal underwear are important protection.

Each type of diving has seen an evolution of preferred equipment and procedures, although many practices will see overlapping techniques. Each presents different mental and physical challenges.

We will discuss the generic considerations for deep diving and urge the reader to seek specific training from qualified sources before attempting the more demanding applications of cave and wreck divers.

PHYSICAL CONSIDERATIONS

Strangely enough, many divers fail to fully recognize the implications that external influences may play in dive planning. This is especially crucial in deep diving activities and we offer the following breakdowns:

Size/Strength:

This is primarily a consideration when the equipment package becomes sufficiently large or heavy to be a performance detriment to women or slightly built men. This is not to say that such divers need to be excluded, but the physical ability to move comfortably on the surface and in the water with heavy, cumbersome gear that may also have considerable drag characteristics, can make certain types of diving very difficult for smaller divers to handle.

Thermal Protection:

Even in tropical waters, the body will rapidly chill after prolonged exposure such as that encountered on extended stage decompression. Be sure to select a suit that will allow a sufficient comfort margin. Dry suits become a requirement for most divers once temperatures drop below 70^0 F (20.9^0 C) due to extended decompression times. Remember, cold is a contributing factor to narcosis, decompression sickness (DCS), fatigue, mental acuity and task performance, and can result in severe dexterity degradation.

Vision:

Surprisingly, many divers fail to recognize the importance of being able to see well underwater. If you wear corrective lenses on land, get a mask with a prescription-ground faceplate. If you wear contact lenses, wear them while you are diving as well. Older divers may require a bi-focal plate to allow comfortable reading of gauges and instruments. It is alarming how many accidents have occurred simply because the diver could not see properly. Divers have missed ascent or anchor lines leading them to decompression stages and some have even missed the dive boat, all due to vision deficits.

Hydration:

The importance of proper hydration has been clearly shown as a means of lessening predisposition to decompression sickness. Avoid carbonated beverages containing caffeine, coffee and alcohol before and after diving. Alcohol has a direct effect tending to shut off Anti-Diuretic Hormones (ADH) and contribute to dehydration. Fresh water and unsweetened apple juice have become the fluids of choice. They should be taken frequently and in sufficient quantity to insure clear urine when passed. If the urination cycle is below normal, you are probably already dehydrated. The old mountain climbers all religiously urinated in the snow before major climbs; dark urine color (and perhaps poor handwriting) were grounds for excluding a climber. The authors highly recommend the excellent series of articles on hydration and flying & diving by Michael Emmerman.

Rest:

This should be obvious. But the benefits of proper sleep patterns and non-stressful relaxation play significant roles in our physical performance. If you are tired or suffering from inadequate rest, your ability to deal with task loading and simple common sense decisions may be impaired. The body needs a break to "charge its batteries" and restore full function. Get a good night's sleep before any deep dives, at least eight hours. This can be difficult in some resort settings with "distractions". If necessary, modify dive start times to get fully rested. Burning the midnight oil has no place in deep diving. Avoid any sleep medications as these have been proven to have latent effects during dives in some cases.

Diet:

Practice a well balanced dietary ethic. Many deep divers have found consumption of heavy breakfasts or hard to digest foods to be a factor in narcosis susceptibility. Many consume only light fare such as toast or muffins followed by a heartier meal post-dive. Avoid orange, tomato and grapefruit juices as they will stimulate seasickness in many persons.

Fitness:

Overall physical fitness is definitely desirable. A combination of strength and aerobic exercise is recommended along with a regimen of regular swimming and swimming with fins. Diving is a demanding physical test of endurance in many cases. You should be in sufficient shape to handle surface swims, rescue situations, the underwater demands placed upon your body to perform against current, equipment drag/breathing resistance and the myriad unseen contingencies that can and will ultimately present.

Alcohol/Smoking/Drugs:

How many nails do you want in your coffin? Choose your weapons... Each of these influences various performance functions from decreasing your reactive and reasoning ability to inhibiting gas exchange in the lungs. Suffice it to say that none of the aforementioned will do anything but make your body less efficient. Some studies suggest enormous potential hazards when combined with the effects of pressure.

History:

Any injury that could contribute to poor circulation such as scar tissue, burns or prior surgery should be regarded as a potential DCS problem and will call for a more conservative decompression schedule. Divers with past histories of decompression sickness (DCS) or arterial gas embolism (AGE) should be cleared by a diving physician before resuming dive activity. Diving doctors will be familiar with the precise parameters and current thinking on guidelines for return to diving. Evaluation of a lung injury or categorizing a Type I or Type II DCS hit will normally be beyond the scope of traditional general practice medical professionals.

Free-diving:

Breath-hold diving has virtually developed into a lost skill in the majority of today's divers. But this is one of the best conditioning exercises known. It promotes proper weighting, breath control, economy of exertion and overall "control", both mental and physical. Such expert deep divers as Tom Mount, Rick Freshee, Bret Gilliam and Billy Deans are all accomplished free divers.

MENTAL CONSIDERATIONS

Herein lies hardest part of screening candidates for deep diving since no objective testing has really been established. The reader should note that he is not only covering this chapter as a guide to self-evaluation, but

Many divers are not comfortable in confined spaces and should avoid them while diving. This inviting wreck may tend to provoke panic in a claustrophobic if suddenly presented with an unanticipated stressful scenario.

Photo by Bret Gilliam

for his intended diving companion as well. Rigorous, demanding training programs are conducted by the U.S. Navy and commercial diving operations with the specific goal of "washing out" unsuitable individuals. No such controls exist within the sport diving community or instructor evaluation programs. If anything, the screening of sport divers and instructors has become less exacting as the industry attempts to broaden its market appeal.

For our purposes, this text is directed at advanced divers, hopefully with sufficient experience (**100 plus dives, in various environments and conditions**) to have mastered the entry level anxieties of dealing with strange equipment, unfamiliar environments and the usual chaos associated with the learning process in recreational divers. Divers should be completely comfortable with equipment handling including assembly, gearing up on a rocking boat or in the water if necessary. The elements of buoyancy control should be routine along with contingency drills for out of air scenarios and other emergencies.

We want to be prudent in identifying and screening candidates with any of the following behavior patterns:

The Panic-Prone Individual:

One must be at home and comfortable in the water. The most common cause of death in divers is panic and inability to deal with stressful situations underwater. Evidence of high anxiety or past "anxiety attacks" should target a prospective diver as unsuitable. This syndrome includes fainting, hyperventilation, claustrophobic tendencies, etc. Close and confined spaces are easily encountered in cave and wreck diving; if such situations cause undue anxiety they should be avoided. Divers should be comfortable with direct facial immersion in water. Many well-experienced divers have proven susceptible to rapidly progressive panic when deprived of their mask. Please refer to Chapter 3 for a more complete discussion of panic and its manifestations.

The Counterphobe:

This individual may possess a deep-seated fear of the water and keep such phobias well hidden from others. Diving may be an avenue of hopefully overcoming these fears. This attempt at boosting self-confidence may be well-intended but lead to tragic consequences in a true emergency at depth. This syndrome is nearly impossible to identify in advance with any degree of accuracy.

The "Dragooned", Reluctant Diver:

Do not let yourself or anyone else be "finessed" into diving activities that you or they are uncomfortable with. The motivation to participate has to be genuine and not the product of coercion or peer pressure. Likewise, motivation to dive that can be identified as an effort to please a spouse or close friend rather than for the individual's pleasure or satisfaction must preclude involvement in deep diving. If any doubt arises as to the diver's willingness to participate, question him or her privately to determine their true state of mind.

The Buccaneer/Top Gun Candidate:

Typically self-centered, impetuous, cocky and headstrong. Incapable of following directions. Sometimes difficult to separate from a confident, qualified diver that is highly motivated but lacks patience with others less skilled. The former cannot be relied on due to typical selfish diving practices and general disregard for accepted diving plans. Avoid them!

Psychotic Disorders:

Totally a crapshoot here... but a few latent suicidal types do appear from time to time. Beware the diver signing up for the deep wreck dive trip to Truk Lagoon... who didn't buy a round-trip airline ticket.

Ideally, we are looking for divers with maturity (not a function of age, incidentally), intelligence, self-control, common sense and confidence. Our candidate should understand the importance of overlearning skills and procedures, reflex response conditioning and a finely-honed ability to deal with stress.

Mentally, our diver will be logical and motivated to excellence in every phase of dive planning and execution. The diver must be at ease with the situation and anticipate in advance every reasonable contingency. Ultimately, deep diving is more a mental discipline than a physical one. Mount (1979) has suggested an ideal balance to be 60% common sense (mental) and 40% physical ability for overall diving skills, and this applies well for advanced deep diving.

CHAPTER 3

Stress

*I don't want to participate in any sport
in which my species is not at the top of the food chain.*

Ken Fonte

*Stress in diving is probably the central problem
in the accidents and resulting injuries and fatalities
that occur to divers . . .*

Art Bachrach and Glen Egstrom

STRESS

Many divers do not seem to place traditional activities in the context of stress-inducing scenarios. Diving is supposed to be fun, right? The following passage is excerpted from Bachrach and Egstrom's (1987) Stress and Performance in Diving:

> "We will cover your nose and eyes with a rubber and glass cup that will give you tunnel vision and prevent breathing through your nose. A snorkel which is partially filled with water will increase breathing resistance, especially when you work harder. A rubber suit will increase your surface area and your buoyancy while creating a restriction over each of the body's joints. (A partial adjustment will be made by fastening 15-20 pounds (6.8-9.1 kg) of lead to your waist.) Fins for your feet will make walking more difficult and require more energy when swimming. A buoyancy compensation device will pro-

vide additional drag, especially when it is inflated to increase your buoyancy. Approximately 40-50 pounds (18.2-22.7 kg) of steel or aluminum will be fixed between your shoulder blades by means of a backpack with a series of straps and buckles, which will terminate somewhere under the buoyancy compensator near the weight belt buckle. A regulator with various and sundry hoses and gauges will be attached to the tank and will cause you to breathe against an added resistance both during inhalation and exhalation. Various other items, such as knives, gauges, goody bags, cameras, spear guns, gloves, hoods and booties will be added for your comfort and convenience."

These learned authors (by this humorous accounting) have accurately placed into perspective the realities of the stressful environment that scuba divers willingly subject themselves to. By necessity our sport is equipment intensive and simply donning that equipment can produce levels of stress far in excess of what the average person may be comfortable with. Indeed, divers have been observed to reach heart rates approaching 200 beats per minute, nearly 3.5 times the normal rate, just gearing up!

Deep diving not only subjects the participants to added stress but the deeper environment also makes coping with such performance detriments critical. In our discussions we are most concerned with recognizing the early effects of stress and dealing with the effective management of these stimuli underwater.

Stress is variously defined: McGrath (1970) describes it as "a result of an imbalance between the demands placed upon an individual and the capacity of the individual to respond to the demands." Sells (1970) states "for a situation to be stressful the individual must perceive the consequences of his failure to be important." These two views provide perspectives from both the physical and mental effects and clearly shows the potential for compound stress stimuli to be at work simultaneously in the diver. Smith (1979) provides a succinct overview, "in the context of human behavior, stress might be regarded as a force that tends to break down an individual's ability to perform. Physical stress tends to weaken or injure the diver; psychological stress leads to behavior impairment."

The role of stress in deep diving applications cannot be ignored. Typical reactions to stress include such signs as rapid breathing or hyperventilation, the consequence of which should be immediately apparent to our readers. Importantly, stress is so varied to individuals that even what may be considered a "routine" problem can be highly stressful in some divers. Bachrach and Egstrom (1987) describe stress as "basically learned" and this perception is learned through "modeling" behavior. If your mother was afraid of reptiles, this phobia may well be passed along to you subconsciously. Likewise, much of the public has an inherent dread or horror of sharks or moray eels with no actual experience to justify such fear. Experienced resort guides think nothing of handfeeding eels or swimming with sharks but to the uninitiated the mere appearance of such a creature can rapidly induce stress reactions that can lead to near panic.

We all probably have a few skeletons rattling around in our mental closets, some that we may not have even a vague recognition of. Well experienced divers have reported extreme anxiety in their first encounter with "silting- out" situations in caves or wrecks. Willful control of this stress anxiety through discipline and fall-back on training can prevent escalation to a threat scenario.

SOURCES OF STRESS

Photo by Bret Gilliam

"**Time pressure**" is a classic method used by psychologists to alter experimental testing and induce error by test subjects. Problems that are easily accomplished become increasingly difficult and sometimes impossible if the element of time is introduced as an opponent. Diving, especially deep diving, is time dependent: we only have so much allotment due to constraints of decompression and/ or gas supply.

This emphasizes the importance of dive planning so that orderly progression of the dive is maintained within the dive envelope calculated. De-

Exploration of confined passages in wrecks or caves can be a potential source of stress to some people with phobias about dark or confined spaces.

The energy necessary to manage unwieldy and heavy gear on a bouncing dive boat can result in equipment induced stress.

viations from the plan can cause rapid acceleration of time pressure stress inducements. This is true not only for the dive itself but for pre-dive activities such as gearing up. Do not allow yourself to be hurried into mistakes. How many times have you observed divers entering the water without a mask or without fins? Simply putting the gear on an empty cylinder without checking its pressure happens too often.

"Task loading" is another factor well known to produce errors in performance. Simple enough: give the diver more projects (tasks) to do than he reasonably can accomplish in the time period allotted. Or give him competitive, multiple jobs that require him to do two or more things at the same time. Divers are already burdened with monitoring gauges, keeping track of their position underwater (pure navigation and also depth trim), noting the performance of a buddy, etc. Add to this equation an underwater camera system or duties requiring written observations and we have a fairly well "task loaded" diver before any contingencies may arise. And let's remember that all this activity is being attempted in water deep enough to have effects from narcosis and gas density for breathing purposes.

Environmental considerations such as current, cold water or reduced visibility will all contribute to stress loading. Further, physical exertion to deal with such environmental detriments *and* any normal exertion on the dive will lead to compounding of stress factors.

Equipment alone can be a primary source of stress inducement simply due to its bulk, weight, drag etc. Take note of the experienced diver whose gear is streamlined and well organized. This individual will be wearing a BCD selected for its suitability for the dive situation. Tropical wall diving in warm water is far more easily accomplished with a light wet suit (2mm) or dive skin with a neoprene vest. Combining this with the newer editions of BCD's that feature less volume, form fitting styles and a full-foot power fin eliminates the needless bulk of heavier wet suits, booties etc. Gauges conveniently mounted in a single console with a dive computer provide easy viewing and no distractions of arm or wrist attached devices. Combining the "octopus" second stage into one of the inflator/second stages such as SCUBAPRO's AIR II or SEAQUEST's AIR SOURCE further streamlines the diver. A lightweight belt sized for neutral buoyancy at low tank pressures (to facilitate safety and/or decom stops) completes the package.

Obviously, this equipment package must be modified as we deal with cold water, cave or wreck situations but the emphasis on effective management of equipment should be obvious. Consider the equipment stress of the diver outfitted for deep water mixed gas wreck diving: we see him in a dry suit, dual 120 cu. ft. cylinders, redundant regulators and gauges, redundant BCD's and inflators, heavy weight belt, lift bags, decompression reels, and, in many cases, stage bottles of NITROX and O_2 clipped to his rig. This individual may well have in excess of 200 pounds (91 kg) of equipment strapped to him.

All this adds up to a diver who is heavily predisposed to performance- limiting detriments before he ever leaves the surface. Indeed, as mentioned in the previous chapter, this individual may already have exceeded his physical limits to safely conduct a dive simply due to the equipment load he has strapped on. Is this a comfortable, relaxed diver? Maybe... but add a rough sea and a pitching boat with a violently surging swim platform or ladder, and unless this diver is a superior physical specimen it will be a major stress loading activity to deal with the equipment and get into the water safely.

This leads into the current debate about what equipment is necessary for deep diving. The authors *do* have some concerns about recent trends that exhibit a fascination for equipment-intensive outfitting far in excess of the practical requirements of the dive. At some plateau, the point of diminishing returns is reached: is carrying 300 cu. ft. of gas effective if the performance detriment by the sheer weight/size/drag of such gear requires the additional gas supply? Gilliam (1990) deliberately chose a single cylinder (100 cu. ft.) and regulator package to lesson his equipment load on his record 452 fsw (137 m) AIR dive. With proper breathing techniques etc. he was able to comfortably complete the dive on this reduced rig. He relates, "some would argue that redundancy is a requirement at such extreme depths but with DIN fittings I was not concerned with a regulator failure at the valve. Therefore, the physical stress and distraction of extra equipment to me was not justified. I wanted to carry enough gas with me to do the dive, obviously, but the single 100 provided that for me and I was far more comfortable in the water."

Logically, deep divers must carry the gas volumes necessary to do the dive plan with an adequate safety margin. Extended decompression in colder water will dictate larger gas storage carried by the diver but we caution our readers to carefully weigh the equipment stress load with operational requirements of the dive site. There will always be debate on what equipment *is* necessary but a perspective on what is realistically matched to the dive plan must be encouraged.

An experienced diver dresses for the occasion as it were. A tuxedo is not required for a backyard barbecue. Veteran divers who have access to the most advanced "technical gear" will not hesitate to simplify a gear set when conditions allow. Gilliam's record dive to 452 feet was focused on a specific goal and was of limited duration. In such extreme depths on AIR he balanced his gas volume needs based upon vast experience against his performance ideals dictated by a stripped down and low-drag configuration gear set. In contrast, Sheck Exley's record mixed gas dive to 881 feet had totally different requirements due to cold water, multiple gas switches, extreme depth and drastically extended decompression time. Both dives were extremely hazardous and conducted solo, but both were successful, in part, by balancing equipment packages to the precise operational need.

Mitch Skaggs demonstrates a well-balanced and efficient equipment package at 175 on the wreck of the Hydo-Atlantic in Florida.

Divers should be aware in intimate detail of their personal gas consumption rates at a range of depths and dive situations. Likewise, a consideration of their thermal comfort and suit needs must be plugged into the equipment equation. For Caribbean divers conducting multi-level drop-off wall excursions to depths up to 200 fsw, a single BCD is probably adequate with an oversized single cylinder and a regulator with DIN fittings. Some would like the redundancy of a Y-valve for regulator backup. Fine... we are still dealing with a manageable gear package. The same dive conducted on northeast wreck will obviously call for an expanded gear set including doubles, dry suits etc. But let's always keep in mind the common sense rule of equipment stress: Match your gear set to your operation.

Ego threat stress is significant as well in our dive planning. Smith (1979) notes, "An individual can be effectively destroyed by tearing down self-esteem, pride or ego. . ." The overextension of capabilities by personal challenge or peer group pressure is a leading contributory factor to deep diving accidents. Individuals must seek at all times to do dives within their own limitations. Gentile (1988) relates the case of an experienced northeast coast wreck diver who elected to sit out the last dive of the day as conditions worsened. Unconcerned by any supposed negative peer reactions, Gentile praises this individual for his good judgment in knowing when to quit.

We must not let perceived ego threats intrude on our good judgment. Divers should not encourage others to participate in deep diving activities with which they are uncomfortable. The emotionally mature diver can abstain from diving in any situation with no attendant ego damage. Smith (1979) puts it best: "The truly mature person can do this even when others may extend themselves further into the situation because of either their superior ability or their own foolishness. The threat to one's ego when one must back away from a challenge can be quite stressful, and tolerance to this stress is important in diving. . . A diver who is incompetent and knows it may be stressful. An incompetent diver may also be stressful to other divers who know about the incompetency. A diver may even stress companions into death by threatening their ego through constantly challenging them to test their limits to save their pride."

EFFECTS OF STRESS

Even a passing review of the material will demonstrate that sources of stress are varied and quite probably unlimited. Now we shall briefly look at the behavioral mechanics of stress and the resulting mental narrowing. As we heap stress loads on our diver he becomes less sensitive to his environment and less able to intelligently focus on problems. These interferences with mental thought processes manifest in several classic ways:

"Perceptual narrowing" whereby the diver is unable to notice or deal with subtle developing aspects of a situation and perceives only the grossest or more obvious elements of a problem. At depth, the effects of such narrowing are more serious. A diver who finds himself unable to maintain neutral buoyancy and continues to fixate on depressing the inflate button of his BCD to no avail has lost the intellectual ability to perceive another solution to his problem.

"Cognitive or analytical narrowing" whereby the diver is hampered in his ability to analyze a problem. Example: a diver barely reaches his decompression stage bottle because he was low on air. As he begins his 20 foot (6.1m) stop, he has trouble breathing but the indicated pressure is 2500 psi. Under sufficient stress he may not realize

Simply the act of going deeper without proper experience can be a source of stress to the untrained diver. Do not attempt dives to depths beyond your capability.

Watch for signs of stress such as "contact maintenance" when a diver will not let go of the safety line at the surface.

that the valve is not open all the way or that switching to the "octopus" would solve the problem.

"Response narrowing" occurs when the diver is unable to focus skills and knowledge upon problems. This typically manifests with loss of poorly learned skills or behavior. Overlearned, reflex action type skills are retained longest. The obvious importance of drills and skill repetition until reactions to certain situations are second nature cannot be overemphasized.

"Panic" is usually described as unreasoning fear, the ultimate plateau of mental narrowing. Smith (1979), "As stress increases, the diver's ability to diagnose and respond to them properly may diminish accordingly. In any stressful situation, it is critical for the individual to break out of this escalating cycle as quickly as possible.... early detection is important. Thus, it is desirable to recognize the early symptoms of stress in your own behavior and in the behavior of others before these symptoms reach panic proportions. Panic is the end of the line. It is usually terminal and contagious."

Signs of Stress

- Rapid breathing, hyperventilation
- "Wild-eyed" look
- White-knuckle gripping; muscle tension
- Rapid, jerky, disjointed movements
- Irritability, unreasonableness
- Fixation, repetitive behavior
- High treading, attempts to leave the water
- "Escape to the surface" behavior
- Stalling – taking too long to suit-up
- Imaginary gear problems or ear problems
- Contact maintenance (e.g. clutching swim ladder, anchor line)

SUMMARY

The anticipation of problem situations in a dive and the ability to adopt contingency plans calmly and rationally are vital in deep diving. Experience plays a great role in the individual's ability to deal with stress and to formulate alternative reactions to threat scenarios presented. Overlearning of all relevant skills and complete familiarization with equipment is necessary. If overlearning can be taken to its highest level, then much of the reactive behavior in an emergency will be reflexive and not require conscious thought processes. Smith (1979) notes, "Overlearning takes all doubt out of human performance under stress as far as that particular skill is concerned. This not only greatly reduces the probability of human error on certain tasks but also frees the diver's mind to deal confidently with more complex aspects of the problem."

Stress accompanies us everywhere and is magnified in deep diving activities. Know yourself, know your buddy and/or your diving team. Dive within your limits.

CHAPTER 4

Nitrogen Narcosis

"It was hard to admit at the time, but my first face-slamming
experience with narcosis occurred at just 160 feet.
I was crushed; demoralized. Eventually, after about 20 dives,
I had worked my way past 200 feet. I was finally the victor;
I had beaten narcosis, or so I thought . . ."

Wes Skiles

Within the context of air diving, the effects of inert gas narcosis are second only to acute CNS oxygen toxicity in hazard to the scuba diver. Commonly known as "nitrogen narcosis", this condition is first described by Junod in 1835 when he discovered divers breathing compressed air: "The functions of the brain are activated, imagination is lively, thoughts have a peculiar charm and in some persons, symptoms of intoxication are present." Early caisson workers were occasional victims of befuddlement on otherwise simple tasks and some were reported to spontaneously burst into singing popular songs of that period. Much of the mysteries of compressed air impairment remained speculative until Benke zeroed in on elevated partial pressures of nitrogen as the culprit. His observations were reported in 1935 and depicted narcosis as "euphoric retardation of the higher mental processes and impaired neuromuscular coordination".

Other studies confirmed this phenomena and U.S. Navy divers reported narcosis a major factor in the salvage efforts on the sunken submarine Squalus in 1939. Working in depths of 240 fsw (72.7 m) in cold water, these divers reported loss of clear thought and reasoning. Several unusual entanglement scenarios resulted and in the normal work process at least one diver was reported to unexpectedly lose consciousness underwater on the wreck. Because of this, the Navy switched to then experimental HELIOX mixtures marking the first major project with this gas. Bennett (1966) first related narcosis to the Greek word "nark", meaning numbness. The Greeks used this in association with the human reactive process to opium which produces drowsiness, stupefaction and a general feeling of well being and lassitude.

At any rate, the best explanation appears to be the Meyer-Overton hypothesis relating the narcotic effect of an inert gas to its solubility in the lipid phase or fat. This is postulated to act as a depressant to the nervous system proportional to the gas amount going into solution. Mount (1979) has expressed the narcotic effect as determined by multiplying the solubility by the partition coefficient. By examining tables of various inert gases compared by solubility and partition coefficient it becomes abundantly clear that nitrogen is one of the least desirable gases in a breathing mixture for divers at depth. The relative narcotic potency is expressed as a number value with the highest number reflecting the least narcotic effect. Argon is extremely narcotic with a value of .43, nitrogen is rated at 1.0 with helium one of the least narcotic at 4.26.

As experienced divers more frequently dive to deeper depths in pursuit of wreck, cave exploration and photographic interests, the subject of inert gas narcosis becomes more ardently debated. Much discussion of narcosis theory among scuba divers has been conducted "underground" by a close-knit community of "high-tech" professional divers without a public forum of information exchange. Narcosis was regarded as an occupational hazard that had to be dealt with in order to gain access to new cave systems, more remote wrecks or the most spectacular drop-off walls.

Due to the controversial nature of deep diving within the traditional sport diving industry, an understandable reluctance to discuss actual diving practices was perpetuated. Little actual "field work" was published and a word of mouth grapevine developed to compare different diving techniques in widely diverse areas. In the late sixties and early seventies three distinctly different segments of emerging "technical" diving were conducting deep air dives. On the cave diving scene indi-

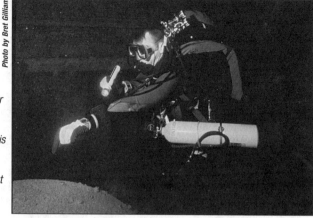

Make sure your instruments are easy to read at depth under the influence of narcosis. Here Norm Brinsley illuminates his wrist mounted computer to check dive status at 210 feet on the wreck of the Lowrance.

viduals such as Sheck Exley, Tom Mount, Frank Martz, Jim Lockwood and Dr. George Benjamin pushed ever deeper with their explorations, while Bahamian and Caribbean groups led by Neil Watson and Bret Gilliam pushed beyond the 400 fsw (121.2 m) barrier for the first time in open water. Simultaneously, a whole new wreck diving cult with Peter Gimble, Gary Gentile, Hank Keatts and Steve Bielenda was coming out of the shadows in the northeast to assault previously unreachable sites such as the *Andrea Doria*.

Published accounts of narcosis experiences were largely limited to cave diving newsletters although Gilliam presented a quasi "how-to" paper on deep air methods in 1974. This presentation at the International Conference on Underwater Education in San Diego stimulated some limited exchange of information between the diverse communities but also focused criticism from national training agencies, etc. The "underground" once again retreated from the harsh glare of sport diver scrutiny and new breakthroughs and techniques reverted to word of mouth communiqués. As veteran deep wreck explorer Gary Gentile put it, "you can always tell a pioneer by the arrows in his back!"

In 1990 for the first time, the "technical diver" began to come out of the closet and stay a while, and in-depth discussions of narcosis went public.

Some of the earlier accounts by Cousteau (1947) relate instances of near total incapacitation at depths of only 150 fsw (45.5 m) and cite the supposed "Martini's Law" and the classic broad generalization of "Rapture of the Deep". In reality, the severity of impairment is drastically reduced in well equipped and experienced/adapted divers at greater

Factors contributing to narcosis onset and severity include:

- Increased partial pressures of CO_2 (hard work, heavy swimming, etc.)
- Cold
- Alcohol use or "hangover" conditions
- Drugs
- Fatigue
- Anxiety or apprehension, FEAR
- Effects of motion sickness medications
- Rate of descent (speed of compression)
- Vertigo or spatial disorientation caused by no 'UP' reference such as in bottomless clear "blue water" or in severely restricted visibility
- Task loading stress
- Time pressure stress
- Another lesser known contributory factor is increased oxygen partial pressure

depth. Narcosis is certainly a factor to be dealt with responsibly by divers, but many texts suggest levels of impairment that are far exaggerated for seasoned practitioners.

Today's diver has the advantage of high-tech scuba gear that can markedly increase his performance. Design evolutions in buoyancy compensating devices (BCD's), scuba regulators, instrumentation, less restrictive and more efficient thermal suits etc., all contribute to his ability to work deeper safely.

The authors would like to emphasize that deep air diving below 220 fsw (60.6 m) is generally not recommended given the alternatives available in today's industry. On high risk or particularly demanding dive scenarios this depth should be adjusted shallower. Many veteran air divers now opt for mixed gas to virtually eliminate narcosis problems. What is the cutoff depth on air? This is clearly subjective and must be answered by the individual diver who considers his own narcosis susceptibility, his objective and his access and financial commitment to mixed gas equipment.

TABLE 4-1

Relative Narcotic Potencies

Helium (He)	4.26	*(least narcotic)*
Neon (Ne)	3.58	
Hydrogen (H_2)	1.83	
Nitrogen (N_2)	1.00	
Argon (A)	0.43	
Krypton (Kr)	0.14	
Xenon (Xe)	0.039	*(most narcotic)*

Photo by Bret Gilliam

Buddy teams need to be more aware of each other on deep dives. Get used to looking for overt symptoms of narcosis and monitor your partner's instruments during phases of the dive. Don't hesitate to abort your dive plan if you feel unduly affected. Lynn Hendrickson and Scott Lockwood on Caribbean deep wreck.

Wes Skiles (1990), a highly experienced and respected cave diver, has expressed his preference for mixed gas on any penetrations below 130 fsw (39.4 m). Members of the scientific diving community still practice air dives to 190 fsw (57.6 m) officially (with far deeper dives reported "unofficially"). Gentile, Mount and Gilliam suggest practical air limits of between 250 and 275 fsw (75.7 and 83.3 m) for trained individuals, but it must be clearly understood that such depths place the diver outside the recommended working limits for oxygen exposures. Mixed gas solves some problems for some people, but it adds several new problems and operational considerations to the equation: expense, extended decompression time etc. For many experienced air practitioners, deep air diving remains a viable choice simply because done with the proper disciplines and training it is a reasonable exercise. That is to say it can be approached with an acceptable level of risk. But new divers venturing beyond traditional sport limits must be fully cognizant of the elements of risk, that deep diving will reduce the margin for error, and the accompanying increased chance for injury or death must be understood. Diving within one's limitations should be etched firmly in the deep diver's memory. Depths below 130 fsw (39.4 m) can be safely explored but such diving cannot be taken lightly.

ADAPTATION

Narcosis can be controlled to varying degrees specific to individuals but tolerances can change from day to day. Almost any experienced deep diver will tell you that "adaptation" to narcosis takes place. Bennett (1990) notes, "the novice diver may expect to be relatively seriously effected by nitrogen narcosis, but subjectively at least there will be improvement with experience. Frequency of exposure does seem to result in some level of adaptation." The actual mechanics of adaptation are not clearly understood or proven but most deep divers agree that they will perform better with repeated progressively deeper penetrations on a cumulative basis.

Gilliam (1990) relates no significant impairment at 452 fsw (137 m) for his brief exposure, approximately 4.5 minutes in the critical zone below 300 fsw (91 m). He was able to successfully complete a series of higher math and thought/reasoning problems while suspended at the deepest level. But this is probably the extreme end of adaptation; he dived every week for over a year with never more than a six day layoff. His 627 dives during this period included 103 below 300 fsw (91 m).

Particular attention needs to be paid to buoyancy control and awareness of surroundings when diving deep. This wreck penetration can be conducted using available light techniques but strict observation of depth, time and "no silt" dive behavior is necessary.

For the diver who regularly faces deep exposures, a tolerance far in excess of the un-adapted diver will be exhibited. A gradual work-up to increasing depths is the best recommendation. (This should not be mis-construed as an endorsement of "reverse profile dives". We refer to making each first dive of the day progressively deeper than the day before to build tolerances, i.e., Day 1: first dive to 150 fsw, Day 2: first dive to 175 fsw, etc. Subsequent dives on Day 1 and Day 2 would be shallower than the first.) This process should be over several day's time if the diver has been away from deep diving for more than two weeks. Adaptation appears to be lost exponentially as acquired so no immediate increased narcosis susceptibility will necessarily be evident but divers are cautioned to exercise great conservatism if any layoff is necessitated.

THE DIVING REFLEX

Back in the mid-1800's Paul Bert observed pronounced brachycardia (lowered heartbeat) in ducks while diving. Suk Ki Hong (1990) describes "a reflex phenomenon that is accompanied by an intense peripheral vasoconstriction, a drastic reduction in the cardiac output, and a significant reduction of O_2 consumption". Hickey and Lundgren (1984) further noted aspects of the mammalian diving reflex to include "muscular relaxation, astonishing levels of brachycardia, e.g., heart rates 13% of pre-dive levels in harbor seals... and depressed metabolism. All of these adaptations conserve the body's energy stores." Simply put, this reflex serves to apparently slow down most vital, internal functions such as heartbeat and shunt blood from the extremities enabling the diving seal or dolphin to more effectively utilize it's single breath oxygen load while underwater.

Similar responses have been noted in human subjects. Several divers stumbled onto this in the late sixties and began to effectively incorporate facial immersion breathing periods prior to diving. Exley and Watson practiced such techniques and Gilliam became a leading proponent of surface and ten fsw (3.03 m) level extended breathing with his diving mask and hood removed before dives below 300 fsw (91 m) in 1971. He has recorded dramatic reductions in his heart rate and respiration rate by following a protocol of ten minutes facial immersion breathing at the surface, then five minutes at ten to fifteen fsw (3.03 to 4.5 m) from a pony bottle. His pulse has been measured at twelve to fifteen beats per minute and respiration rate dropped to two a minute at deep depths (dive to 405 fsw/122.7 m in 1977). Other divers have adopted varying uses of the diving reflex technique in conjunction with meditation disciplines with significant success. Of the divers using this technique, many report pronounced reduction of narcosis, reduced air consumption and better coordination at depth. Regardless of the scientific proof challenges, the technique is becoming more widespread and its subjective benefits certainly bear closer scrutiny.

EQUIPMENT

At depth the air we breathe has far greater density and can be an operational problem if the scuba regulator is not carefully selected to comfortably deliver adequate volumes upon demand. Breathing resistance can markedly increase onset and progression of narcosis. Many so-called "professional" regulator models will fall sadly short on performance below 200 fsw (60.6 m).

Exhalation resistance is a prime factor in breathing control, perhaps more so than inhalation ease. Studies have shown exhalation detriments to be the most significant fatigue element in underwater breathing tests. So how do you choose between the dozens of models offered? Some benchmark can be derived from perusal of U.S. Navy test reports but sometimes results can offer inconclusive appraisals. The Tekna 2100 series unit basically failed the Navy tests for high performance but has been a popular regulator with many experienced deep divers since its introduction. Gilliam (1990) used it on his record setting 452 fsw (137 m) dive in Roatan and reported complete satisfaction.

Now is a good time to ensure that you select comparable quality instruments compatible with the depths you anticipate exploring. Keep in mind that many depth gauges and dive computers have depth limitations that will render them useless over normal sport diving ranges. Make certain that the information is displayed in an easily understood format. If you have a hard time deciphering what you are looking at on the surface, imagine the problem at 250 fsw (75.8 m) under the influence of narcosis.

Depth gauges should have large faces and well graduated depth increments so they can be read precisely. Many divers report digital gauges as found in computer models to be far easier to read at depth.

ON THE DIVE

Wreck and drop-off wall divers should use descents undertaken with a negative glide to the desired operational depth and BCD used to quickly attain neutral buoyancy. Do not waste energy using leg kicking to maintain position in the water column. Slow, deep ventilations with minimal exertions will keep CO_2 down and reduces onset and severity of narcosis. Narcosis has been reported subjectively to be most strong when first arriving at depth. Allow yourself a stop-activity period to monitor your instruments and let the initial narcosis effects stabilize.

Diving deep properly is more a mental exercise than a physical one. The diver must constantly be aware of his own limitations to narcosis and not hesitate to abort a dive if impairment becomes unreasonable. If narcosis is severe on descent, slow the rate or stop completely until symptoms are controlled. If possible face an "up" reference at all times such as anchor line or face the drop-off to orient the wall perpendicularly to the surface. This affords more accurate references if you are sinking or rising. If necessary, hold on to the descent line or a drop-off wall outcropping to insure of control of depth while narcosis can be evaluated.

SYMPTOMS

In spite of the warnings of various academicians, it is unlikely that the diver will experience "rapture" or the uncontrollable desire to kiss a fish or dance with an imaginary mermaid. However, there is a wide range of individual susceptibility. Almost all divers will be impaired eventually. This will manifest in many ways.

Most divers are acquainted with traditional depictions of narcosis symptomatology (light-headedness, slowed reflexes, euphoria, poor judgment, even numbness, etc.). But many early symptoms are more subtle. Initially divers will notice, in many cases, a reduced ability to read fine graduations in a depth gauge or watch along with increased awareness of sensitivity to sound such as exhalation and inhalation noise. Perceptual narrowing may limit some divers to successful execution of only limited task loading. Short term memory loss and perceptions of time can be affected. With experience, divers can learn to control these deficits to some extent. But these very real dangers cannot be underestimated. A diver unaware of his depth, bottom time or remaining air volume is about to become a statistic!

Buddy teams need to be more aware of each other in deep dives. Just as frequent scanning of instruments is mandated so is confirmation of your buddy's status. Generally, you should look for him about every three breaths and observe him for any overt signs of impairment. Quick containment of a problem situation in its development is vital to prevent a stressful rescue event that may be difficult to perform at depth.

Gilliam (1972) offered an effective narcosis check between divers. "We were frequently diving very deep with long working bottom times on this contract in the Virgin Islands. I had a secret dread of one of our team's divers being overcome without our immediate knowledge. So I came up with a childishly simple hand signal response exercise for use at depth to detect narcosis. If one diver flashed a one-finger signal to another diver, it was expected that the diver would answer with a two-finger signal.

A two-fingered signal was answered with three-fingers; if you really wanted to screw a guy up you gave him all five fingers and then he had to use two hands to come up with a six-finger response. We reasoned that if a diver was not able to respond quickly and correctly to the signal given, then sufficient impairment was presumed to abort his dive. It worked great for us then and I still use it today." Over the years, scores of divers have reported using Gilliam's narcosis signals with success.

Although narcosis effects are generally eliminated by ascent, it is important to understand that many divers will experience some degree of amnesia in their performance at depth. Commercial divers have reported successful completion of a work project to the diving supervisor upon ascent, only to learn later that the objective was not completed at all! Less experienced deep divers will typically not remember their greatest depth or bottom time unless disciplined to record it on a slate prior to ascent.

Again, the experienced deep diver will sharply focus on his job objectives and constantly monitor his instruments. Modern devices such as dive computers greatly improve safety controls with maximum depth and time memories as well as decompression planning models.

DEEP WATER BLACKOUT

An advanced stage of narcosis was first described by Exley in 1971 in which the affected diver simply "went to sleep at depth". Gilliam (1972) also performed a rescue below 300 fsw when he observed his partner drifting way unconscious in what he thought was the aftermath of an oxygen seizure. The diver revived during the ascent with no memory of his experience. During the double fatality of Farfar and Gunderson in 1971, the surviving member of the dive team, Jim Lockwood, succumbed to blackout during the descent and has speculated that Farfar saved him by inflating his BC. Exley made an attempt to save the deceased pair but aborted his rescue somewhere below 400 fsw when he felt himself "passing out". It was not until the mid-1980's that other accounts were documented and the term "deep water blackout" was assigned to this phenomena. Although most described incidents were quite deep (in excess of 300 fsw), more recent cases have manifested in alarmingly shallow depths by comparison.

In 1994 while conducting a deep diving class off Miami, instructor Mitch Skaggs had a student abruptly go unconscious at approximately 190 fsw with no prior warning of any narcosis symptoms or observable impairment. Skaggs was able to replace the diver's regulator and control his ascent where he recovered. His diving was curtailed with a firm recommendation that deep diving below 150 fsw be discontinued completely.

Several deep diving experts have long suggested that a physiological "wall" is met with regards to narcosis impairment that is definable by individuals and the observations of others in their dive teams. That "wall" would appear to be absolute with some variable margins and should not be exceeded. Some divers are capable of recognizing their own impairment while others have to be convinced of their slow reactions, clumsy swim patterns, unresponsiveness to signal or communications etc. by buddies. There is little room for error in deeper depths and every effort should be made to identify personal limits and provide adequate safety factors by limiting exposures to lesser depths. The unpredictability of "deep water blackout" is so potentially dangerous that anyone venturing beyond depths in which their experience is well established should only do so under the direct supervision of a professional technical instructor.

THE MOUNT-MILNER TEST

In 1965 a research project was conducted by professional diver Tom Mount and psychiatrist Dr. Gilbert Milner to determine the effects of anticipated behavior modeling in diving students with respect to narcosis. Three control groups of four students with equal male/female ratios were trained in identical dive classes except:

Group One was taught that a diver would get narcosis at 130 fsw, and much emphasis was placed on the extremely high probability of narcosis with **severe** symptoms.

Group Two was taught of the existence of narcosis, the symptoms and depths of occurrence beginning at 100 fsw, but were not subjected to an intimidating lecture, as in Group One, that narcosis was an absolute barrier.

Group Three was well educated on narcosis with three full hours of lecture on symptoms, risk, danger and known research. They were told that divers with strong will power as postulated by Miles (1961) could mentally prepare themselves and greatly reduce the effects.

Prior to the open water deep dives all students were given two dives to 30 fsw and two dives to 100 fsw to develop good breathing techniques.

Before the actual dives for testing purposes, the students were taken on a 50 fsw dive where the tests were performed so a mental/dexterity familiarity could be achieved with the format of the test problems. Changes were then made in the test so they could not be performed from memory. The tests consisted of handwriting evaluations, peg board testing, math and ball bearing placement in a long-necked narrow bottle, etc.

In the initial test depth of 130 fsw, divers in Group One had minor to above average narcosis problems while Group Two and Three divers had little affect on test scores.

At the 180 fsw test depth, two Group One divers dropped from the exercise due to severe narcosis problems and were removed from the dive. All Group Two divers were affected although still functioning at about 50% test levels. Group Three divers had minor impairment.

At the 200 fsw test depth, all divers in Group One and two from Group Two were dropped due to severe narcosis and apprehension. Group Three divers actually showed slight improvement in test scores.

At the 240 fsw test depth, one diver was dropped from Group Two and one from Group Three due to severe narcosis. The remaining Group Two diver and three Group Three divers showed levels of impairment but again scores and performance showed improvement over the previous depth level. One diver, a female from Group Three, registered her highest scores on all tests at the 240 fsw level.

Concurrent testing of experienced deep divers showed 7 out of 10 divers with no decrease in performance or scores at the 200 fsw test level. The three divers with decreased performance finished the testing (2 with perfect scores) but required additional time than was usual. At 240 fsw, 5 out of 10 performed all tests with no decreased performance. One diver had problems with the ball bearing test but perfect scores on the peg board, math and handwriting. The other two showed up to 42% deficits and had problems completing the tests.

TABLE 4.2

Narcosis Symptoms

- Light-headedness
- Euphoria
- Drunkenness
- Impaired neuromuscular coordination
- Hearing sensitivity or hallucination
- Slowed mental activity
- Decreased problem solving capacity
- Overconfidence
- Short term memory loss or distortions
- Improper time perceptions
- Fine work deterioration
- Exaggerated movements
- Numbness and tingling in lips, face and feet
- Stupor
- Sense of impending blackout
- Levity or tendency to laughter
- Depressive state
- Visual hallucination or disturbances
- Perceptual narrowing
- Less tolerance to stress
- Exaggerated (oversized) handwriting
- Amnesia
- Loss of consciousness
- Retardation of higher mental processes
- Retardation of task performances
- Slurred speech
- Poor judgement
- Slowed reaction time and reflex ability
- Loss of mechanical dexterity

The obvious conclusions include a subjective validation to both "adaptation" and the negative influence of "modeling" behavior in those groups of divers preconditioned that narcosis was inevitable and severe. The Group Three divers with little prior diving experience were satisfactorily still performing a the 200 fsw level and three divers continued to perform (with one showing improvement still) at the 240 fsw test level.

If we teach our children that all dogs will bite, we can safely assume that when presented with a specimen even as lowly as a toy poodle (which should probably be shot on sight anyway), we can expect a high fear index. Likewise, if we teach our dive students that narcosis is a finite, unyielding biophysical wall, then we can logically expect such conditioning to impair their performance beyond a more realistically educated diver lacking preconceived phobias and suggestions. Education is the key to performance and safety.

CONCLUSION

Depth limitation largely becomes a decision based upon narcosis levels and available gas supply (until the O_2 toxicity range is entered). Most divers will be able to function well in excess of the so-called 130 fsw (39.4 m) limit with even a little practice.

Interestingly, the first edition of the NOAA Diving Manual published in the mid-seventies contained this notation on narcosis: "Experience, frequent exposure to deep diving, and a high degree of training may permit divers to dive on air as deep as 200 fsw (60.6 m)..." Although scientific diving programs and university based research groups generally advocated air diving to around this recommended limit, a significant proportion of dives were conducted in far deeper depths if necessary for observation or collection purposes including dives beyond 300 fsw. The proliferation of "Do as I say, not as I do" mentalities still dominate all factions of the industry primarily for fear of critical condemnation by less realistic "experts".

All divers should exercise prudence and reasonable caution in all aspects of deep diving but particularly so when it comes to narcosis. Experience is vital before attempting progressively deeper dives. (Remember this does not imply "reverse profile" dives.) Ideally, the diver should be seeking out the benefit of training by a competent, well experienced deep diving instructor before a penetration below sport diving depths. Don't try to obtain field experience on your own or with another buddy. The historical record provides too many fatalities or near misses due to narcosis to warrant such a risk.

CHAPTER 5

Oxygen Toxicity

"Oxygen... a potent hazard if poorly managed."
John Crea

WHAT IS OXYGEN TOXICITY?

Oxygen is the most basic life support system our bodies employ, and yet also has the capacity to cause great harm. Keller (1946) has called oxygen "The Princess of Gases. She is beautiful but has to be handled with special care". We cannot live without it, but in prolonged breathing exposures or in deep depths on standard air scuba systems too much of a good thing can prove fatal.

Thom and Clark (1990) note, "paradoxically, the same gas that is required to sustain life by preventing loss of consciousness and death from hypoxemia has toxic properties that affect all living cells at sufficiently high pressure and duration of exposure." Most divers are familiar with the basic characteristics of oxygen as it occurs in our atmosphere. It is a colorless, odorless and tasteless gas found free in dry air at 23.15% by weight and 20.98% by volume. For discussion purposes, we will consider its volume percentage to be 21%. Interestingly, the relative toxic effects of oxygen are determined not by the percentage in any mixed gas (including standard air at approximately 21% oxygen and 79% nitrogen), but by the oxygen partial pressure (PO_2).

A review of Dalton's Law of Partial Pressures is helpful (The total pressure exerted by a gas mixture is equal to the sum of the partial pressures of the components of the mixture i.e. P = P1+P2+P3... etc.), but put simply, as depth increases a corresponding elevation in the partial pressure of oxygen is achieved and must be considered by any diver planning deeper exposures. At the surface we are naturally adapted to PO_2 at .21 atmospheres absolute (ATA). This is considered the reference point for "normoxic" conditions.

It is important to be aware of certain ranges of tolerance in normal, healthy persons. Most people can maintain proper blood oxygenation down to .16 ATA (16% oxygen in the mix at surface pressure) but dropping much below this will limit performance/endurance and unconsciousness will likely result approaching .1 ATA (10% oxygen at the surface).

As a physics reminder please note that we commonly refer to the percentage of a gas in any mixture as the Fg (fraction of the gas expressed as the decimal equivalent); thusly the FO_2 at the surface can be correctly expressed as .21; Pg or partial pressure of a gas may be expressed as the Fg multiplied by atmospheres absolute or ATA's. Therefore, the PO_2 at 66 fsw is properly expressed as .63 ATA of O_2. This is derived from multiplying .21 (the FO_2 of oxygen in air) by the pressure in ATA's: .21 X 3 = .63 ATA's of O_2. Though the FO_2 will remain constant, the PO_2 will increase with depth.

The diver may recall the old reference to the "Ten and Ten Rule" wherein it supposed that blackout will occur if the percentage of either oxygen or carbon dioxide (CO_2) reaches 10% in the gas mixture. This was particularly important to competitive free divers and spear fishermen while holding their breath and attaining depths in excess of 80 to 100 fsw (24.2 to 30.3 m). Many of these individuals could reach far deeper depths through applied disciplines of hyperventilation and adaptation in conjunction with techniques employed to precipitate the "diving reflex" to extend time underwater. This practice, however, is a double edged sword: As depth increased CO_2 was produced by the body's metabolism, and absent any other source the "O_2 storage" was depleted. To a certain degree this was counterbalanced by a corresponding rise in the percentage of CO_2 in the system since this gas is a metabolic waste product as O_2 is burned.

The relationship is important because high CO_2 is a major stimulus to breathe while low O_2 is not. As the diver held his breath, O_2 was con-

Photo by Bret Gilliam

Onset of oxygen toxicity symptoms can occur without warning ad with potentially fatal consequences. David Sipperly explores a wreck at 210 feet with strict buoyancy control and close adherence to not exceeding 1.6 ATA PO_2. Deeper dives should be conducted on mixed gas for most divers.

sumed and CO_2 eventually said, "Hey buddy, I'll continue to hurt you unless you get back to the surface and get a fresh breath, you idiot!" Now the insidious danger occurs. As the diver ascended, both partial pressures dropped accordingly. His stimulus to breathe was reduced as PCO_2 dropped while his PO_2 could be dropping to dangerous levels.

At some point, the diver passed out from this "latent hypoxia" syndrome or what became commonly known as "shallow water black out". Typically the diver showed no signs or distress and simply went limp, sometimes within ten feet of the surface. Those who were successfully rescued and revived related no warning of the impending blackout or any major stimulus to breathe. But several fatalities were sustained before the problems were identified and the hazards of deep breath-hold diving were well communicated.

CENTRAL NERVOUS SYSTEM (CNS) O_2 TOXICITY
(Paul Bert Effect)

For the free swimming scuba diver, the most immediate dangers with O_2 toxicity are encountered in deeper depths where the PO_2 exceeds 1.6 ATA (218 fsw); in military, commercial and some scientific applications the ideal method of controlling the toxic effects of O_2 are to keep

DEEP DIVING • 123

TABLE 5.1

Signs and Symptoms of CNS O_2 Toxicity in Normal Men*

Bradycardia	Respiratory changes
Palpitations	Nausea
Depression	Spasmodic vomiting
Apprehension	Fibrillation of lips
Visual symptoms:	Twitching of lips, cheeks, nose, eyelids
Dazzle	Syncope
Constriction of visual field	Convulsions
Tinnitus and auditory hallucinations	
Vertigo	*Table excerpted from DIVING MEDICINE (Bove and Davis, 1990)

the oxygen dose as near "normoxic" as possible. This is accomplished by controlling the gas mixtures. A typical mix would reduce the oxygen percentage in a deep dive usage and let the elevated pressure raise the PO_2 to normoxic levels. For example, if a diver needed a mix for the 300 fsw (91 m) level the O_2 could be used at only 2% with another inert gas. The affect of 10 ATA's at 300 fsw would produce a PO_2 of approximately .21 ATA, the same as we normally breathe at the surface. The dive supervisor could select a single inert gas such as helium (He) or combine two inert gases such as nitrogen and helium while keeping the O_2 percentage constant. The resulting gas mixes are commonly referred to as HELIOX or TRIMIX respectively. Realistically however, this mix would incur a greater decompression obligation due to the elevated inert gas percentages if oxygen was kept at an FO_2 of .10 to .15 FO_2 would be more practical. (See Mixed Gas chapter for a more complete explanation).

Since our text is primarily designed for use by deep divers using standard air as the breathing gas, we do not have the luxury of custom mixing our oxygen percentages. Our gas is going to be 21% O_2 and 79% nitrogen and we are stuck with it unless the diver makes the commitment to mixed gas equipment and its attendant responsibilities. As air divers we will be most concerned with the acute phase of oxygen toxicity (sometimes also referred to as oxygen poisoning). Acute O_2 toxicity for well experienced and "depth adapted" divers will ultimately be the deciding factor in penetration limits, not inert gas narcosis.

The central nervous system is primarily affected in the acute phase and the following table will illustrate typical manifestations.

In **Table 5.2** below the authors have provided a simplified, abridged version to **Table 5.1**. The reader is directed to note that the first letter of each of the symptoms listed in **Table 5.2** spells out the acronym **VENTID**.

Even a cursory examination of these effects should illustrate the seriousness of a CNS O_2 hit in deep water. Onset and severity of symptoms do not follow any particular pattern and may vary in an individual diver from day to day. Of particular note is that there may be no warning with less serious symptoms before full convulsion is precipitated. Thom and Clark (1990) observe that "minor symptoms did not always precede the onset of convulsions, and even when a preconvulsive aura did occur, it was often followed so quickly by seizures that it had little practical value".

Many divers have relied on the incorrect supposition that lip twitching or "eye ticks" would provide adequate notice of impending disaster but this has been disproved by chamber tests and direct observation in actual dive scenarios. It is strongly suspected that CNS O_2 toxicity and/or severe narcosis played the major role in the loss of almost a dozen divers in the last two decades while attempting record dives on standard air.

Oxygen convulsions, per se, are not inherently harmful but imagine the implications for an unattended diver or even one with a buddy near by. Management of a patent airway and rescue in such an extreme situation is near impossible and the diver will almost certainly drown.

Mount (1991) related a near miss accident he was inadvertently involved in during a deep dive in 1971. He was diving at the 330 fsw level and in control of narcosis with no O_2 toxicity problems when he observed an obviously out of control female diver blissfully pass him with

TABLE 5.2

CNS O_2 Toxicity Symptoms (VENTID)

V ision: any disturbance including "tunnel vision," etc.
E ars: any changes in normal hearing function
N ausea: severity may vary and be intermittent
T witching: classically manifest in facial muscles
I rritability: personality shifts, anxiety, confusion etc.
D izziness: vertigo, disorientation

Exercise, heavy leg kicking or rapid swimming can all elevate CO2 and increase the diver's susceptibility to oxygen toxicity. Bob Cunningham demonstrates perfect neutral buoyancy and a relaxed dive style at 220 fsw in spite of wearing "quad" cylinders and carrying a bulky camera system.

Photo by Bret Gilliam

a vigorous kick cycle heading straight down! He gave chase and intercepted her near the 400 fsw (121.2 m) level. Making contact and arresting her plunge required heavy exertion and power kicking strokes to initiate ascent for the pair. "Within seconds after this effort, I had almost complete visual collapse. I found myself looking through a solid red field with black spots; basically blind. I made it up to the 300 fsw level with her and was relieved in the rescue by other divers. By 275 fsw I was getting occasional 'windows' but my vision did not return to normal until past 250 fsw. "

Another account is related by Gilliam (1991) of another close call while diving on a scientific project in the Virgin Islands in 1972. "My regular buddy and I were gathering samples at 290 fsw as part of an ongoing survey. We were both well adapted from daily deep diving and routinely worked this depth without difficulty. On this occasion, another scientist diver had joined us at his request. In prior discussions, he had satisfied us that he was familiar and experienced with deep diving procedures. About seven minutes into the dive we watched him begin hammering away on a coral sample for retrieval and suddenly go limp. I caught him as he started to fall over the drop-off wall and ventilated him with his regulator's purge valve while rapidly ascending. At 190 fsw he completely recovered and began breathing on his own. He was unable to recall anything except beginning work with his hammer. This incident finally stopped the university's practice of forcing outsiders on our professional teams. It was sheer luck that ĭ happened to be looking his way when he passed out".

Most cases of underwater blackout result in death. The dangers of this type of CNS O_2 toxicity cannot be too greatly emphasized. On air, at 300 fsw (91 m) or 10 ATA, the PO_2 has reached 2.1 ATA; this partial pressure will definitely produce toxicity limited only by time and other influences such as elevated PCO_2.

For these indisputable facts, the practice of air diving deeper than 300 fsw (91 m) must be placed in the perspective of assumable risk of sudden death not just injury.

It should be noted that divers routinely push nearly 3 ATA of O_2 in recompression chambers for extended periods. Theoretically, chamber divers are supposed to be at rest but many of the bounce dive profiles practiced by extreme deep air divers include performance plans that essentially have the diver "at rest" in the water with negative descents and controlled buoyant ascents in the toxicity range.

Neither Watson and Gruener (1968) nor Gilliam (1990) suffered O_2 toxicity problems on their record dives to 437 and 452 fsw (132.4 and 137 m) respectively but their times in the critical toxicity zone were limited and they each had practiced exceptional adaptive techniques. (In spite of this, Watson and Gruener reported near total incapacitation due to narcosis.)

Gilliam (1990) believed that adaptation was proven to narcosis as well as to onset of O_2 toxicity and was able to effectively limit narcosis impairment. "But my primary concern from the very beginning was O_2 Toxicity. My tables were based on fast descents and fast ascents in the toxicity zone. I felt I could tolerate up to five minutes below 300 feet and still get out before the high O_2 would hit me. In retrospect, of course, it worked. Would it work again, who knows?"

Other factors in his success include almost absurdly low respiration and heartbeat rates, repeated progressive deep exposures and limited physical exertion. Like narcosis, O_2 toxicity can be precipitated by higher CO_2 levels generated in work tasks or simply swimming harder. Deep divers need to develop strong disciplines for energy conservation and focused breathing habits. The double whammy of sudden onset and

Balancing the oxygen dose demands that the diver plan both his "bottom" and "decompression" exposures. Following a 35 minute dive to 220 fsw, Mitch Skaggs switches to 80/20 nitrox at his 20 foot stop. This allows him to take his decom with a 1.4 ATA PO$_2$ exposure and not violate the 45 minute single dive limit at 1.6 ATA.

increased severity of narcosis and CNS O$_2$ toxicity in a stress situation can rapidly accelerate a borderline control situation into a disaster.

The U.S. Navy still conducts oxygen tolerance tests in dry chambers to screen individuals with unusual susceptibility to O$_2$. However, highly motivated individuals may escape detection anyway. Both Rutkowski and Gilliam have served as chamber supervisors and conducted such tests. In 1991 when interviewed, neither could recall any instances where a pre-screening O$_2$ tolerance test was failed. The validity of such test protocols remains debated.

The following table (see **Table 5.3**) gives the oxygen partial pressure limits during working dives as recommended by NOAA. This will provide some parameters for dive planning and is deliberately conservative. The scuba diver should be safe within these limits presuming good physical fitness and no predisposition to toxicity such as heavy smoking habits or asthma conditions. No guarantee of safety can ever be presumed.

Given the growing usage of NITROX mixtures and other mixed gases that may provide oxygen in the mixture at a greater or lessened percentage than that of air at an FO_2 of .21, the following Table 5-4 has been provided as a handy reference for maximum depths on various FO_2 to remain within recommended limits of exposure.

As in the case of **Table 5-3** these depths are recommendations based on normal working conditions for the diver. In the case of gases mixed for purposes of decompression, it may possible for some divers to use deeper depths on higher FO_2 values. Consult experts before attempting such higher exposures.

TABLE 5.3

NOAA PO_2 and Exposure Time Limits for Working Divers

Feet of Seawater (fsw)	Normal Exposure Limits		Maximum Total Duration, 24 Hr Day in Minutes
	Oxygen Partial Pressure (PO_2) in ATA	Maximum Duration for Single Exposure in Minutes	
218	1.6	45	15
203	1.5	120	180
187	1.4	150	180
171	1.3	180	210
156	1.2	210	240
140	1.1	240	270
124	1.0	300	300
108	.9	360	360
93	.8	450	450
77	.7	570	570
61	.6	720	720
	Exceptional Exposures		
281	2.0	30	
266	1.9	45	
250	1.8	60	
234	1.7	75	
218	1.6	120	
203	1.5	150	
187	1.4	180	
171	1.3	240	

CHRONIC OXYGEN TOXICITY

(Lorraine Smith Effect)

This effect was commonly referred to in the past as pulmonary toxicity; Rutkowski makes frequent reference in his lectures to the diver's "pulmonary clock", etc. Recently, the term "whole body" toxicity has also come into use.

This phase of O_2 toxicity is less a problem for divers except in prolonged in-water oxygen decompression or in actual recompression therapy. This "chronic" toxicity is generally associated with longer, low pressure exposures as compared to the high PO_2 values encountered at depth. Due to the limits of extended hyperbaric oxygen breathing, a method of calculating the individual total O_2 exposure incurred during all phases of a dive was developed. This can also be used to factor decompression and O_2 treatment breathing periods. This measure is known as the Unit Pulmonary Toxicity Dose (UPTD) and tables are available for calculating UPTD's for AIR, pure O_2 and mixed gases.

Hamilton (1989) notes in his REPEX paper, "The Pennsylvania unit (UPTD) has served well and is based on empirical data; it is the basic unit used in the REPEX method. For two reasons, however, we prefer to use an alternative term: OTU or Oxygen Tolerance Dose. First, since we are dealing with operational physiology in managing exposure to oxygen in diving we prefer to refer to these as techniques for 'tolerance' of O_2 exposure, rather than for avoiding O_2 'toxicity'. They are the same thing, but we feel it offers a more positive approach."

The OTU and its predecessors are calculated by the following expression:

$$OTU = t \left[(PO_2 - 0.5) / 0.5 \right]^{0.83}$$

where t is the duration of the exposure in minutes and PO_2 is the oxygen partial pressure in ATA. The 0.5 ATA is the "threshold" below which no significant symptoms develop; even oxygen injured lungs can recover below this level. (Bardin and Lambertsen 1970 and Eckenhoff et al. 1987) The exponent 0.83 was determined to give the best fit to the data on reduction of vital capacity as a function of oxygen exposure. An important benefit of this method is that the units are additive, and the net result of multiple short exposures can be totaled.

TABLE 5.4

FO$_2$	*1.4 ATA fsw*	*1.6 ATA fsw*
0.15	275.00	319.00
0.16	255.75	297.00
0.17	238.76	277.59
0.18	223.67	260.33
0.19	210.16	244.89
0.20	198.00	231.00
0.21 (normoxic)	187.00	218.43
0.22	177.00	207.00
0.23	167.87	196.57
0.24	159.50	187.00
0.25	151.80	178.20
0.26	144.69	170.08
0.27	138.11	162.56
0.28	132.00	155.57
0.29	126.31	149.07
0.30	121.00	143.00
0.31	116.03	137.32
0.32	111.37	132.00
0.33	107.00	127.00
0.34	102.88	122.29
0.35	99.00	117.86
0.36	95.33	113.67
0.37	91.86	109.70
0.38	88.58	105.05
0.39	85.46	102.38
0.40	82.50	99.00
0.41	79.68	95.78
0.42	77.00	92.71
0.43	74.44	89.79
0.44	72.00	87.00
0.45	69.67	84.33
0.46	67.43	81.78
0.47	65.30	79.34
0.48	63.25	77.00
0.49	61.29	74.76
0.50	59.40	72.60

Maximum Depths for a Given FO$_2$ Given a Limiting PO$_2$

TABLE 5.5

OTU DOSE BY PO$_2$ AND AIR DEPTHS

PO$_2$ Atm or Bar	Depth FSW	Depth MSW	OTU / Min.
0.50	45.6	13.8	0
0.55	53.4	16.2	0.15
0.60	61.3	18.6	0.37
0.65	69.1	21.0	0.37
0.70	77.0	23.3	0.47
0.75	84.9	25.7	0.56
0.80	92.7	28.1	0.65
0.85	100.6	30.5	0.74
0.90	108.4	32.9	0.83
0.95	116.3	35.2	0.92
1.00	124.4	37.6	1.00
1.05	132.0	40.0	1.08
1.10	139.9	42.4	1.16
1.15	147.7	44.8	1.24
1.20	155.6	47.1	1.32
1.25	163.4	49.5	1.40
1.30	171.3	51.9	1.48
1.35	179.1	54.3	1.55
1.40	187.0	56.7	1.63
1.45	194.9	59.1	1.70
1.50	202.7	61.4	1.78
1.55	210.6	63.8	1.85
1.60	218.4	66.2	1.92
1.65	226.3	68.6	2.00
1.70	234.1	71.0	2.07
1.75	242.0	73.3	2.14
1.80	249.9	75.7	2.21
1.85	257.7	78.1	2.28
1.90	265.6	80.5	2.35
1.95	273.4	82.8	2.42
2.00	281.3	85.2	2.49

R.W. Hamilton, HAMILTON RESEARCH LTD.

Chart of OTU dose by PO$_2$ and air depths. The values in the Table from left are the PO$_2$, depth in fsw or msw diving with air to give that PO$_2$, and the number of OTU per minute at the indicated PO$_2$ level. To calculate a dose, multiply the value in the chart for the exposure PO$_2$ by the number of minutes of the exposure. For exposures at different PO$_2$'s, calculate the dose in OTU for each exposure at a given PO2 and sum the OTU's to get the total exposure.

These dose tolerances were calculated originally for divers in multi-day saturation missions; scuba divers are urged to consult with experts in O_2 management before attempting any dives where significant OTU doses will be accumulated. Because of the nature of the REPEX operation its algorithm does not devote much attention to acute CNS toxicity specifically. It is intended that divers just stay out of the CNS toxicity zone by staying below 1.5 ATA PO_2. As a general rule of thumb, the daily OTU dose should always be calculated to allow the diver to sustain a full treatment **Table 6** (approximately 650 OTU/UPTD) if necessary. Refer to Table 5-3 for suggested exposures at specific depths/ATA PO_2 for scuba divers. By referencing between these two tables, the accumulated OTU dose can be accurately tracked.

Many divers like the extra security of a full face mask when breathing oxygen during long decompressions. This should preclude drowning in the event of an oxygen seizure.

For isolated or single day exposures, an 850 OTU dose can be tolerated. The reader is referred to Hamilton's original REPEX work for additional information.

Symptoms of chronic pulmonary O_2 toxicity include shortness of breath, fatigue, dry coughing, lung irritation and a burning sensation in the breathing cycle. Pulmonary edema is most common and a marked reduction in vital capacity. In treatments in recompression chambers, patient tenders also look for irritability in the patient or unreasonable disposition as early warning signs that dictate an air break in the schedule to allow some relief period.

TABLE 5.6

Oxygen Limits for Life Support Systems

ATA O_2	
3.0	50 / 50 NITROX Therapy Gas @ 6 ATA (165 fsw)
2.8	100% O_2 @ 2.8 ATA (60 fsw)
2.5	Decompression for Operation Diving (maximum)
2.4	60 / 40 NITROX Therapy Gas @ 6 ATA (165 fsw)
2.0	U.S. Navy Exceptional Exposure to Working Diver
1.6	U.S. Navy Maximum Normal Exposure to Working Diver
.5	Maximum Saturation Exposure
.35	Normal Saturation Exposure
.21	Normal Environment O_2 (normoxic)
.16	Begin Signs of Hypoxia
.12	Serious Signs of Hypoxia
.10	Unconsciousness
<.10	Coma / Death

PLANNING

From a practical standpoint, pulmonary or "whole body" effects are virtually impossible to sufficiently accumulate using open circuit equipment so that they become a factor in diving planning. Some instructors with an incomplete understanding of tracking the OTU dose have mistakenly concluded that precise measurement of such units is necessary. Hamilton emphasizes that this REPEX tracking theory was designed for divers in saturation with no opportunity to return to the surface and normal oxygen pressures during the multi-day period. Thus the importance of multi-day dose accumulations became crucial to planning. However, open circuit divers eventually will have to return to the surface if only to sleep and eat. That period is adequate to allow sufficient "blow off" time to reset the pulmonary clock to, essentially, *zero* each day. In almost any foreseeable dive plan, the CNS limits will always be the controlling oxygen clock. You can prove this yourself by simply adding the OTU's for any given dive and you'll find that just to obtain 300 OTU's or more would require a superhuman dive profile that violates the exposure recommendations for the CNS clock so grossly as to make the pulmonary considerations moot.

However, it must be emphasized that accurate tracking of the CNS clock is crucial. This includes both the bottom depth exposure *and* the decompression phase. Several accidents have occurred because divers planned only for the "depth" phase of the dive and forgot the consequences of breathing oxygen or high O_2 percentage nitrox during decompression.

Here's an example:

A dive to 220 fsw on air for 30 minutes is allowable while staying inside the 45 minute single dive exposure for oxygen at 1.6 ATA. However, 88 minutes of decompression will be required (using U.S. Navy tables). Assuming the deeper stops were taken on air, it would be a common mistake for some divers to think they could safely switch to pure oxygen for the 20 foot stop. The table calls for 23 minutes at this depth. But wait: oxygen at 20 fsw brings the diver right back to 1.6 ATA again and this would place him 8 minutes over the maximum recommended limit. Convulsive events have been precipitated for precisely these types of failures to calculate the *total dosage*. What's the solution? Drop the decompression phase PO_2 by utilizing an 80/20 nitrox mix which will keep the exposure at or below 1.4 ATA.

So what's happening with the pulmonary "whole body" clock? Not much. The bottom phase of the dive on air loaded about 60 OTU's and even if the entire decompression phase was taken on varying mixtures to yield a uniform 1.4 ATA O_2 exposure, only about 140 OTU's would be added there. This totals right about 200 OTU's for what is a decidedly aggressive dive by any criteria. Remembering that you can take up to 850 OTU's per day (and still provide an allowance of 650 OTU's should you need to reserve them for a DCS treatment), 200 OTU's doesn't really amount to anything. In fact, you could do this same profile four more times before you ran out of exposure time on the pulmonary clock. However, the reality is that you would blow the CNS limits off the gauge and probably bend yourself as well.

So if you've been staying up nights worrying about calculating OTU's, relax. They'll take care of themselves just fine if you stay within the CNS guidelines.

SUMMARY

Both manifestations of oxygen toxicity can play a role in the deep diver's plan. Of most concern is the extremely dangerous and unpredictable CNS O_2 Toxicity hit at depth. Divers should exercise extreme caution when venturing beyond the 1.6 ATA range and penetrations beyond 275 fsw (83.3 m) on air are ill-advised except in the most experienced and adapted diver.

Unlike narcosis impairment, where a quantifiable possibility of rescue exists from an alert buddy or self-recognition of problem levels can be relieved by ascent, an O_2 hit can quickly progress to uncontrollable convulsive states and drowning. As divers become more attuned to management of inert gas narcosis, the O_2 toxicity barrier will be the ultimate depth limit.

CHAPTER 6

Staged Decompression

*"It would go a long way toward promoting diver safety
if everyone would finally accept that ALL dives
are decompression dives."*

John Crea

As you venture longer and deeper into the watery depths, you leave the realm of sport diving and along with it the no-decompression limits that you were taught to dive within. Longer and deeper diving moves you into the realm of decompression diving, a realm where planning and careful preparation is essential, and inadequate planning and preparation can literally be fatal.

This chapter will discuss staged decompression, some background physiology, planning considerations, equipment requirements, equipment configuration, utilization of oxygen during decompression, and emergency procedures.

PHYSIOLOGY AND PHYSICS REVIEW

During diving, using compressed air for the breathing mixture, the body takes up the inert gas nitrogen when exposed to higher ambient pressures (resulting in elevated PARTIAL PRESSURES OF NITROGEN). This nitrogen is stored as a dissolved gas in all of the body tissues, with the amounts stored in each type of tissue determined by the blood supply to that tissue and by the solubility of nitrogen in that tissue (these parameters determine the "half-time" for that tissue). After the body has taken up this nitrogen while diving, it must be safely released from the body during ascent in a slow, controlled manner to prevent the development of decompression sickness (consisting of the formation of **bubbles** that can cause great damage to the body, and possibly even permanent disability or death if allowed to occur).

The technique used to allow the controlled removal of nitrogen from the body during ascent is called **Decompression**. Decompression may be accomplished in one of two ways:

I. By a continuous ascent at varying rates (very difficult for most divers to follow precisely).

II. By ascending to pre-calculated depths, and remaining at those depths for a specified length of time to allow excess nitrogen to be removed from the body tissues (as indicated by various decompression tables) until it is safe to ascend to a shallower depth. This procedure is repeated in carefully defined steps until it is safe to ascend to the surface. This is the procedure most commonly used today by the vast majority of divers, the military and commercial dive companies and is referred to as **Staged Decompression**.

Many different tables (DCIEM, U.S. Navy, Royal Navy, etc.) spell out the procedures for this staged decompression, in which the diver stops at predetermined depths and waits for a specific amount of time to allow nitrogen to exit the body tissues. These tables specify the ascent rate to the first stop, ascent rate between stops, and the body position for decompression. (The U.S. Navy tables specify that the decompression stop depth be measured at mid-chest, as the tables were originally designed for hard-hat divers who ascended in a vertical position. Many articles have discussed the optimal position for decompression, with the consensus being that a horizontal position appears to be best, but if a vertical position is required the decompression stop depth should be measured and maintained according to the U.S. Navy requirements.) These standard tables are almost always designed for use by divers who are breathing air both during the dive and the decompression. (Custom tables are available that incorporate the utilization of other gas mixtures during decompression to produce more nearly optimal inert gas removal.)

Photo by Bret Gilliam

Decompression is an exacting discipline that requires attention to ascent rates, stop depths and times, and oxygen exposure management.

It has often been stated that decompression diving carries an increased risk of DCS compared with dives that do not require decompression. Although this is true for many profiles in the U.S. Navy tables (and possibly other tables), it is not necessarily a general truth, as many variables come into play with these dives (however, the U.S. Navy has reported that their tables are inadequate for longer and/or deeper dives requiring significant decompression times). Selection of conservative tables that have been extensively tested should result in a DCS rate during decompression diving comparable to that found during dives not requiring decompression.

If decompression diving is planned it is essential to choose a table that accounts for the conditions of the divers, and of the dive site. If the divers are required to work hard during dive, more decompression will be required. If the dive conditions will result in the divers becoming cold, this will also increase the decompression required. Again, it must be emphasized, a conservative, well-tested decompression table should be utilized during all decompression dives. "I personally recommend either the DCIEM tables or proprietary tables to divers performing deep dives requiring significant amounts of decompression" (Crea, 1991).

PLANNING FOR STAGED DECOMPRESSION

The essentials of staged decompression are readily enumerated:

1) Ascent from the maximum depth to the first decompression stop at an ascent rate as defined by the decompression tables or dive computer in use.

2) Upon reaching the first decompression stop, the diver holds this depth for a given time. After completing the required "hang time," the diver then moves up to the next stop (at the required ascent rate) and repeats the procedure until he reaches the surface.

As seen from the above, the basics of decompression diving appear quite simple. You make your dive and you carry out the required decompression. However, failure to properly perform these "simple" steps can result in injury and/or death. Proper planning is what keeps this procedure a safe and reliable one.

The major areas of concern are:

1) Adequate gas supply;
2) Equipment considerations;
3) Ability to control ascents; and
4) Rate of ascent.

GAS CONSUMPTION CALCULATIONS

It is essential that enough gas be available to allow the diver to complete his scheduled decompression (aborted or omitted decompression increases the risk of development of DCS, and has been known to "ruin a diver's day"). Thus, gas consumption calculations need to be made prior to the dive to assure that adequate amounts of gas will be available for the dive plan. Since you will probably be diving with a buddy, each diver should plan his gas supplies to take into account the possibility of "problems" in which each diver has enough gas for his planned dive decompression, and sharing with his partner. Planning for two times the minimal amount of gas calculated is recommended.

How do you calculate gas requirements? The deep diver should have a good idea of his gas consumption (at the surface at rest). This gas consumption rate (expressed as RMV—respiratory minute volume) is utilized in the rest of the calculations presented here. Surface consumption rates may vary from 0.3 cu. ft./min to as much as 3.0 cu. ft./min.

In order to calculate your air consumption, you must first understand the following term: The "Respiratory Minute Volume (RMV)" is the amount of air consumed in one minute on the surface.

RMV's vary from diver to diver, and a diver's own RMV will change due to variations in his breathing rate. Obviously, if we are anxious, cold, or just out of shape, our breathing rate will be greater than expected. Also, if we are swimming against a strong current, we will be breathing more than at rest.

It follows from the ideal gas law and Boyle's Law, that our RMV will vary with depth. If we double the ambient pressure, we will double our RMV. Thus, if an 80 cu. ft. tank will last 60 minutes at the surface, then it will only last 30 minutes at 33 fsw, 20 minutes at 66 fsw, 15 minutes at 99 fsw, and only last 10 minutes at 165 fsw. The following relationship holds:

RMV x Ambient Pressure (ATA) = Consumption At That Depth

The aspiring deep diver will be well rewarded for taking the time to evaluate his surface consumption rate, as this is the only effective way to estimate his gas requirements for any given deep dive.

Once a RMV has been determined, then the surface equivalent consumption is easily calculated by the following equation:

Total Gas Required = Sum of the Gas Required at Each Stage of the Dive
and
Gas Required at Each Stage = ATA x RMV x Time x Work Modifier

ATA = Pressure at each Stage (ATA) = (Depth x 33)+1
RMV = Respiratory Minute Volume (expressed in cu. ft./min.)
Time = Time in minutes spent at that stage/depth
Work Modifier = A factor by which the gas requirements are multiplied by – reflecting the fact that gas consumption increases with increasing work levels. Suggested work modifiers are as follows:

AT REST	=	1
MILD WORK LOAD	=	1.5
MODERATE WORK LOAD	=	2.0
HEAVY WORK LOAD	=	3.0 – 5.0

Now, the dive is planned (bottom time and decompression requirements). Gas requirements are calculated based on the RMV and anticipated work load. Descent times are treated as if they were included in the bottom time. Ascent rates are calculated by using the average depth and the ascent time as below:

$$\text{AVERAGE DEPTH} = \frac{(\text{Maximum depth} + \text{1st Stop depth})}{2}$$

This Average Depth is then used in your calculation for gas consumption during ascent (and can be used for extremely deep dive descents). These calculations need to be carried out for every different gas utilized during the dive.

Once you have calculated your gas requirements for your planned dive, then consideration must be made for the "unplanned." Gas supply amounts should be "padded" to allow for emergencies. If you are diving with a partner, then **each diver should plan on having enough gas to support both divers in case of a catastrophic gas supply failure by one of the divers**.

This reserve supply can be calculated by doubling the amount of gas originally calculated. However, this allowance is not enough if you are planning a dive with significant penetrations (i.e., wreck and/or cave diving). For these situations, the cave divers "thirds rule" is more appropriate. One third of the gas supply is allowed for the penetration, one third for the exit, and one third reserved for emergencies. This should allow adequate gas to provide gas for your partner if he suffered a total gas supply failure at maximum penetration or depth.

EQUIPMENT CONSIDERATIONS

Decompression diving can require additional pieces of equipment that are not usually required during no-decompression diving. The key concept in safe deep diving is the concept of **Redundancy**. Simply put, this means that you carry backups of any equipment that is critical for that dive. Usually this refers to redundant regulators, decompression bottles, dive computers or tables, etc. It should not have to be said that **only reliable equipment should be used for deep diving**. If there is any question as to the reliability or performance of any piece of equipment, then it should be serviced prior to utilization for deep diving and tested on a simple dive before being used for deep diving. Failure of dive equipment is usually only irritating during sport diving, but can be critical during deep diving. Deep diving is not the time to be trying out new equipment or borrowed gear. The following is a brief list and description of some of the more common pieces of **extra** equipment used during decompression diving. (Please refer to the Chapter 7 for material on regulator selection, tank valves, etc.)

Bail-Out Bottle (Also known as a **Pony Bottle**) – This is a small scuba cylinder (40 cu. ft. or less) with regulator attached. Usually this is carried by the diver as an emergency gas source for emergency use during wreck penetrations and/or other "out of air emergencies."

Decompression Line – A decompression line is a line that the divers follow during their ascent and decompression. Quite often, this is the same as the dive boat's anchor line, but ideally is a separate weighted line with 10 foot increments marked. Extra equipment is quite often clipped off on this line (safety bottle, decompression bottles, surface supplied oxygen regulators, fluids and/or food, etc.).

Jonline – A three to six foot long line with one or more hand loops that can be clipped to the decompression line. This line is named after its inventor, Jon Hulbert. By attaching one end of this line to the decompression line and hanging on to the other end, it serves to smooth out the changes in depth that could occur if you were directly attached to the decompression line.

Lift Bag with Line – This is a small (25 - 50 pounds of lift) bag with enough line to reach from your maximum dive depth to the surface. It is utilized whenever the standard decompression line is not available. Upon starting your ascent, the lift bag is inflated and sent towards the surface while you pay out the line. You then ascend this line, and utilize it to allow you maintain a constant depth at each planned stop. This is an extremely comfortable method to use during decompression. If a standard yellow lift bag is used, it not only allows ease of decompression, but it marks your position for the boat that is hopefully searching for you.

Line Reel – A reel with 150 - 1000 feet of braided nylon line. Used by cave divers as a guide line to assure a known exit path, it is also used in this manner by wreck divers when penetrating a wreck. It can also be used during decompression to supply a guideline back to the anchor line or decompression line.

Stage Bottles – These are extra single scuba cylinders with regulators. In the usual sense of the phrase, stage bottles are extra cylinders and regulators carried by cave divers to allow farther penetration into cave systems. In decompression diving, stage bottles usually refer to either scuba cylinders attached to the decompression line for use during decompression or carried by the divers to allow the diver to carry out decompression independent from the dive boat.

Tables or Dive Computers – These decompression tools are the heart of safe decompression diving. If diving using computers, then it is highly suggested that two similar computers be utilized (what would you do if your only computer "dies" while inside a deep wreck? Especially if this is the third day of diving utilizing the computer.)

Dive tables should cover the planned dive depths and planned bottom times, plus a good safety margin on either side of the planned depth and time. Also, dive tables used for deep diving should be conservative and well tested over the range of dive depth-bottom times that you are planning to perform.

OXYGEN AND IN WATER DECOMPRESSION

In the last few years, the use of oxygen during decompression has become one of the most discussed topics in the technical diving community. Why use oxygen during decompression? Is in water use of oxygen during decompression safe? How do you set up your equipment to be able to utilize oxygen for in water decompression? These are just a few of the questions that are being asked and although many of the answers are found in medical and diving physiology texts, they are often buried in medical terminology, and sometimes open to interpretation or misinterpretation.

First, some background information on oxygen. Oxygen is a colorless, odorless gas, that comprises 20.99% by volume of the air you breathe. Oxygen has a molecular weight of 31.999, and has a density of 0.08279 lb./cu. ft. All materials that are flammable in air will burn much more vigorously in oxygen. Some combustibles, such as oil and grease, burn with near explosive violence in oxygen if ignited. However, pure oxygen is **Nonflammable** and **Nonexplosive**. Gaseous oxygen is usually stored in metal cylinders at a pressure of 2000 psi to 2400 psi. Both steel and aluminum cylinders have been used for storage of gaseous oxygen. (However, Air Products has recently stated that they will not fill aluminum cylinders with oxygen, due to concerns over aluminum oxide formation and potential explosion hazards.) Care must be taken to

Nitrox decompression cylinder being deployed in advance of dive for use at 30 foot deco stop in area of no current.

remove all oils, greases and other combustible contaminants from delivery systems and storage cylinders or replace then with oxygen compatible lubricants before being placed into oxygen service.

The removal of nitrogen from the body after exposure to elevated ambient pressures is based on the **Gradient** between the partial pressure of nitrogen in the tissues in question and the partial pressure of nitrogen in the blood (and ultimately the partial pressure of nitrogen in the lungs). The partial pressure of nitrogen in the blood is in equilibrium with the partial pressure of nitrogen present in the lungs. As you surface, the

Photo by Bret Gilliam

Oxygen and Nitrox
decompression cylinders
rigged and labeled for use.

partial pressure of nitrogen in the tissues and blood exceeds the ambient pressure, and when this pressure difference becomes great enough, then bubble formation occurs (The development of decompression sickness is really much more complex than this, but this simplistic approach is adequate for this discussion. Readers are referred to any of the many diving physiology texts for further discussion of this topic). The pressure of the gas mixture that you are breathing is in equilibrium with the ambient pressure, such that as you ascend, the partial pressure of nitrogen in the lungs is lower than that in the blood or the tissues. When this occurs, gas diffuses from the tissues into the blood, and then is carried to the lungs. At the lungs, the partial pressure of nitrogen in the alveoli is lower than the partial pressure in the blood, and the nitrogen diffuses from the blood into the alveoli and is exhaled.

Any technique that will decrease the partial pressure of nitrogen in the breathing mixture will increase the rate of removal of nitrogen from the blood, and thus from the tissues. This is the rationale behind the use of various gas mixtures that are low or totally lacking in nitrogen during decompression. With a large nitrogen gradient between the blood and the lungs, you remove nitrogen from the body as rapidly as possible. The

Cathy Castle uses a special decom station rigged with 330 cubic foot oxygen bottle and backup 80 cubic foot cylinder during film project. One regulator mounted on the main tank could supply several divers with a huge supply of oxygen and provide a stable "deco bar" at the same time.

Oxygen can be supplied from the surface as well. Here Bret Gilliam rigs a thirty-foot supply hose to be tethered at the 20-foot stop for contingency use.

easiest way to achieve the greatest nitrogen gradient during decompression is to totally remove nitrogen from the breathing mixture used during decompression.

However, this raises the question of with what gas do you replace the nitrogen? You can replace it with another inert gas, such as helium, but then you are presented with the extremely complex problem of calculating the uptake of another inert gas while removal of the nitrogen is going on, and its influence on our decompression schedule. It is actually possible to accumulate enough helium during decompression from an air dive (if breathing Helium-Oxygen during decompression) to have to consider decompression from the absorbed helium taken up during its use in decompression.

Or, you can replace the nitrogen with a non-inert gas (one that is metabolically active). Oxygen is the metabolically active gas we utilize. Oxygen has several advantages going for its use in this scenario. These are:

I. Using 100% oxygen allows us to have the largest possible nitrogen gradient between the lungs and the blood/tissues, so that nitrogen is removed at the greatest possible rate.

II. Oxygen is used metabolically by the body, and as such is not usually stored in the human body. Thus, you do not usually have to worry about these elevated tissue partial pressures of oxygen contributing to the development of decompression sickness. (In theory, with extremely high partial pressures of oxygen, some contribution to the development of decompression sickness is felt to be possible. However, the partial pressures required are much higher than those encountered if oxygen is utilized only during the 20 ft. and 10 ft. decompression stops.)

III. Oxygen has approximately the same density and thermal characteristics as air, so work of breathing is not changed and heat loss is not a problem. Helium has a high thermal conductivity and chilling is a potential problem with the use of helium in the breathing mixture. (Especially if helium is used to inflate your dry suit.) Not so when oxygen is used for dry suit inflation. (The use of 100% oxygen for dry suit inflation is, however, NOT RECOMMENDED.) No extra insulation needs to be used in the dry suit, and the heat loss via the respiratory tract is approximately the same as with air (heat loss from the respiratory tract is mainly a function of the body supplying humidity to the dry breathing gas, and the heat needed to vaporized the water to provide this humidity must be supplied by the body).

IV. Oxygen is relatively inexpensive compared to most other gases that might be considered for use.

V. Oxygen is the immediate treatment of choice (other than recompression) for decompression sickness, and as such, if you should develop "bubble trouble" during decompression, you are already treating it.

Photo by Rob Palmer

Norm Brinsley drifts easily under his lift bag while decompressing in the 6 knot current of the Gulf Stream. By drifting, all effects of the current are negated and the diver is not subjected to "flags in the breeze" scenarios. This method also allows the boat captain the freedom to maneuver in an emergency.

VI. There is a concept called the "Oxygen Window" or "Inherent Unsaturation" that comes into play when oxygen is used to replace the inert gas in a breathing mixture. This refers to several physical laws and the fact that oxygen is utilized metabolically in the body. What it basically means is that you can actually remove **more** inert gas (nitrogen when talking about air diving) for the same gradient when breathing oxygen than when breathing any other gas mixture that produces the same gradient for off-gassing. The reasoning behind this is somewhat complex, and we do not have the room in this chapter to cover it adequately. The reader is referred to one of the good diving physiology texts for further explanation.

The use of oxygen to shorten the time required for safe decompression was mentioned as early as 1878 by Bert and again by Ham and Hill in 1905. It has been discussed by Behnke (1969) and used in Japan in caisson workers. Use of oxygen during decompression has been a mainstay of the U.S. Navy's HELIOX procedures. A reduction in decompression time of about 40% is theoretically possible by switching from air to oxygen during shallow decompression stops.

Photo by Bret Gilliam

The use of oxygen by many advanced divers is not routinely done to shorten the decompression times that are required (although this is possible with custom designed decompression tables). It is used to increase the reliability of the tables used and thus reduce the probability of developing Decompression Sickness. Many of the dives made by cave and wreck divers today are in the realm approaching the tested limits of

Back-mounted inverted decom cylinders are easier for a diver to open and close the valve. This 45 cubic oxygen cylinder is mounted to Rick Thomas' primary 160 cubic tank and remains "off" during the dive to eliminate accidental switching to oxygen at depth.

the U.S. Navy air decompression tables, and many dives are into the **Exceptional Exposure Tables** (which are poorly tested, and have an unacceptably high incidence of developing DCS when used). When a diver moves into the deeper or longer schedules of the U.S. Navy Tables, the incidence of Decompression Sickness increases (Thalmann, 1985), and many of the Exceptional Exposure profiles have been tested only on a very limited basis (if at all), and the actual incidence of Decompression Sickness may be much higher than that for the rest of the Navy tables. Thus, by increasing the efficiency of the decompression schedule, the use of oxygen during in water decompression can improve the reliability of the decompression schedule utilized and reduces the risk of developing DCS.

Photo by Bret Gilliam

All regulators and pressure gauges used with over 40% oxygen mixtures should be properly cleaned for oxygen service and labeled or color coded.

In summary, the use of oxygen during decompression has much to recommend it. It increases the rate of nitrogen off-gassing, and thus increases the reliability and efficacy of the decompression schedule used (if used with standard air tables or with dive computers that were designed for use with air).

Breathing oxygen during decompression increases the gradient for nitrogen removal, and will therefore increase the rate at which preexisting bubbles will be reduced in size, thus "treating" any bubble formation that might occur during a decompression.

Finally, the use of oxygen in water is not without dangers, and should only be under taken by those divers who have the education and knowledge to utilize this advanced technique safely.

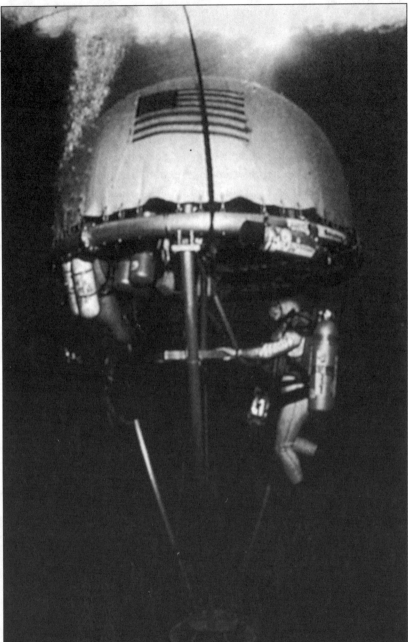

The use of dry chambers for decompression has been popularized on some cave diving projects requiring extended hangs. This allows the diver to drink fluids comfortable, talk with the dive team, and relax.

NITROX AND DECOMPRESSION

Along with oxygen, the use of NITROX (within its depth limitations) to "optimize" decompression has seen an increased use in the last few years. The major advantage of NITROX use is that it allows you to get off of compressed air when decompressing at deeper depths, where uptake of nitrogen into the slower compartments continues. Refer to Chapter 10 for more information.

SUMMARY

Ideally, during decompression, we would breathe a different gas at each decompression stop. These different gases would be selected based on the reduction of the amount of inert gas in them and how they are within oxygen toxicity constraints. Since gas switches at every decompression stop are usually not logistically feasible, many divers choose to make one or two gas switches during decompression.

However, the savings from this technique can be slight if the times at deeper decompression stops are minimal. Also, utilization of NITROX and oxygen during decompression must take into consideration of oxygen toxicity limits. Refer to any of the experts in our reference section for advice on the utilization of different gases for decompression.

Jim Baden uses a "jon-line" to give himself more room at a crowded decompression line.

CHAPTER 7

Equipment Considerations

*"Remember, darling, it's more important to look good
than to feel good. And you look marvelous!"*

Billy Crystal as Fernando

DRESS FOR SUCCESS

Diving, like skiing, is undeniably an equipment intensive sport. Twenty-five years ago we can remember struggling to get divers to use submersible pressure gauges instead of their "trusty" J-valves. "Nah, I don't need anything hanging off me like that," they argued, "this is supposed to be a single hose regulator isn't it?" But once the unenlightened experienced the singular pleasures of abruptly running out of air at a hundred feet or so when the reserve lever had been accidentally activated, we started to see a reluctant stream of customers in to grudgingly make the investment. In many cases it was like watching a kid trying to buy condoms in a pharmacy the first time. The diver would enter the store, pace the aisles while rummaging through fins, masks, spear guns etc. never once owning up to his true mission. Finally after inventorying the store, he would approach the counter carefully avoiding any direct eye contact. "Gimme a snorkel keeper, three o-rings, four feet of surgical tubing, one of them tee shirts, and, of yeah, maybe one of them new 'seaview gauges' I been hearing about." The sale was a struggle for both of us but the interests of safety were served no matter how circuitous the route. Safe sex, safe scuba, it's all the same.

The divers that took up the sport in the 1950's and 1960's were pretty much a rugged bunch of individualists who disdained any "gadgets" that broke up the fashion of the minimized ethic. Mask, fins, weight belt, tank and a regulator. That was it, thank you very much. If someone had tried to ease one of these guys into a hot pink matched set of gear... well, you probably remember that scene in the movie *Deliverance*. Gradually though, divers recognized that equipment evolutions made diving easier, more efficient and more fun. Modern BC's with power inflators caught on after some initial skepticism and fears that they would replace swimming skills. The single hose regulator became the four hose regulator as inflators, submersible pressure gauges, and additional second stages were added. Compact electronic dive computers are now replacing bulky depth gauges and watches.

As instructors we managed to finally overcome the resistance of that era to purchasing proper equipment and by the 80's divers started to look fairly standardized. It was a relief not to argue with Joe Macho any more over whether his safety vest with 10 pounds of lift from a 12 gram CO_2 cartridge was suitable for making deep wall dives.

Then a peculiar phenomena surfaced in the 90's and caught many of us completely by surprise: it was now fashionable to be absurdly over equipped. Many professionals are continually amazed at the lengths some divers go to equip themselves beyond all reasonable expectation for perceived necessities underwater. On some dive boats we've had trouble identifying a living breathing human entity under the load of scuba gear attached to their back, hung from their shoulders, and dangling from various hooks and D-rings in resplendent array. It's great to own all the latest stuff but it's not necessary to wear it all at once!

The mainline recreational diver wasn't the problem now, but rather the advanced or technical diver had emerged looking like some mutated version of a Navy SEAL crossed with the Sharper Image catalog!

Perhaps the authors will have to shoulder part of the blame since they published books and articles that contained photos of divers decked out in high volume doubles with multiple regulators, double BC's, and a couple of full sized cylinders as stage tanks. Never mind that these divers were engaged in extremely deep mixed gas exposures. And their dive plans with long bottom times called for extra primary breathing gas and oxygen/nitrox decompression and/or travel mixes. Now other divers wanted to look like these guys even if their diving called for far less cumbersome rigs. Why? Because it was cool, it was neat, and it caught the diving high tech fashion wave. Forget about your dinky Rolex watch when you could wear three dive computers and some impressive tekky wrist slates. The age of Neo-Tek chic had dawned.

Front view of a diver fully geared in redundant system for deep diving.

"It all sort of caved in on me when I did some diving in Key West in 1991 and witnessed this preposterous scenario," Gilliam remembers:

"There will always be debate on what equipment is necessary but a perspective on what is realistically matched to the dive plan must be encouraged. On a 60 to 90 fsw multi-level dive in May with air and water temperatures in the eighties, one dive team wore the following equipment: two members used full 1/4 inch wet suits with hoods, one member a full dry suit. All three wore fully redundant double 105 cu.ft. cylinders with isolation manifolds and all were employing NOAA NITROX I as dive mix. The three divers were demonstrating marked pre-dive equipment stress-loading just in the process of gearing up and moving around on the dive boat. Additionally, all were severely affected by the discomfort of the thermal suits while waiting to get in the water. In spite of the high ambient temperatures, one diver even made use of a separate suit inflator bottle filled with ARGON as an insulating gas.

Meanwhile, eight other divers dressed in conventional scuba rigs and lightweight wet suits or dive skins performed the same dive far more efficiently and they probably had a lot more fun.

A diver's performance is directly affected, either for better or worse, by his equipment selection. Certainly, the diver team discussed above

Harry Wenngatz wearing OMS 160 single cylinder and oxygen E bottle. Note reduction in mass, drag, and weight.

Back view of diver in doubles.

was drastically over equipped for the site conditions and any reasonable expectation of contingency. But they liked using the "high tech" gear even though it was not justified in this application. Given circumstances that presented cold water, extensive wreck or cave penetration etc. and the gear makes sense. As it happened, the gear set only lessened their performance.

An experienced diver dresses for the occasion as it were. A tuxedo is not required for a backyard barbecue. Veteran divers who have access to the most advanced "technical gear" will not hesitate to simplify a gear set when conditions allow."

This trend to pack the equivalent of a local dive store inventory on the diver's back has serious downsides. Sure, you may have more gas volume than the Goodyear blimp, but you also may have sacrificed your ability to swim with any degree of safety and efficiency. At some plateau, the point of diminishing returns is reached: is carrying 300 cubic feet of gas effective if the performance detriment by the sheer weight/size/drag of such gear requires the additional gas supply? We don't think so.

A lot of this overloading within the open water fraternity came from watching what the cave divers were doing. Many of their long deep dives in restrictive overhead environments dictated exceptional gear packages to handle their site specific contingencies. Cave divers also had the luxury, in most cases, of not having to factor currents, marine life, surface wave conditions, and boats that broke loose into their decompression plans. Basically, if they made it back to the first decom stop, they were pretty much home free.

Unfortunately, well meaning but inexperienced tech divers adopted much of their equipment packages for open water dives without giving much thought to the practical reality of their own operational dive plans. And this worries us a bit. We've seen divers who could barely even stand up under the weight of their doubles and twin full-sized stage bottles stagger to the back of the dive boat and crash in the water like an Apollo space capsule on reentry from orbit. Without double BC's to counteract the excessive negative buoyancy of this rig they would sink faster than a Texas Savings & Loan's cash reserves. Some divers have carried this so far that they are incapable of moving in the water without a diver propulsion vehicle. This is no joke, we're serious. What happens if an equipment or DPV failure calls for self rescue swimming skills? It's not a pretty picture.

The authors encourage divers to take a long look at some alternatives. Recently several manufacturers have introduced high volume cylinders that can provide single tank options instead of doubles. Ocean Management Systems has a 161 cubic foot cylinder (@3500 psi) that offers the equivalent of double eighties with less than half the weight and drag. Beuchat is importing a 190 cubic foot cylinder (@4300 psi) that should meet most diver's demands for dives to 200 feet or so easily. Although both high volume tanks are heavy, at least in the case of the OMS tank it can be dived safely with a single BC. Sherwood and Scubapro both offer cylinders in the 120 and 95 cubic foot range. Most divers that we have persuaded to try the single tank mode have found that their breathing consumption improved so dramatically with the lessened load that they actually use far less air on the same dive plans. And most importantly, they have achieved a greater mobility and swimming capability in the water. Even with single cylinder configurations you can provide a reasonable redundancy factor with isolation Y or H valves and a back up regulator.

Another place to examine for cutting the load is on decompression/ stage tanks. Most divers seem to grab whatever is handy and end up with standard 72 or 80 cubic foot sets. These are bulky, heavy and difficult to swim with. And for most typical dive plans, they provide far in excess of the needs of decompression. Gilliam uses a medical E cylinder fitted with a half-inch pipe thread scuba valve for dives requiring 25 minutes or less of hang time. These cylinders hold about 25 cubic feet of oxygen at 2015 psi and that's plenty at 20 and 10 feet. These are also long and skinny making them easy to mount on your primary cylinder so your hands are free for photography or collecting. If your stops are going to be longer or deeper (remember to observe O_2 depth limits), then there are a variety of selections in the 40 to 50 cubic foot range that can still be back mounted.

Just like adding weight and drag degrades your car's fuel and handling efficiency, your scuba equipment set impacts your physical ability to perform optimally in the sometimes hostile ocean environment. We'd

Mitch Skaggs with rig set up for side mount on 25 cubic foot deco cylinder which will allow him up to 30 minutes of deco at 20 feet with far less bulk than a larger cylinder.

Tom Mount rigs an OMS 45 cubic foot deco cylinder to his shoulder harness. This will provide more than enough oxygen for most anticipated decompressions and is less than half the weight and size of an standard 80.

like every diver to have the ability to "swim away" from an accident or malfunction scenario. Ask yourself if your present gear configuration will allow you this vital luxury.

AIR MANAGEMENT SYSTEMS

The issue of air management for the deep diver is a first-line, first-order, concern. No matter what environment one happens to be diving in, not enough air means big trouble. In addition to cylinders being carried in doubles and triples, larger tanks with an increased capacity are also utilized. Specialized valve manifolds and independent systems are quite common. And as one would suspect, it is vitally important for these specialized systems to be managed properly and safely.

• DIN Fittings:

As far as the high-tech, deep diving vanguard is concerned, the old standard yoke fittings are a thing of the past. Virtually all deep diving rigs incorporate DIN fittings (DIN is an acronym for Deutsches Institut fuer Normung, the German equivalent of the United States' CGA - Compressed Gas Association). These are fittings that are screwed directly into the cylinder valve (also a DIN connection) and thereby "mating" the regulator's first-stage with the tank valve.

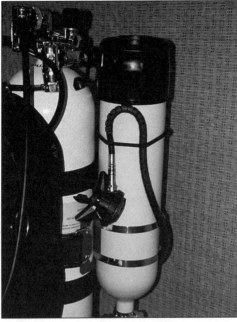

Another configuration with the OMS 45 mounted upside down directly to the primary back tank allowing easy access to valve.

Aside from the fact that this type of connection allows for the use of a higher pressure cylinder, typically 300 bar (1 bar = 14.504 psi; 300 bar = 4351.2 psi) is used on 3500 psi service. Also no external o-rings are necessary (DIN fittings incorporate "captured" o-rings) thus decreasing the possibility of a blown o-ring that could conceivably lead to a catastrophic air loss.

• Single Cylinders (Singles):

With the introduction of a plethora of high volume single cylinders, the diver now has almost and unlimited choice to choose from.

Diving cylinders come in a variety of shapes and sizes from the ubiquitous aluminum 80's (80 cubic feet) that have a working pressure of 3000 psi, to the newer high pressure (HP) steel cylinders (80's, 102's, 120's) that have a working pressure of 3500 psi. The high pressure cylinders come with a standard DIN fitting, whereas aluminum cylinders are not compatible with some DIN equipment due to their lower rated working pressure (as mentioned above, DIN rigs typically utilize 3500 psi/300 bar cylinders). Another generation of low-pressure (by comparison) cylinders such as the OMS line feature up to 120 cubic foot volumes at only 2650 psi. Although not specifically endorsed by the manufacturer, these cylinders are commonly used slightly higher pressures of up to 3500 psi to gain increased volumes. It is now possible to purchase single cylinders capable of holding nearly 200 cubic feet.

Keep in mind that in addition to the above-mentioned cylinder sizes, there are many others that are in use—some that are no longer being manufactured. The cylinders discussed here, particularly the HP models in connection with deep diving, were chosen because of the fact that they are perhaps a bit more common than others.

• Doubles:

Also referred to as twins or duals, this is a cylinder configuration that involves two cylinders (typically dual 80's, 102's, 105's, or 120's). The cylinders are "linked" or "joined" together via a manifold that is mated to the neck of each tank. A standard twin manifold incorporates a single first-stage regulator connector seat and an on/off valve. The latter serves as an on/off mechanism for both cylinders.

Doubles are used to provide the diver with twice the amount of a particular breathing medium than would normally be allowed. Although heavy and bulky, they make it possible for the deep diver to remain at depth for an extended period of time as well as providing him with additional gas for emergency use. The reader is reminded that the use of twins does not negate the need for an additional Emergency Breathing System (EBS).

One particular *disadvantage* of using doubles is that they are comparatively bulky, much heavier, and cumbersome than a single, requiring a little getting use to before an individual will feel comfortable.

• Independent Doubles:

Independent doubles (two cylinders, each with a separate set of regulators and instruments) are composed of a similar configuration to twins. The primary difference is that instead of the manifold providing a single valve and single regulator seat, it supplies the diver with dual valves and two regulator seats. This provides the diver with two completely independent systems: One for primary use and one for emergency backup. By allowing an individual to turn on or off either regulator independently (thus making it possible to keep one regulator and its cylinder shut off and in reserve), it adds an additional margin for safety.

Independent doubles have gained limited popularity due to the additional "air insurance" that their use provides as well as the fact that they supply the diver with a reserve regulator and cylinder. They are an excellent combination of primary air source and EBS in a single configuration. The down side is that the diver must continually switch between the two primary cylinders to ensure even usage. Having to remove a regulator at depth is not a procedure that many technical divers recommend and the added mass of equipment resulting from two complete independent packages can get a bit confusing for many divers.

• Benjamin Conversion:

Dr. George Benjamin in collaboration with Ike Ikehara designed the first double cylinder isolation manifold in the late sixties. A crossover bar plumbed into the cylinder valve below the valve orifice allowed two regulator systems to be mounted. In the event of a regulator failure or o-ring blowout, the diver could turn off the supply valve on that cylinder, effectively "isolating" the defective gear. However, the air in the cylinder could still be used via the crossover supply plumbing. *(NOTE: Benjamin Conversions are rarely used today and the reader is advised to have any such rig thoroughly inspected by a qualified equipment technician or someone who is expert in their use and function before the equipment is utilized.)*

• Isolation Manifolds:

Essentially this is the "manufactured version" of the original Benjamin modification. Originally produced in the late 1970's with a standard valve system it was the first industry response to the need for an isolation manifold. This manifold was produced in response to requests from the active cave diver community and was standard equipment for NOAA's *Hydro Lab* saturation system for scientist aquanauts. First designed and manufactured by Sherwood, this is a system that goes one step further than the typical independent doubles setup. Now officially called the **DIN Double Genesis Manifold**, it employs a unique isolation valve that can be used to isolate either cylinder. The added factor of cylinder isolation represents a truly independent EBS that allows for maximum redundancy. Since Sherwood's original isolation unit was introduced, a variety of similar manifolds have followed from Dive-Rite, OMS etc. Most are available in DIN fittings with conversion threaded plugs that can be removed to allow conventional yoke usage.

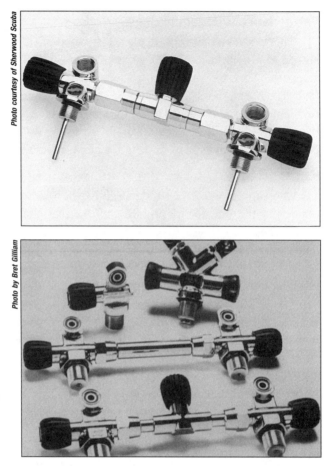

*Sherwood
Genesis DIN
isolation
manifold.*

*A variety of OMS
DIN valves and
isolation manifolds.*

•Crossover Manifold/Yoke:

These were originally designed to quickly equalize the pressure in the cylinders of two divers. They were built for use with 2250 psi tanks and when they were eventually used with 3000 psi tanks they malfunctioned due to the increased pressure. There was a 3000 psi model manufactured, but they were not as common as the 2250 psi model. They were also used to make "doubles" out of two tanks. The danger presented by the use of this type of rig is that if the manifold is accidentally knocked against an overhead obstruction, etc. an air leak could occur, or the seams of the manifold may be damaged and become separated. The crossover manifold/yoke is rarely used today and the reader is advised that they are potentially dangerous and belong on the shelf and not in the water.

Valve/Manifold/Regulator Cage:

This is a cage that is normally constructed of stainless steel and designed to protect the cylinder valve/manifold and the regulator's first-stage from abrasion and/or damage caused by contact with hard surfaces (rocks, wrecks, cave/cavern surfaces, etc.). If the valve/manifold or regulator first-stage were to be accidentally slammed into a hard surface, the end-result could be a catastrophic air loss. With the addition of a protector cage this type of emergency can be avoided.

REGULATORS

Choosing a regulator for deep diving is somewhat more involved than choosing one for traditional sport/recreational diving. In *Aqua-Corps: The Journal for Experienced Divers* (Volume 3/Winter 1991), an excellent article by Ron Russell, a diving equipment manufacturer's representative specializing in high-tech gear, offers a few parameters to consider before purchasing a regulator:

"What's important in a regulator anyway? Apart from the overriding concern in some quarters with the way your regulator color-coordinates with the rest of your gear, I would like to suggest a few basic criteria:

- Performance: how well does the regulator deliver air under various conditions?
- Reliability: how failure-prone is it within your intended parameters of use?
- Maintainability: how easy is it to service and what needs to be replaced at overhaul?
- Safety design: what design features have been included to minimize potential hazards?
- Ergonomics: how well does the regulator fit with human physiology? (Ed. physical requirements?)
- Compatibility: how will the regulator work with the diving system you now have or may acquire in the future?"

The six points listed above are certainly critical considerations for deep divers. Let's now take a closer, more definitive look at the particulars involved with each.

Performance:

This applies to how well the regulator breathes or "performs" at depth. As depth increases it becomes considerably more difficult for the regulator to deliver the air, which has become more dense. Additionally, the more arduous a divers' activity (harder working), the greater the exhalation resistance. (These are both factors which contribute to increased diver fatigue and carbon dioxide buildup.) Another influencing factor involves cylinder pressure; as tank pressure decreases, it becomes more difficult for the regulator to supply air at an efficient rate.

All of the above considerations dictate that the regulator chosen must be able to perform adequately no matter which of them come into play. Any regulator used for deep diving should have a balanced first-stage (diaphragm or piston) and a matched/compatible first- and second-stage. Additional second stages should be designed to work at the same intermediate pressure that the first-stage delivers. (*If the second-stage is designed for a lower intermediate pressure and is used with a first-stage that delivers a higher intermediate pressure, then it is likely to free-flow.*)

Reliability:

This refers to the unit's dependability as well. Does its track record show that it can perform well, and without incident, at depth? It is critically important for the regulator to be mechanically reliable. Particularly at greater depths, even a small malfunction can turn into a catastrophic air loss.

An excellent means of gaining information about a particular regulator's reliability is to consult a deep diving training facility (See **Training Facilities** in back of book).

Maintainability:

Is the regulator easily repaired if, prior to a dive, a malfunction is detected? This applies to both minor field repairs as well as in-house repairs, overhauls, etc. Also, it is important that spare parts for field repairs and parts for regularly scheduled maintenance be readily available from the distributor or the manufacturer. Other important considerations are: How often does the unit have to be overhauled (once every six months or once every year)? How durable are the second-stage seats? Is it necessary for the regulator to be retuned if the diving environment changes (i.e. going from warm, tropical water to cold water)?

Safety Design:

If a problem does occur at depth (such as a first- or second-stage failure or malfunction) are there any safety features built in that would help to avert a full-blown emergency? One such example is the Poseidon regulators that have a built-in overpressure relief device in the LP hose that connects the first- and second-stages. With this system, if

Comparison of the OMS 120, Sherwood 120, and Beuchat 140 cylinders.

the second-stage should malfunction resulting in free-flowing, the free-flowing air would be vented from the relief device in the hose. In this way, the regulator would still be breathable.

The reader should keep in mind that most, if not all, downstream designed regulators will automatically free-flow and continue to deliver air in the event of a malfunction. However, if this should occur, the diver's air would then be depleted at a much faster rate than normal. Conversely, upstream designed regulators will lockup and no longer deliver air to the diver in the case of a malfunction.

Ergonomics:

This is a term that has recently been exploited by the automotive industry. It refers to how well the design of a particular product matches the "physical" needs of the consumer. In the case of automobiles, it is usually the comfortability of how the overall car design fits with the human body, to which the term is applied. In the case of a regulator, it again refers to the degree of physical comfort that the device affords. Does the unit contribute to jaw fatigue due to its' design and weight? After extended periods of time in the water (particularly after a long dive and during an even longer decompression) does the unit continue to feel comfortable?

Compatibility:

Is the regulator compatible with the rest of your diving equipment and if you should decide to "upgrade" will it remain as such? Also, is it compatible with the type of diving that you'll be conducting (deep, cave, wreck, ice, etc.) or, in consideration of the above five points, would another choice be more prudent?

EMERGENCY BREATHING SYSTEMS (EBS)

Remember your Open Water/Entry Level class and the various "rules of scuba" that your instructor taught you? Well if not, here's a brief refresher:

Rule number one – BREATHE CONTINUOUSLY. This can be a difficult rule to follow if your regulator (first/second-stage or cylinder

Selection of OMS low pressure, high volume cylinders rigged as doubles.

OMS cylinders and dual bladder BC.

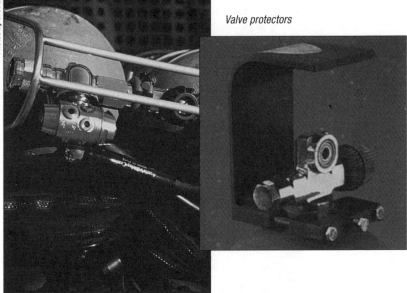

Valve protectors

valve) decides to malfunction. It is therefore necessary to provide yourself (or perhaps another member of the dive team who may require assistance) with some form of a backup system.

(Note: Although sharing air via an Octopus/Alternate Air Source is certainly a viable option, it is not addressed to any length in this text due to the fact that the authors believe in a more logical, realistic line of defense— self-sufficiency and equipment redundancy.)

All deep divers should provide themselves with at least an extra second-stage regulator. Additionally, some means of emergency backup should be provided for a catastrophic air failure (e.g. first-stage malfunction/failure, torn LP hose, blown cylinder valve o-ring, etc.). The emergency backup is not only for the diver who is carrying it, but, as referred to above, another member of the dive team may need it as well. The alternate air source, as per the general consensus of the high-tech deep diving community, should be equipped with a hose of at least 5 feet in length - particularly in overhead environments. This is to insure that an out-of-air team member will have sufficient hose length to safely function during ascent or, should the scenario arise, during a decompression "hang". Additionally, when diving in a constricted environment such as a cave or wreck it is often necessary for the divers to exit in single file formation due to the "constriction" of the cave/wreck. A safe-second hose of sufficient length will allow this type of single file exit.

Emergency breathing systems (EBS) are categorized into two groups: Type I Alternate Air Supply and Type II Redundant Air Supply. Type I emergency breathing systems are very different from Type II in that they do not offer air supply redundancy. However, they do offer one form of redundancy – a backup second-stage regulator. Due to the fact that they don't provide an additional air supply, they are referred to as alternates. Their primary function in the recreational diving community is one of supplying an out-of-air buddy with an octopus/safe-second, or in the case of a primary second-stage failure, to supply the diver with an emergency backup. Type II systems are referred to as redundant because they offer a completely separate air source. An example of a Type II EBS would be a pony bottle with attached regulators.

In order to select the appropriate backup system it's important for the diver to examine exactly what type of coverage and redundancy is needed and then decide which Type II system would best fit the situation. The ideal Type II system would allow the diver to extricate him/herself from an out-of-air situation by ascending at a safe, normal rate (60 feet per minute, or appropriate rate of ascent if a dive computer is used) and avoiding a possible lung overexpansion injury. Another consideration would be staged decompression diving. If a particular backup system did not allow the diver enough reserve air to make a required stop(s), then it would be considered insufficient. A missed decompression stop is certainly less severe than drowning, but if both can be avoided by diving with the proper equipment, so much the better.

It is also important to take into consideration the *amount* of air that is necessary for the diver to carry. Limiting factors in this equation would be: Personal air consumption, depth, water temperature, overhead environments, arduous activity involved, etc. After considering all of the various factors, the proper Type II EBS could then be selected (e.g. size of pony/bailout bottle, etc.).

THERMAL PROTECTION SYSTEMS

The deep water environment requires a diver to be properly suited and thus protected against the affects of cold water. Cold water as it is referred to in this text means water that is 75^0 F (26^0 C) or less.

In addition to wet suits, the standard fare of non-cold water divers (Caribbean, South Pacific, etc.), dry suits with thermal underwear are

DUI thermal underwear for dry suit.

OMS argon gas dry suit inflation system.

the obvious alternative. They provide the diver with exceptional protection against the elements by keeping all but his hands and head dry (some suits are designed to keep hands and head dry as well) and also allow the individual to be dry at the end of a dive. This is particularly important for repetitive dives, especially if the diver's surface interval takes place in an environment that is less than warm and comfortable.

Affects of Cold Water:

Body heat loss via conductivity in water (water has approximately 25 times the conductive capacity of air) contributes physiologically to a number of negative factors that influence a diver's efficiency. A few of these factors are:

1. Loss of flexibility in the limbs (arms, hands, legs).
2. Overall fatigue and sluggishness.
3. Loss of short-term memory.
4. Greater susceptibility to inert gas narcosis (nitrogen narcosis).
5. Greater susceptibility to decompression sickness.

Affects of Increased Pressure:

With an increase in pressure comes an increase in wet suit compression. This in turn results in the suit providing less and less thermal protection.

The use of a dry suit requires that the diver adjust the amount of air (gas) that is contained inside the suit. Most sport divers have an additional low pressure (LP) hose routed from the first-stage, that is connected to the primary cylinder, to the inflator mechanism on the suit. However, for more advanced types of diving activities such as that involved in deep diving it may be more prudent, due to the more disciplined air regulation parameters, to carry a separate cylinder (usually a 13+ cubic foot pony bottle) for the sole purpose of suit inflation. This method allows for the air in the primary cylinder to be used for respiration and BCD inflation, without the added drain of supplying air to the dry suit.

In addition to the use of air for dry suit inflation it is becoming more common for specialized gases such as Argon to be substituted. Due to the fact that Argon is very dense, it is an excellent insulator.

DIVER PROPULSION VEHICLES (DPV'S)

Efficient, air-saving maneuverability is a very definite concern for the deep diver. One particular piece of specialized equipment often used

Photos courtesy of Florida Speological Researchers

Rick Nicolini and Dustin Clesi of Team Diepolder '91 made the farthest and deepest penetrations in that system to pass lines laid by Dale Sweet and Jim Lockwood almost eleven years earlier.

by deep divers is a diver propulsion vehicle (DPV), also known as a "scooter". From the state-of-the-art workhorse Aqua Zepp, that is manufactured in Germany and has a working depth in excess of 300 feet, to "beefed-up", altered Tekna and Dacor scooters (they normally have a maximum working depth of approximately 160 fsw/48m, but can be rigged for use in deeper water) deep divers are taking advantage of the benefits of these devices.

DPV's allow the diver to conserve energy and thereby decrease air/gas consumption, which in turn allows for more bottom time. In the case of cave divers, DPV's allow cavers to penetrate further into a cave or cavern system than would normally be permitted if the diver were merely using fins for propulsion. Scooters, primarily the Aqua Zepp due to its larger size, are also utilized as sites of attachment for additional cylinders, lights, cameras, videos, etc.

WEIGHT SYSTEMS

Weight systems used by deep divers vary depending on the type of diving being conducted as well as the type of equipment used. The deeper one ventures into the depths the less weight needed due to the increase in hydraulic pressure (the pressure being exerted upon the diver by the overlying water column). Also, many deep divers who utilize double HP steel cylinders do not wear a weight belt due to the weight of the tanks. Another limiting factor is water temperature (i.e. geographic location). Warm water divers who wear 3mm or less wet suits and do not require a thicker suit or a dry suit can often avoid the need for a weight belt.

One concern that the reader is advised to be cognizant of is the fact that as the dive progresses and the cylinders are depleted of air/gas, the diver will be somewhat more buoyant due to the loss of the air/gas. This means that even though a weight belt wasn't necessary for the beginning of the dive, it may now become necessary (particularly when decompressing) due to the additional buoyancy. Because of this factor some divers will hang a weight belt with the appropriate amount of weight on the anchor line or the decompression line.

DIVE COMPUTERS (DC'S)

The utilization of dive computers as applied to deep diving is a very technical and involved subject. The reader is therefore referred to Chapter 8 for further information about their use.

ABOVE: The Dive Rite Wings system for back mounted BC designs. LEFT: The Dive Rite back plate

DEPTH GAUGES

If an individual has elected not to use a dive computer, a depth gauge is necessary. Those gauges constructed of metal (not plastic) are the only acceptable choice for deep diving. Additionally, the gauge should be graduated every 5-10 feet for more accurate reading.

Helium-Filled Depth Gauges:

Aside from the depth gauges incorporated into dive computers, the helium-filled gauges made by SOS Italy are by far the most accurate. These are available in two editions: a 250 ft. model and a 500 ft. model. Long distributed in the U.S. by Scubapro, they are now only available through SOS of Italy. Considered by most experienced deep divers to be the most accurate depth gauge ever built, they are still in wide demand. Many divers still refer to these gauges as the #503 and #507 gauges respectively from Scubapro's catalog.

THE SELF-SUFFICIENT DIVER

In *Solo Diving: The Art of Underwater Self-Sufficiency,* von Maier (1991) notes, "For an individual to be completely self-sufficient underwater is certainly the most desirable end result of diver training. Realistically, not all divers are either capable of this (in a complete, definitive sense), or have a desire to achieve it. In fact, for many sport divers, solo diving just doesn't present the same appeal as it does for others. Perhaps they prefer a buddy for personal reasons such as companionship, or they simply feel more comfortable having someone along for the dive. These are reasons that, in this author's opinion, are valid and present no real problems. The problems arise when a buddy is desired to maintain an individual's safety (i.e. to compensate for poor watermanship or inadequate training)."

And so it is with deep diving. Before individuals enter into the deep water realm it is critically important for them to be self-sufficient. It is also imperative that they possess excellent watermanship along with better-than-average skill levels.

If it is important for the normal, everyday recreational diver to be self-sufficient, it is even more important for the deep diver to fit this definition. Aside from the obvious prerequisites – excellent health and watermanship;

BELOW: The Seapro Tech BC. RIGHT: This unit comes with well designed d-rings and accessories to allow mounting a variety of extra gear easily. Note regulator retainers worn around neck.

Photo by David Sipperly

above-average skill levels; proper training and education - it is necessary for the deep diver to be self-reliant in terms of equipment emergencies as well. This is exactly what equipment redundancy is all about.

EQUIPMENT REDUNDANCY

Proper, quality equipment and deep diving go hand-in-hand. If a diver experiences a second-stage failure at 170 fsw (51.5 m), he'd better have some form of backup. And the backup should be a high quality

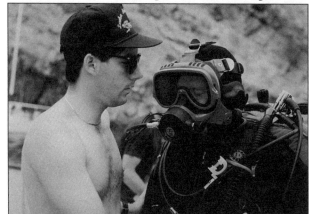

Full face mask with communications unit.

Dive Rite explorer reel

Photo by Bret Gilliam

second-stage, not the typical, inexpensive "octopus" that so many sport divers carry. The same goes for several other pieces of equipment. Not only does the deep diver need to possess backup systems (i.e. redundant), but these systems must be of the same high quality and proven performance as the equipment that they are meant to replace.

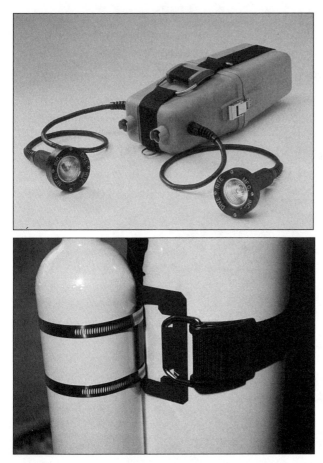

Dive Rite high powered lighting system with dual heads.

Dan Berg's Aqua Explorer mounting system for attaching pony or stage bottles directly to primary cylinders. This is a particularly well designed unit and can accommodate up to 50 cubic tanks.

SUMMARY

Specialized equipment and deep diving go hand-in-hand. Longer exposures and greater depths not only require that the diver be physically and mentally prepared, but that he also possess the proper equipment (as well as the knowledge to utilize the equipment) to safely perform the dive.

Diving equipment has evolved so quickly to service the technical market that it is impossible for us to adequately review or illustrate the many choices a diver now has when outfitting. This subject will be covered in detail in a training program with specific recommendations and examples that will meet your local environmental site conditions. If you are already trained and experienced, make a habit of dropping in to your local tech dive store to get updated periodically. There's usually something new and interesting out every few months. The latest advances have come in high volume cylinders, computers and BCD's. We should be seeing affordable rebreather units in 1995. Stay informed and educated about equipment. You may find you want to rent an item before purchase. We regard this as an excellent practice. If you encounter resistance, shop around until you find a dealer with a more enlightened attitude.

And finally, don't be afraid to innovate and customize your package to effect the most practical outfit possible. Beware of instructors who will pontificate that there is only one proper way to do something. The authors have learned from experience, and even students, that different solutions to the same equipment problem are widespread. We don't necessarily believe that there is a "wrong" way to configure equipment unless it is obviously dangerous. How you wear your decom cylinder is more a personal choice: back-mounted or side carried? It's your call, it's what works best for you and is most comfortable for your swimming style and site conditions. But use the excellent advice and counsel of professional tech divers and instructors along with store staff to help formulate your decisions. But remember... you're the diver that has to dive with this equipment in the water. What works for you and your size, fitness, age, and objectives is most important.

Photo by Wes Skiles

A fully equipped technical diver ready for adventure.

CHAPTER 8

Dive Computers and Deep Diving

*"For those of us who love the underwater world,
the advent of dive computers has greatly enhanced our
recreation. Using computer-assisted multi-level diving
techniques will allow divers to spend more time underwater.
It is important to remember, however, that dive computers are
a tool that must be understood and used properly."*

Ken Loyst

To discuss the role of dive computers in deep diving necessitates a preliminary overview of the validity of these devices in standard diving. Like many new evolutions in equipment, dive computers were initially met with skepticism and outright condemnation by some members of the diving community. In retrospect, much of this hostile reception was not deserved. The most vocal critics tended to be the so-called experts who were never fully cognizant of the theory of multi-level diving that was widely applied as far back as the late sixties.

The SOS Decompression Meter was introduced in 1959 but did not gain widespread U.S. distribution until Scubapro gained import rights in 1963. Although not a "computer" by any stretch of the imagination, this relatively simple device provided the first basis of practical underwater calculation of multi-level diving and became popular with professional photojournalists, film makers and divers who were tired of being boxed in to the confines of historical "square profile" table plans. Although many simply dismissed the "decom meter" as invalidated and branded it the "Bend-O-Matic", thousands of divers used it without incident and only grudgingly parted with their well-worn units to make the switch to electronic computers.

Obviously, the old "meter" users were comfortable with multi-level profiling and the transition to modern computers was a natural progression. Some early computer models failed to live up to expectations or suffered from design failures that led to flooding, power failures, etc. These initial problems were almost completely eliminated and as we go to press in the fall of 1991, today's diver has over two dozen highly accurate and reliable computers to choose from.

So why use a computer? Quite simply, they are more accurate in measuring depth and time, and virtually every model available incorporates a decompression algorithm more conservative than the standard U.S. Navy tables. Most divers use computers to gain more time underwater safely since the units are "active" devices that compute theoreti-

---

Dive Computer Book

Dive Computers: A Consumer's Guide To History, Theory and Performance *by Ken Loyst with Karl Huggins and Michael Steidley* is specifically designed for any diver that either owns a dive computer or is considering purchasing one. **Dive Computers** is a diver's guide to using dive computers safely and to making an intelligent decision as to which dive computer would best fit your diving needs. Get the straight facts about dive computers currently available. Information includes history of dive computers, historical references of the pioneers in decompression theory, explanations of decompression theory and multi-level  diving, and a systematic computer comparison and performance section with 24 dive computers.

Dive Computers: A Consumer's Guide To History, Theory and Performance can be purchased through your local dive retailer or through Watersport Publishing, Inc., P.O. Box 83727, San Diego, CA 92138, (619) 697-0703.

cal tissue/compartment inert gas loading and outgassing based upon actual depths and times. This provides an obvious benefit to "square profiles" where the diver's uptake and release are modeled on assuming that the entire dive was spent at the deepest depth for the total dive time.

But even if you have a problem accepting the theory of multi-level diving, then modern computers will give you a safety edge based upon their highly accurate depth measuring sensors and timing devices. Using them solely in this application can provide a safety buffer for the strict table user. Some models are significantly more conservative than the Navy tables. For instance, we can all remember that the U.S. Navy tables allow 60 minutes at 60 feet (18.2 m) with no decompression. By comparison, the Dacor Micro Brain Pro Plus computer allows only 44 minutes for the same depth based on its Buhlmann model and program that presumes diving at slight altitude.

The acceptance of diving computers has literally swept through the industry in the nineties. Just a glance around any liveaboard vessel will confirm this, and more and more entry level divers are purchasing computers during or immediately after training.

Although any piece of equipment can fail, modern dive computers are extraordinarily reliable. Additionally, the safety of their decompression models has been proven. In Gilliam's study (1989-90) of 77,680 dives by sport divers, he had zero cases of DCS among computer users (who made up over 50% of the data base).

Recent workshops and symposia have seen respected experts predict such a dominance by computers that dive tables as a primary dive planning protocol may well become obsolete. Although not willing to go on record officially, the majority of professional underwater photographers, resort guides, etc.., have already abandoned tables and use computers exclusively. Mount (1991) stated "All my dives since 1983 have been on dive computers. I use two computers in case of a failure. I decompress by the most conservative one. The only time I look at dive tables is when I teach classes, I feel they (tables-Ed.) are ancient history with today's technology."

SELECTION OF A DIVE COMPUTER FOR DEEP DIVING

Not all computers are suited for deep diving due to their depth limitation. Exceeding a depth barrier or incurring a decompression obligation of more than five minutes was sufficient to put many models into "error" or "out-of-range" modes. In this condition, the diver was locked out by some models and diving could not be resumed for 24 hours.

This book does not have space for an expansive subject treatment of all diving computers and their functions. The authors strongly recommend the text *Dive Computers: A Consumer's Guide to History, Theory and Performance* by Ken Loyst, with Karl Huggins and Mike Steidley (Watersport Books, 1991). Also, it is prudent to consult other experienced deep divers for their input on computer selection.

Computer application should be based on several criteria:
Algorithm

As any diver whom has spent some "hang time" can tell you, there are vastly different decompression models incorporated in the various units. This will involve an informed, educated choice as to what model is most appropriate for your age, water temperature, physical condition, level of deep diving adaptation, etc. Some computers using the Buhlmann algorithm will require substantially more decompression time than others based on more liberal models. Many divers consider this an added safety factor and others consider it a damn nuisance. Take the time to research a computer before buying it and definitely insist on diving a "loaner" before making the investment. Once the unit is selected, conform to its decompression schedule. Never cut "hang times" short.

Depth Range

You can't very well plan a dive to 220 fsw (66.6 m) if your computer isn't designed for that depth. Some very popular and well-de-

Photo by Bret Gilliam

Lynn Hendrickson checks dive computer for decompression status at 20 foot stop. Computers have made it possible to more accurately plan decompression while actually underwater and allow for contingencies.

TABLE 8-1

Deep Diving Dive Computers						
Dive Computer	Model Type	Dive Timer Range (in minutes)	Full Function Range (in feet)	Depth Gauge Range (in feet)	Decompression Stop Limits (in feet)	Decompression Stop Time (maximum in min.)
Beuchat Aladin Pro	Buhlmann ZHL-16	199	330'	330'	80'+	99
Dacor Micro Brain Pro Plus	Buhlmann-Hahn P-4	199	270'	330'	98'	90
Parkway Legend	Buhlmann ZHL-16	199	330'	330'	80'+	99
Scubapro DC-11	Buhlmann-Hahn P-5	199	300'	300'	70'	90
Suunto Solution	Nikkola SME	999	325'	325'	140'	99
U.S. Divers Monitor II	Buhlmann ZHL-16	199	330'	330'	80'+	99

signed computers that are appropriate for normal sport diving depths are absolutely ruled out for deep diving. ORCA's workhorse, the Edge, introduced in 1983, was never designed for use beyond 165 fsw (50 m). Likewise, Dacor originally unveiled the 1988 version of the Micro Brain Pro Plus with a depth limitation of 330 fsw (100 m), but in Gilliam's field testing (1989) it was discovered that the unit's case was sufficiently compressed into the internal components so as to render it incapable of true depth registration much below 290 fsw (87.9 m). Dacor modified the depth recommendation to 270 fsw (81.8 m) thereafter. Although not officially sanctioned by the manufacturer, similar experimental dives revealed that the Beuchat Aladin Pro would accurately read out depths well beyond the range in the manual. It is doubtful that the unit is computing gas loading beyond its stated range, but it still offers the benefit of a digital depth gauge. How deep will it read? Gilliam (1990) took one to 467 feet (141.5 m) as indicated in feet of fresh water (ffw) and at least one other has been taken to 480 (145.5 m) as indicated on a mixed gas dive. For the purposes of any reasonable dive exposure, this unit will perform.

Decompression Display

Unless you are comfortable with a computer that tells you a decompression or "ceiling" obligation has been incurred but does not tell you for how long you must remain at that stop, we suggest using a computer

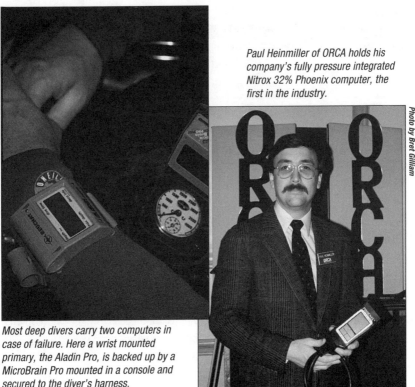

Paul Heinmiller of ORCA holds his company's fully pressure integrated Nitrox 32% Phoenix computer, the first in the industry.

Most deep divers carry two computers in case of failure. Here a wrist mounted primary, the Aladin Pro, is backed up by a MicroBrain Pro mounted in a console and secured to the diver's harness.

that gives decom stops displayed in minutes. This is particularly important for the shallow hangs which can get quite long. Air management is far easier if you know exactly how much time you are obligated to for decompression.

Ascent Rate

Few computers use ascent rates in excess of 60 feet per minute (18.2 m/minute) and most incorporate far slower rates. This is fine for most divers and leads to a more controlled "continuous ascent decompression" within normal sport diving ranges. However, it can be a problem in deep diving where a slow ascent rate can actually contribute to more inert gas loading. The diver is then faced with a difficult decision: increase the ascent rate at least to the 100 fpm (30.3 mpm) level in the deeper segments of the dive (over 100 feet), and then slow down in the

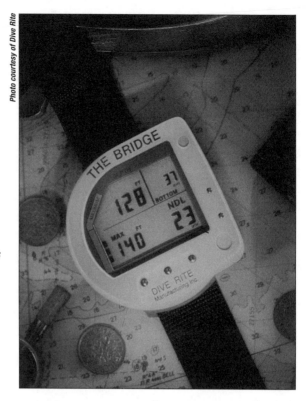

Dive Rite's nitrox computer, The Bridge, is fully programmable for oxygen percentages from 21% to 50%.

shallower segments of the dive, but risk throwing the computer into "error" or confusing it by excessive speed of ascent (at least as far as the computer model is concerned).

SUMMARY

Dive computers have a valid role in deep diving if used correctly and within their model limitations. The authors advocate redundant computers per diver if tables are not used. During the Ocean Quest experimental studies by Gilliam (1989-90), extensive deep (200+ fsw/ 60.6+ m) diving was done using the computer models as the sole basis of decompression with no incidence of DCS. These dives were of relatively short duration at depth, however (usually exposures of 30 minutes or less). As divers involved in wreck and cave penetration become involved with more extensive bottom times, the potential of pushing the limits of the decompression model become greater and increase the attendant risk. Custom tables should then take precedence with comput-

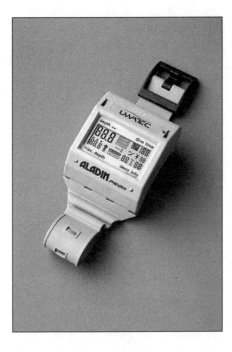

The Aladin Pro dive computer is considered to be one of the best units for technical diving applications.

ers primarily used as digital depth/time instruments and their decompression information used in a backup role.

Computers have increasingly altered traditional dive planning practices since the diver now has an effective means of calculating deviations from a fixed plan while underwater. We recommend that divers have a working dive plan scenario prior to water entry, but deviation to take advantage of unexpected marine life appearances or dramatic coral formations discovered at deeper depths is reasonable and will not compromise safety. The computer (and backup) will allow far more flexibility and yet keep track of no-decompression or decompression obligations.

It is good practice for divers to familiarize themselves with the manufacturer's recommendation for computer failure. Each model applies different "Murphy's Law" procedures and are provided in the computer manual. There is a described protocol for at least one computer (ORCA models) so that the diver may reenter Navy tables. Michael Emmerman authored this suggested procedure and does offer the only viable return to tables scenario.

Computers, like any instrument, can fail but their track record is extremely good in retrospective. Divers must also bring a personal helping of common sense to the table. As it has been pointed out ad nauseam by some critics, it is theoretically possible for a computer to "allow" a potentially hazardous dive profile. However, even a mild grip on reality will suggest that computers be used conservatively much the same as

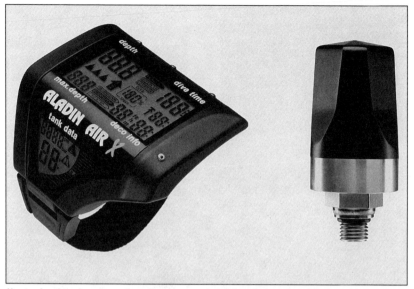

Uwatec has introduced an extraordinary compact air integrated version of their workhorse Aladin computer. Called the Aladin Air X, this unit retains the reliable decompression algorithm but incorporates a wireless, hoseless transmitter that eliminates the need for a high pressure hose. Cylinder pressure is displayed (along with the usual dive status information) on a small streamlined wrist unit. The unit also displays remaining dive time based upon present depth and the divers breathing rate. Dive profile memory can be downloaded to a PC for record keeping and dive planning simulations. In our tests, the Aladin Air X performed without a hitch. This is one of the best innovations brought to market.

safety buffers have been added to tables (next greater depth or time) for years by divers seeking a cushion. Don't run your computer to the edge (no pun intended) of its decompression model.

Use computers as the valuable tool they can be but don't expect any device to think for you.

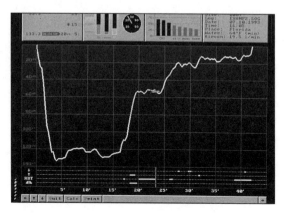

Sample of dive profile downloaded to a PC from the Aladin Air X by Uwatec.

Bill Gardner rigged with two BC bladders in case of accidental puncture while deep on a wreck. The negative weight of his doubles and stage bottles require a minimum of 35 pounds lift from his BC to maintain neutral buoyancy in the first phases of the dive.

CHAPTER 9

Contingencies

"What could happen? I've covered everything."

John Wayne Bobbitt

It goes without saying that sooner or later even the best laid dive plans go awry. And usually when you least expect it. But even when the worst occurs, a well trained diver can manage his new circumstances if he is conditioned to always have a contingency plan to implement. "Murphy's Law" has an infinite series of disasters lurking for divers whatever environment they choose to explore: caves, rivers, quarries, deep walls, or even shallow reefs on drift dives. Let's examine a few curve balls that get tossed the way of these intrepid explorers, particularly deep wreck divers.

Most scenarios will involve low or out of air situations or isolation from surface support. Low air crises are typically initiated by one or more of a combination of events that often involve entanglement, getting lost inside or outside the wreck, equipment failure, poor observation of gas management rules, or unpredictable natural catastrophes such as breakdowns of the wreck structure itself. How the diver reacts to these types of stress may determine his ability to survive.

Generic guidelines in gas management may involve various implementations of the cave diving community's "rule of thirds" (one third of starting gas volumes for initial penetration, one third to come out on, and one third in reserve), or less conservative rules if no penetration or decompression ceiling is anticipated. Key to all gas volume planning is matching the plan to the diver with the highest breathing rate and the smallest volume of breathing gas carried by the team. This should allow a reasonable margin of safety in most circumstances.

Entanglements in fishing line, old nets, electrical wire, wreck debris etc. are a matter of routine for many divers. The assistance of a buddy diver can be invaluable in extricating a trapped diver but individual self-rescue should be the first order of priority. That includes an attitude of "defensive diving" and an awareness of one's surroundings at all times. At least two sharp knives worn on the arm or chest area within easy reach should be standard gear. Many divers have found that carrying a pair of wire clippers capable of quickly cutting through such hazards are invaluable. Your macho-looking "broadsword" strapped to your calf won't do you much good if you can't reach it or if it isn't sharp enough to do the job.

Most divers can easily cope with entanglements that snag them from the front, but can you deal with a wad of monofilament hung in your valve manifold where you can't see it? Familiarization with your own equipment is absolutely essential. You may have to remove it in a confined area to deal with the problem and then replace it. This can take time and throw your air consumption and bottom time calculations out the window. Self control and smooth logical reactions to stress are survival tools not practiced enough by most divers.

The OMS H-valve allows two regulators to mounted on a single cylinder and each can be isolated in the event of failure or free-flow.

Photo by Bret Gilliam

The Sherwood Genesis isolation manifold for doubles allows dual regulators with the ability to let one regulator draw from both cylinders if one fails. Here Bill Gardner closes the isolation manifold shut-off.

Well, now you've managed to cut away the entanglement but in the process the wreck interior has silted out from your bubble stream and movements in the confined space. Your powerful dive light can only reflect a blinding backscatter of suspended particles rendering your vision to zero. One school of thought advocates "progressive penetration" whereby, at least theoretically, the diver "memorizes" the wreck interior by gradual excursions over many dives until the diver can effect an exit by touch and learned landmarks. I happen to think that this is a bit overly optimistic especially if you are four decks down inside the *Andrea Doria*, and some veteran wreck divers whom I greatly respect swear by this method. But after some thirty years of diving and having wrecks cave-in on me, lights fail, and other dive teams silt-out rooms for me once too often, I'm a firm advocate of employing a reel with line to provide me a continuous pathway to the safety of the wreck's exterior. One thing is for sure, you can't start up to the surface until you get outside the wreck. You make the call on which method will provide the most reliable exit.

Almost all deep wrecks will call for planned decompression. Some divers elect to carry all necessary gas volumes for the dive itself and the decompression on themselves in the form of doubles or extra "stage tanks" reserved solely for ascent and hangs. Others plan to return to the anchor or ascent line and rendezvous with extra cylinders hung off at the first decom stop or supplied from hoses attached to large cylinders on the boat. Since a growing number of divers are using oxygen or nitrox mixtures for more efficient decompressions, it's vital that these extra gas supplies can be located and accessed. That's usually not a problem if ocean currents are not a factor or if the diver can guarantee his underwater navigation will return him to the ascent line.

However, if your dive buddy is named Murphy, you can count on getting disoriented due to reduced visibility and missing the up line or simply getting blown off the wreck by a strong current. Even if you do everything perfectly, the boat itself could break free if its anchor line parts or breaks out of the wreck. That's why the prudent diver will leave his decom tanks clipped into the wreck at the nearest point to his penetration entrance. If unexpected events delay his exit or make it impossible to return to the anchor line, he will still have the necessary gas supply to make a controlled ascent and complete his decompression.

On a large wreck without strong current he could elect to fasten his reel line to the wreckage and ascend to his decompression depth. This would still keep him in a fixed vicinity and his bubble stream would identify his position for the surface observers. However, in a strong current an "up line" can be impractical and it will be necessary to deploy a lift bag on the reel line to mark his position and then complete his decompression schedule while free-drifting beneath it. This is a less desirable scenario since the diver will move away from the wreck with the current, but an alert surface crew will be on the lookout for the lift bag and send a chase boat or recover the diver after the other team members are aboard. Most divers carry the lift bag in a BC pocket or attach it with shock cord to the cylinder where it's out of the way until needed. To ensure it will be spotted, a high visibility color or painted reflective markings along with the diver's name are added.

Okay, you've survived entanglement, silt-out, and gear failure while you made it to your stage tanks. And, in spite of being blown away in the current, you've deployed your lift bag and completed your decompression. Now you surface expecting the boat to waiting for you. But Mother Nature has teamed up with Murphy to yank your chain a little more: fog or dense rain limits visibility to a wispy thirty feet or so. Aren't you glad you brought that sonic alarm and a high intensity signaling strobe? In areas where fog can materialize quickly like the north-

LEFT: A reel is an essential piece of equipment allowing use for navigation and to deploy surface floats during free drifting decompression. BELOW: Many divers feel that use of a guide reel on wreck dives is essential to provide a path to safety in the event of visibility failure due to silting. Scott Lockwood runs his reel from a point on the wreck main deck before penetrating the interior.

east, we recommend a collapsible radar reflector that can be held up on a "safety sausage" to aid the boat in finding you.

The investment in a few peripherals such as a reel, line, lift bag, signal device etc. are probably less than your bar bill on New Year's Eve. These devices combined with a healthy dose of common sense and some defensive diving skills, will enable you to cope with most contingencies. It's rare that everything goes wrong at once but it's nice to be prepared and have the confidence to implement safety plans quickly and efficiently. Training, experience, and an anticipation for the unexpected mark the diver who will manage effectively when a stressful situation presents. Never expect things to go right and you'll rarely be disappointed.

RUNNING ON EMPTY

Gilliam reflects, "Thirty-four years ago when my dad consented to let me learn to dive in Key West, my "course" was short and sweet. It basically consisted of learning to remove and replace my gear in about thirty feet of water in the boat basin and the stern admonition to "breathe out on the way up". This intensive curriculum was covered in about an hour and my instructor, a charter fishing captain and part-time salvage diver, never interrupted his routine of rebuilding a recalcitrant outboard motor to actually bother getting into the water with me.

But he was concerned enough to put down his screwdriver briefly and reemphasize what he considered the essence of survival advice. "When you run out of air," he intoned, "just don't hold your breath or your lungs will explode!" That conjured up some pretty graphic images for a nine year old imagination in the fifties. I mean they already had us hiding under our desks as part of the atom bomb air raid safety drill in school. It didn't take us long to figure out that if this was the key to their survival plan, then any further serious contemplation of memorizing the multiplication tables was going right on the back burner. But the mental picture of a small mushroom cloud escaping from my mouth as a consequence of breath-holding stuck with me like Michael Jackson at a choir boys' picnic."

The operative word in dive planning of that era was *"when"* you ran out of air, not *"if"*. In the absence of submersible pressure gauges, the

Photo by Bret Gilliam

Jim Mims has clipped his decom tanks to the wreck and will retrieve them prior to ascent. This ensures adequate decom gas should the boat break loose and he has to handle his decompression independently.

Lynn Hendrickson tests a "Come-To-Me" safety float. Such devices make a diver far more readily seen in rough water.

This reel and lift bag are comfortably carried behind the diver mounted to his primary cylinder. If needed he can access them with one hand to complete drifting decompression with the bag marking his location.

dive was concluded when the regulator began to breathe hard or when the air abruptly ceased. This was not as big a deal as it might sound today simply because divers experienced the out of air scenario routinely and were conditioned to dealing with it.

With the evolution of modern dive equipment, we no longer have to guess at how much air is remaining in our tanks. Today's gear can even give you a digital readout of the exact psi left and predict how many minutes it will last based upon your breathing rate. Regulators no longer begin to perform like garden hoses sucked on from the pool bottom when cylinder pressures drop below 600 psi. Divers can select extra capacity tanks up to nearly 200 cubic feet to match any dive plan. In fact, given the tools available from the industry in 1994, it's hard to really justify running out of air at all. But it still happens occasionally, though not nearly with the frequency of the earlier stalwart explorers.

So what do you do if the needle locks up at zero because you were concentrating on getting the perfect photo when you should have been monitoring your instruments? Let's look at some options in order of preferred priority.

1. **Emergency Swimming Ascent:** Most experts agree that if you can solve a problem yourself then the chances of screw-ups are dramatically lessened. Therefore in any routine out of air situation, it is desirable to make a direct ascent to the surface under your own power while retaining the regulator in your mouth and continuously exhaling slowly. And remember that you will probably get a couple of breaths on the way up as the ambient pressure is reduced during ascent. Well, what is routine? Certainly most divers can comfortably deal with ascents from around thirty feet or so. Bob Halstead, a vastly experienced professional dive guide, has suggested that you should never dive deeper than twice the depth from which you can comfortably free dive. (The active theory here being that if you can free dive to 60 feet, it's really a round trip of 120 feet. So you should be able to come up from that depth on a one-way mission.)

Almost all dive professionals have witnessed someone run out of air as shallow as 15 or 20 feet and then frantically engage the nearest unsuspecting diver in a mad attempt to share air that more closely resembles the mating act of porcupines on really bad acid. When asked why they didn't simply swim unassisted to the surface, they usually confess they were so conditioned to seeking an air donor that the obvious solution never occurred to them.

Of course, an ESA will not allow the luxury of a safety stop or a required decompression stop. But if you're not charmed by the idea of a solo ascent from deeper depths, then we need to look a little farther down our option list.

2. **Independent Back-Up Reserves:** These are secondary air sources that can be carried with a diver and used like normal scuba for limited duration life support. One of the simplest and most popular devices introduced in the '80's is the SpareAir. This unit is available in several volume sizes and incorporates a small cylinder with an integral tiny regulator & mouthpiece. If needed, it is retrieved from a lanyard or carrying pocket/pouch and the diver can breathe normally during his ascent. This is a distinct advantage over an ESA deeper than 100 feet and it also allows the option of handing the unit off to another diver if they ran out thus avoiding the close personal involvement of sharing air.

However, it must be kept in mind that SpareAir units even of the largest size volume manufactured are still decidedly "spare" on how long you can breathe off one. And you have to have the confidence to smoothly locate and use the unit in a potential stress situation. We know some divers who can easily complete a safety stop following a 60 foot ascent with one of these units, but other divers are hard pressed to get more than three or four breaths coming up from only slightly deeper. It's all a matter of breathing rates and self-contained "cool", but we recommend opting for the company's largest model if adding a SpareAir to your gear package and then practicing with it to see how it meshes with your personal comfort zone.

By employing a larger "pony bottle", long popular with the North Atlantic wreck community, the diver can provide more than adequate backup air for a safe ascent and deco stops. These are typically sized from about 12 cubic feet up to nearly 45 cubic feet. Most are designed to be mounted to the primary cylinder package and are equipped with a conventional regulator though without pressure gauges, inflators, etc. To aid a buddy, the "pony bottle" second stage can be handed off and a tandem ascent accomplished including decompression if necessary. In this use, divers must now recognize the added risk and responsibility of act-

Photo by Bret Gilliam

In addition to his stage deco tank, this diver carries an independent 25 cubic foot "Bailout" cylinder with standard air that can be used for an emergency ascent in case of total primary system failure.

ing as a team once the need is communicated by the diver needing air. This is one step more difficult than the independence of a "give away" unit, but still attractive and reasonable to most dive plans.

Certainly, smaller "pony bottles" can be limited in their applications in deeper depths. And divers should take a close look at ensuring a cylinder volume appropriate for the deepest expected contingency. But the advantage of a diver-carried independent breathing source is undeniable.

One instructor recently dismissed the relevance of these units by sarcastically declaring, "A pony bottle at 250 feet will only last you long enough to say the Lord's Prayer." Gilliam counters, "I suggest that most divers can get back to the surface or damn close to it in less time than reciting that Bible passage or singing the national anthem, for that matter. By his reasoning, I guess we'd have to shoot every football player that banged up his knee. 'Looks like Montana's pulled up lame. Damn shame, we'll have to put him down.' I'm more a subscriber to the Yogi Berra school of higher thought: 'It ain't over, 'til it's over!' I'll take all the tools I can get and give a pony bottle ascent a shot rather than adopting some fatalistic acceptance of my fate while scratching my Last Will and Testament on a dive slate."

3. **Redundant Second Stage:** Call it what you want: octopus, safe second, alternate air source, etc. it still amounts to an extra breathable mouthpiece coming off the first stage of your regulator. It won't do *you* any good, but it could make your buddy's day if he needs to borrow it for a while. Virtually all dive training programs now require such safety equipment and its explanation during entry level courses. These can take the form of another conventional second stage or an integrated inflator/second stage such as Scubapro's AIR II or Sea Quest's Source.

Commonly accepted usage involves giving the out of air diver the extra second stage while retaining your own primary in your mouth. In the case of integrated units, it will usually be necessary to give away the primary and breathe from the alternatives since their hoses are too short for comfortable passing. Either way, both the donor and the recipient have got something to breathe all the time during the ascent phase. This eliminates the need for even intermittent breath holding and removes the questions of disease transmittal associated with traditional buddy breathing.

That's the "up" side of the deal. On the "down" side, we still have two divers breathing from one air supply. And it's probably likely that if one buddy is out of air, the other is pretty low as well and is now sharing what-

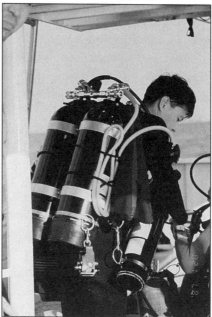

A seven foot long hose octopus second stage is carried for emergency use secured with surgical tubing on the primary cylinder set. If needed, it is quickly released simply by a tug and given to another diver.

ever he has got left. Not a great scenario. It's kind of like an fighter plane already on reserve deciding to do a midair refueling with another plane that just ran out. "Don't worry Skipper, you can sip off my gas until we're back to the carrier!" Profound movie stuff, bad in real life.

We also have to add the element of two divers swimming together cooperatively which can be exceedingly difficult in many situations involving depth, current, or differentials of size or fitness. By adding longer hoses to the "give away" second stage, divers have made it easier to manage these circumstances. But there still is no accepted single method of standardized location, securement or deployment of these devices. But, no matter how you use them they still beat buddy breathing hands down...

4. **Buddy Breathing:** Although still retained as a required skill by several training agencies such as PADI and YMCA, others no longer include a specific reference to single regulator sharing. NASDS stopped teaching buddy breathing in 1977 and NAUI recently refined their standard to require "sharing air" but leaving the method up to their individual instructors after objections were raised.

Buddy breathing is so far down on the list of preferences that it has been relegated to a vanishing art form. Yes, given no other alternatives, it can you back to the surface if both divers are skilled in its practice. Sadly, the record of double fatalities for divers engaged buddy breathing is disproportionately high.

The grim reality is that the skill is difficult to master initially and then quickly lost unless practiced often in the field. Even the most accomplished practitioners will suffer from CO_2 buildup if long distances must be covered or extended durations are required due to overhead conditions or decompression ceilings incurred.

In a perfect world, the authors would like everyone to be proficient in buddy breathing to cover the situations where octopus use is still not uniformly accepted. But as realists, we also recognize that this option in out of air contingencies has been eclipsed by equipment evolution.

So what works for you? Analyze your dive habits, depths, partners, and site conditions. If you're primarily a warm water resort diver within recreational limits, octopus style second stages will probably fit your needs. If your diving is not always done within easy reach of a buddy, take a look at the security of a SpareAir. If you plan more demanding exposures in wrecks or deeper diving, then some serious consideration of "pony bottles" ought to be in your future. And if you simply enjoy a challenge, get a double hose regulator and keep practicing those buddy breathing skills.

CONCLUSION

We've covered just a few scenarios in contingency planning. Believe us... there are an infinite list of others. With careful planning most foul-ups can at least be categorized by general headings such as entanglement, out of air, busted decompression, lost, etc. You will never be able to anticipate every series of events that may result in one or more of those situations presenting. But if you have covered what to do in each presentation no matter how it manifests, you'll be better prepared to cope in a real field situation.

You should always be asking yourself: "what if?" When you can deal with the question through a logical combination of skill, experience and equipment, then you're well on your way to being able to responsibly deal with the reality and harshness of an unforgiving ocean environment. Forewarned is forearmed.

CHAPTER 10

Nitrox

"Mother Nature provided the planet Earth with a NITROX atmosphere known as air. She never said that air was the best breathing medium for divers. Here, as in many other fields of endeavor, human beings have used their knowledge of natural laws to go one step beyond what Nature has provided for them."

J. Morgan Wells, Ph.D.

OVERVIEW

One of the hottest issues in recent years within the diving industry has been debate on the proper role that Oxygen Enriched Air, commonly known as Nitrox, will play in the recreational diving community. Some diving veterans view this gas as a logical next step to increased diver safety and reduction of the incident rate of decompression sickness (DCS). Other experts have raised questions as to its appropriateness for inexperienced sport divers and whether or not dangers exist due to misuse or equipment incompatibility. Some historical perspectives are in order to see the arguments from both sides more clearly.

Dr. Morgan Wells, Chief Diving Officer for NOAA, has been largely credited as the "godfather" of Nitrox and was responsible for standardizing two generic mixtures and implementing the first training and operational guidelines for usage. He remembers, "Nitrox goes back

Nitrox braintrust: Tom Mount (IANTD President), Bret Gilliam (TDI President), Rob Palmer (Director TDI Europe) and Richard Bull (NAUI England).

quite a long way. In fact, my own initial interest in it was back in the mid-sixties during Mark 6 (a rebreather) training with the U.S. Navy. In 1977 when I was writing up the justification and the data base for what we now know as NOAA Nitrox I,

I researched it a little bit more and found a reference to Dr. Chris Lambertsen back in 1943. He was quoted then as suggesting mixtures of nitrogen and oxygen be used to reduce decompression."

The use of Nitrox by the sport diving community is relatively new. However, commercial divers and the U.S. NAVY have been using it successfully for decades. Dr. Wells included tables and procedures for its use in the 1977 edition of the NOAA Diving Manual and from that source grew the initial interest in other applications of the technology.

Part of the problem for many divers with understanding Nitrox is that it seems impossible for even the experts to agree on what to call these mixtures. Technically, the term Nitrox can be used to describe any combination of nitrogen and oxygen (N_2/O_2). The air around us is Nitrox. Your first dive on compressed air was a Nitrox dive. Standard compressed air is a 79/21 Nitrox mixture (79% N_2/21% O_2). This is referred to as a normoxic Nitrox mixture; that is, the oxygen percentage is normal as it occurs freely in air. A Nitrox mixture with less than 79% nitrogen and more than 21%

oxygen is generally called Oxygen Enriched Air or simply Enriched Air Nitrox (EANx). The "x" represents the oxygen content of the mix i.e. EAN 32, EAN 36 etc. Due to the decreased amount of nitrogen, an inert gas that is responsible for decompression sickness, significant safety and operational advantages may be gained.

Dr. Wells makes this observation, "Air has been used as a breathing gas by divers since the beginning of diving. Its principal advantage is that it is readily available and inexpensive to compress into cylinders or use directly from compressors with surface supplied equipment. It is not the 'ideal' breathing mixture because of the decompression liability it imposes. Since decompression obligation is dependent on *inspired nitrogen partial pressure* and time, not *depth* and time, this obligation can be reduced by reducing the nitrogen content of divers' breathing gas."

NOAA currently recognizes two standard Nitrox mixes: NOAA Nitrox I (68% N_2/32% O_2) and NOAA Nitrox II (64% N_2/36% O_2). Due to operational oxygen toxicity limits, NOAA Nitrox I has a depth limit of 130 feet and is the most commonly used mixture, whereas NOAA Nitrox II, has a depth limit of approximately 110 feet.

Nitrox/EANx allows the diver a whole new approach to managing his dive plan through increased bottom times, shorter surface intervals and reduced nitrogen narcosis. The decompression liability of compressed air is a distinct limiting factor. A review of the U.S. Navy No-Decompression Tables will show that at a depth of 60 fsw the no-stop time is 60 minutes. On the other hand, the no-stop limit for 60 fsw with NOAA Nitrox I (EAN 32) is 100 minutes. According to the Navy Tables, a dive to 60 fsw for 100 minutes would result in the diver being required to make an obligatory decompression stop at 10 fsw for 14 minutes. The benefit in this particular example is obvious: more bottom time, less decompression obligation.

Many divers have mistakenly thought of Nitrox as a deep diving gas perhaps due to its technical sounding name similar to Heliox or Trimix. This blurring of distinction has led noted diving physiologist Dr. R.W. "Bill" Hamilton to urge, "call it Enriched Air. That sounds a lot less threatening to the uninitiated and more accurately describes the gas. Don't let this relatively benign breathing gas be forever branded as a 'high-tech' science. On the user level, it really is quite simple."

Several areas of interest for EANx have appeared in the traditional recreational diving community. If we were to accept the national training agencies' recommendations for less experienced divers to be 130 fsw, then EAN 32, would really be the obvious choice.

Three agencies dedicated to training both users and instructors for EANx have developed in the last six years. American Nitrox Divers Inc. (ANDI), the International Association for Nitrox and Technical Diving (IANTD), and Technical Diving International (TDI) have all published standards, manuals, certification cards, and support materials to effectively teach the safe use of EANx to recreational divers. Additionally, these agencies have more technical courses of training to educate and credential professional blenders, mixers and dispensers of the gas.

Dick Rutkowski, well known hyperbaric expert and ex-deputy Diving Director for NOAA, is the President and founder of IANTD. Rutkowski has probably done more to promote Nitrox diving outside of traditional scientific and commercial use than any other individual. He has published the NITROX MANUAL and set up the first large scale dispensing facility in Florida.

In the north Atlantic area, Ed Betts, founder of ANDI, has made equal inroads into the recreational diving community from his Long Island, New York headquarters. Betts is a graduate engineer with a commercial diving background and has owned several dive stores on Long

Photo by Bret Gilliam

Dick Rutkowski, founder of IANTD, analyzes nitrox mixture.

Island for over two decades. Both men have devoted themselves to widening the industry's understanding of Nitrox.

To avoid the stigma of mixed gas jargon and any tinge of "high tech" confusion, ANDI is promoting EAN 32 in this market as "SafeAir". They have aimed the program squarely at entry level divers and encourage the use of the gas in conjunction with standard air tables or air diving computers. With the elevated oxygen percentage and subsequent reduced nitrogen percentage, the mathematical probability of decompression sickness has been significantly reduced.

1994 saw TDI introduced by technical community veterans Bret Gilliam, Dr. Bill Hamilton, Mitch Skaggs and John Crea. TDI has produced a new line of support texts and a low priced instructor liability insurance program.

IANTD and TDI provide a second level of more advanced training that explains the use of the special Nitrox/EANx tables and use of other special mixtures containing higher oxygen percentages. All offer training in the computation of Equivalent Air Depth (EAD) theory, an equation that allows the diver to calculate his "equivalent depth" for any conventional air table based on the nitrogen percentage of his mix. This is more complicated than using pre-calculated EANx tables and has led some critics to question if divers can be trusted to retain this knowledge and accurately handle the required math functions.

The standard entry level course by these agencies consists of approximately four hours of lecture followed by practical diving. There is new material to be assimilated by divers, but most will find the transition fairly easy and well within their reach. Phil Sharkey, Diving Officer for the University of Rhode Island, sums it up, "Boiled down to its simplest form, the Nitrox diver needs to know three things: breathe in, breathe out, don't go below 130 feet."

One thing is for certain, the use of Nitrox/EANx is growing at a remarkable pace. ANDI, IANTD, and TDI have over 1000 active instructors and over 100,000 dives have been logged with a safety record that exceeds that of conventional air dives.

So where then lies the controversy? Dr. Peter Bennett, executive director of the Divers Alert Network (DAN), has raised several questions. "Breathing 32% oxygen/68% nitrogen in NOAA Nitrox I, for example, will give you more bottom time than with air because the extra oxygen does not contribute to DCS. It sounds great, but as often occurs,

TABLE 10-1

DEPTH (FSW)	NO-DECOMP. LIMITS	EAN 32 No-Decompression Limits														
		A	B	C	D	E	F	G	H	I	J	K	L	M	N	O
20		35	70	110	160	225	350									
25		25	50	75	100	135	180	240	325							
30		20	35	55	75	100	125	160	195	245	315					
40		15	30	45	60	75	95	120	145	170	205	250	310			
45	310	5	15	25	40	50	60	80	100	120	140	160	190	220	270	310
50	200	5	15	25	30	40	50	70	80	100	110	130	150	170	200	
60	100		10	15	25	30	40	50	60	70	80	90	100			
70	60		10	15	20	25	30	40	50	55	60					
80	50	5	10	15	20	30	35	40	45	50						
90	40	5	10	15	20	25	30	35	40							
100	30	5	10	12	15	20	25	30								
110	25	5	7	10	15	20	22	25								
120	25	5	7	10	15	20	22	25								
130	20		5	10	13	15	20									
140	15		5	10	12	15										
150	10		5	8	10											

when you reduce one problem, another shows up, in this case, oxygen toxicity of the brain. The danger of brain oxygen toxicity is epileptic-like convulsions. Oxygen convulsions are insidious, often occurring with little warning... convulsions underwater make death by drowning almost inevitable. According to the U.S. Navy guidelines, the depth during short duration air dives at which convulsions become a hazard is 218 feet. Yet with NOAA Nitrox I, the convulsion hazard begins at 132 feet... thus, careful depth control is absolutely essential."

Tom Mount, President and training director for IANTD, notes in rebuttal, "Dr. Bennett's warning is valid but the depth limit for Nitrox is a primary thrust in our training programs. Realistically, divers have been conditioned to 130 feet as a limit on air for years. Our course and those of ANDI and TDI were designed to educate divers specifically to the special considerations of Nitrox use. There has yet to be a case of oxygen toxicity or bends in any of our divers."

A second consideration of Nitrox use that Bennett has identified concerns post dive treatment in a DCS accident. "Potential for further complication due to oxygen toxicity of the lungs exists if a Nitrox diver develops decompression illness. Oxygen toxicity of the lungs occurs when oxygen is breathed for extended periods at partial pressures above half an atmosphere. Its symptoms are similar to those of pneumonia, and the only treatment is to breathe less oxygen. Since the best therapy for decompression illness is 100% oxygen during transport to a chamber followed by recompression with 100% oxygen on the U.S. Navy treatment tables, prior Nitrox diving gives a physician less freedom in using oxygen during therapy when it is needed most. This could make a difference in achieving full recovery."

This argument requires a more thorough understanding of the physiological relationship of oxygen tolerances. There is a computational method of tracking "oxygen dose" commonly referred to as Oxygen Tolerance Unit or OTU. At a recent conference on Enriched Air Technology held in Houston, Dr. Bennett's concern was specifically addressed by NASA hyperbaric medical expert, Dr. William Norfleet. A "worst case" scenario for Nitrox diving in repeated repetitive exposures for a single day of diving was detailed and the accumulated OTU count noted. In Dr. Norfleet's opinion, "I am unable to agree with Dr. Bennett's conclusion. It would take an unrealistic and probably unattainable dive profile to have a consequential effect on post-dive treatment."

Not all of Dr. Bennett's comments on Nitrox are so negative. He is most concerned with improper use by untrained individuals. "While Nitrox and oxygen can be used with reasonable safety in diving, extra equipment and training are required as well as the recognition of the additional risks. What are your goals in diving? Are they worth the added training and equipment? If so, the fine, proceed. But do so with a fair recognition and acceptance of the added risks," he concludes.

The consensus opinion from leading experts at the 1992 Enriched Air Workshop included this passage in their concluding summary: "Hosted by the Scuba Diving Resources Group, the Workshop brought together training agencies, manufacturers, retailers, instructors, technical and scientific experts, the academic diving community, and experienced enriched air users from commercial, government, and scientific organizations. The Workshop concluded that enriched air nitrox has been established as an alternative breathing medium to compressed air and is considered suitable for recreational diving with proper equipment, gas mixtures, training and certification. Current EANx certification agencies... for training users, instructors and dispensers of the gases are adequate and in place."

EQUIVALENT AIR DEPTH (EAD)

The specific decompression procedure that must be followed when diving NITROX is based on the concept of "equivalent air depth" (EAD). This is a procedure that equates the inspired nitrogen pressure of a NITROX mixture at one depth to that of standard air at another depth, the EAD. This is a procedure that has been used extensively by the military and commercial diving industry for over 30 years with both semi-closed and closed-circuit mixed-gas underwater breathing systems. It is highly recommended to use a pre-calculated EAD table and several are widely available.

By using the following formula, any combination of nitrogen-oxygen mixtures can be applied to the standard U.S. Navy Air Decompression tables:

$$EAD = \left[\frac{(1.0 - FO_2)(D + 33)}{.79} \right] - 33$$

1.0 = **Fraction of the total gases at 1 ATA**
FO$_2$ = **Decimal equivalent of percent of O$_2$ in mix**
.79 = **Inert gas content of air**
D = **Depth in feet of salt water (fsw)**

Sample Problem: A diver wishes to make a 120 fsw (36.4m) dive on EAN 32 but does not have the NOAA NITROX I tables with him. What EAD can he use to relate into the USN Air Decompression tables ?

Solution: EAD $= \left[\frac{.68 \times 153}{.79} \right] - 33$

Answer: EAD = 98.7 fsw or 100/25 (USN Air Decomp. table)

SAFETY CONSIDERATIONS

One concern that some divers have is whether or not specialized equipment is required with NITROX. The best answer is: standard equipment is OK for use with up to 40% oxygen mixtures or follow manufacturers specific product guidelines. There is a lot of confusion about using "straight from the manufacturer, out of the box" scuba gear. The author recommends that divers contemplating using various enriched air mixtures take a proper course in NITROX usage as a prerequisite.

NITROX can be obtained by several mixing or blending methods. The preferred method is via the Continuous NITROX Mixer in conjunc-

*Ed Betts,
President ANDI,
at his gas panel.*

tion with an oil-free compressor. In this system, the scuba tank and regulator are never subjected to the hazards of high pressure oxygen. If all NITROX filling systems were using this blending method, then it would be acceptable for regular scuba gear to be used without special handling as long as the O_2 percentage did not exceed 40% (FO_2 = .4 maximum).

The most common mixing method is still by the Partial Pressure Method. This involves transfilling pure O_2 into the scuba cylinder first to a certain pressure, and then topping off the cylinder with AIR. **This is potentially extremely hazardous and should never be attempted by untrained users!** Since partial pressure mixing does exist, the author recommends that **all** cylinder components be oxygen cleaned prior to NITROX service unless fills are obtained from a pre-mixed storage bank.

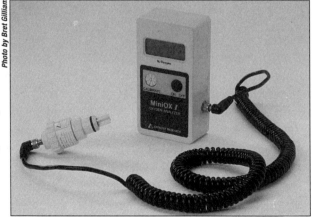

*Digital read out
shows 31.9% oxygen,
as close as possible
to measure for EAN
32. Accuracy of given
nitrox mix should be
within 1% of desired
oxygen content.*

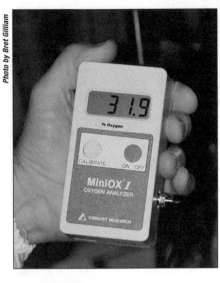

Photo by Bret Gilliam

Portable oxygen analyzer
for determining oxygen
percentage of a nitrox
mixture.

CLEANING

It would be beneficial to discuss at this time the following terms:

oxygen clean

oxygen compatible

oxygen service

These terms are unclear and misunderstood by the majority of divers. **Oxygen clean** refers to the absence of contaminates. These contaminates are varied but the most serious are hydrocarbons such as: machine oils and thread lubricants, cleaning solvents, paint or marking crayons, oily finger-prints or grease, airborne dust or soot, metal scale or burrs, metal filings and

Dedicated nitrox
storage bank for
dispensing to scuba
cylinders.

some metal oxides, rust dust, lint from cloths used to remove any of the above, pipe thread sealants and soapy water used for leak checking.

Scuba equipment shipped from the factory is **never** rated oxygen clean; however, equipment may be rendered so by means of a variety of cleaning processes. Such services can be obtained through a professional facility. The diver has the option of having his original equipment cleaned or purchasing pre-cleaned and labeled NITROX (or O_2) regulators and cylinders. Again remember, conventional regulators *can* be used with NITROX mixtures up to 40% oxygen without any special cleaning or preparation.

Oxygen compatibility involves both combustibility and ease of ignition. Materials that burn in air will burn violently in pure oxygen and explosively in pressurized systems. Also, many materials that do not burn in air will do so in pressurized systems. In oxygen systems, the selection of materials is of paramount importance. Some common materials used in scuba equipment that are not compatible with pure oxygen are teflon seats, buna-N o-rings, silicone grease and neoprene diaphragms to name a few.

Briefly stated, **compatibility** means that all the materials that are in contact with the gas are compatible with the gas at the working pressure of the system.

Oxygen service refers to a product's or component's suitability for use in conjunction with oxygen. Oxygen service requires **BOTH** oxygen clean **AND** oxygen compatible components.

From the above explanation we can see that a component may be oxygen compatible but contaminated (not oxygen clean). Likewise, we could have an oxygen clean component that is not oxygen compatible (pressure rated). This may be a bit confusing at first, but you're in good company. Even most diving instructors have little working knowledge of these terms.

When utilizing oxygen enriched mixtures it is recommended that all components are first oxygen cleaned before entering service. As long as the percentage of O_2 does not exceed 40%, most conventional scuba equipment is considered compatible. .

CODING AND LABELING

Each piece of equipment must now be dedicated to NITROX service and labeled accordingly. This includes the regulator system if

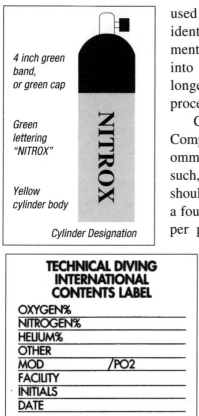

4 inch green
band,
or green cap

Green
lettering
"NITROX"

Yellow
cylinder body

NITROX

Cylinder Designation

used above 40% O_2. Tags are available to identify such gear as NITROX equipment. If the regulator system is put back into conventional AIR service it is no longer considered oxygen clean and the process must be repeated.

Cylinders can be marked as per the Compressed Gas Association (CGA) recommendations for cylinder coding. As such, a scuba cylinder in NITROX service should be color coded (yellow body with a four inch oxygen-green band at the upper portion; some NITROX tanks are

TECHNICAL DIVING INTERNATIONAL CONTENTS LABEL

OXYGEN% _____
NITROGEN% _____
HELIUM% _____
OTHER _____
MOD _____ /PO2
FACILITY _____
INITIALS _____
DATE _____

WARNING
This Cylinder May Contain Mixtures Other Than Air. Proper Training And Analyzing Are Required Prior To Use. Any Questions Please Contact T.D.I. At (305) 853-0966

TECHNICAL DIVING INTERNATIONAL OXYGEN SERVICED CERTIFICATION

This Cylinder And Valve Have Been Visually Inspected & Cleaned In Accordance With Current T.D.I. Standards And Is Suitable For Use With Mixtures Up To And Including 100% Oxygen For A Period Of One Year From The Date Indicated.

| 94 | 95 | 96 | JN | FB | MR | AP | MY | JN |
| 97 | 98 | 99 | JL | AG | SP | OC | NV | DC |

WARNING
The Use Of Gases Containing More Than 0.1 mg Per Cubic Meter Of Hydrocarbons In This Cylinder Will Void This Certification. Any Questions Please Contact T.D.I. At (305) 853-0966

Facility _____
Facility # _____ Date _____

Proper labels for cylinder contents and cleaning as provided by Technical Diving International

coded with the entire neck portion of the cylinder painted oxygen-green instead of a band; either coding is acceptable). More recently it has become accepted practice for divers to use cylinder wrap bands labeled "Nitrox" without regard to specific color coding. These are typically green and yellow in color and may list the oxygen percentage and maximum depth of the mix. In some cases, a separate "mix" tag is used in conjunction to specifically designate the O_2 content etc.

Each cylinder should be tagged with a NITROX identification tag that lists its pressure, FO_2, FN_2, date filled and the name of the filler/

analyzer. No **NITROX mixture should ever be used by a diver without analyzing it** *immediately prior to use!* If a cylinder is returned to AIR service be sure to remove the NITROX coding.

OTHER USES OF NITROX

50/50 NITROX is a popular decompression gas that is used as a safety buffer instead of standard air as a "wash-out" mix due to its elevated oxygen percentage. 80/20 EAN mixtures are also common as an alternate to pure oxygen during decompressions. 50/50 and 40/60 mixes are also utilized in recompression chamber environments when the patient and tenders must be subjected to treatment depths in excess of 60 fsw (18.2 m). This effectively limits the inert gas loading on chamber occupants and still allows proper oxygen balance for the best gradient across the tissue-bubble interface. It also allows tenders a clearer head due to significantly reduced narcosis.

The benefits of NITROX can clearly be seen in the case of a patient/tender at 165 feet (50 m) on Treatment Table 6A. On standard air, the no-decompression time is very limited, but on 50/50 NITROX a tender

Photo by Bret Gilliam

Photo by Bret Gilliam

ABOVE: Color coded NITROX cylinders with yellow bodies and green bands. LEFT: Plain cylinder properly labeled for NITROX use.

is subjected to an EAD of only 92 feet (28 m) allowing him 25 minutes without decompression. This allows him to "lockout" before his no-decompression time and before another tender replaces him. It also markedly lessens the risk of "bending" the tenders on deep treatment or saturation tables.

NITROX DIVE COMPUTERS

The growing interest in Enriched Air/Nitrox (EANx), has prompted several manufacturers to turn their creative talents to refining a dive computer that can handle the increased oxygen percentages in such breathing mixes. ORCA, now a division of EIT Industries, was the first to introduce a nitrox dedicated computer model by modifying their integrated Delphi edition.

This project was headed by diving engineer Paul Heinmiller and was specifically limited to one nitrox mixture: 32% oxygen and 68% nitrogen. Their original Delphi for nitrox has now been upgraded and is offered as the "Nitrox Phoenix". It retains all the features of the "air" version but will be programmed for the 32% oxygen mix. All multi-level decompression computations will be the same except for allowing the model to use the proven NOAA Nitrox I Tables. This will afford nitrox users an even greater advantage over "air" dives since they will not be

Diver using nitrox doubles showing prominent sticker.

forced to use "square profile" dive formats derived directly from tables. Nitrox divers on a 32% oxygen mixture already can enjoy as much as *twice* the bottom time allowed by U.S. Navy air tables down to 50 feet. As depth increases, the bottom time advantage falls off and the 32% mixture has a depth limit of 130 feet. But for the diver working above 100 feet, the advantages are significant. (Navy Tables allow 60 minutes at 60 feet; NOAA Nitrox I allows 100 minutes at the same depth!)

Since there are an almost infinite number of potential nitrox mixes as the oxygen content is increased, two other manufacturers have decided to release nitrox computers with *adjustable* oxygen percentages built right into the software programs. This would allow for such mixtures as EAN 36, another popular blend, which is comprised of 36% O_2 and 64% N_2. This mix affords even greater bottom times and has a depth limit of approximately 100 feet.

Mark Leonard of Dive Rite Mfg. in Florida has collaborated with a major instrument manufacturer in Japan to finalize a joint venture to produce yet another futuristic nitrox computer. His model, The Bridge, has even more bells and whistles including the ability to set any oxygen percentage between 21 and 50%, to adjust O_2 percentages between dives, and will allow interfacing with a PC for downloading and logging

Photo by Bret Gilliam

Lightweight portable after-filter for use with standard compressed air to blend nitrox. This device can be ordered in any size for use with regular oil lubricated compressors to remove hydrocarbons before mixing with oxygen to produce any variety of nitrox. Available though Technical Diving International.

of dives directly to a computer disc or printout. Leonard, an active cave diver who has specialized in state of the art manufacturing for advanced buoyancy systems and underwater lights, has been directly involved in the design process for his prototype.

A CLOSER LOOK AT POST DIVE THERAPY

In 1992 there were some rather disturbing misconceptions promulgated about possible post-dive complications after the use of EAN 32. Most of this has centered on whether breathing such a mixture would somehow preclude a standard recompression treatment if the diver suffered from decompression sickness (DCS). One chamber facility in Grand Cayman had even stated that they would not treat a diver if he was diving on a nitrox mixture. This is a sobering message from a medical facility and bears further examination to get to the actual facts.

Apparently some well meaning, but inexpert, people have suggested that a diver breathing this slightly elevated oxygen mixture would accumulate a sufficiently high pulmonary oxygen dose to the extent that standard treatment tables using oxygen would be unusable. This is categorically false! Any qualified chamber operator would treat a nitrox diver by exactly the same methods as a regular compressed air diver. The incorrect argument that divers could not be treated on conventional recompression tables has already been rebutted by a long list of NASA and NOAA physicians, hyperbaric supervisors and technicians, and noted diving physiologists. Even DAN (Divers Alert Network) training staff have taken the initiative to write chamber facilities to correct this misconception.

Let's examine the relevant oxygen limits as they apply. There are two types of oxygen toxicity, commonly referred to as central nervous system (CNS) and pulmonary (or whole body) effects. CNS toxicity manifests when oxygen is breathed at high partial pressures for certain time frames and can produce a variety of symptoms including convulsive states. Pulmonary toxicity results from prolonged periods of exposure and is typically manifested by shortness of breath, dry cough, or an irritation/burning in the breathing cycle.

There are clearly established limits and guidelines for both types of oxygen exposure or "dose". For CNS involvement, NOAA recommends specific time/pressure limits expressed in oxygen partial pressures atmospheres absolute (PO_2 ATA). For example, a diver can tolerate up to two hours on a single dive at 1.5 ATA PO_2, but only 45 minutes at 1.6 ATA. As the partial pressure is reduced the length of the exposure may be increased. There are also guidelines for daily exposure so dosage can be cumulatively tracked. It's important to realize that oxygen doses are received irregardless of whether the diver breathes nitrox or air.

Pulmonary oxygen toxicity risk can be calculated by oxygen tolerance units (OTU) in a method developed by Dr. Bill Hamilton for use originally in saturation diving. Again, the dose is tracked by PO_2 and operational planning is designed to keep the diver within comfortable limits without significant pulmonary deficits. An OTU is roughly equivalent to breathing pure oxygen at the surface for one minute. There are published OTU tables available to calculate the dose at any depth while breathing air, oxygen, or any nitrox blend.

It is generally accepted that a diver can take up to approximately 1500 OTU's day. Several leading hyperbaric experts have suggested that this could be extended to 2000 OTU's a day while in recompression therapy. So what does all this mumbo-jumbo mean?

Divers are normally treated on U.S. Navy Treatment Table 6 which is 4 hours and 45 minutes long and will produce approximately 650 OTU's. Logically a diver would want to limit his diving exposure so that this type of treatment could be accommodated should the need arise. That means that he has 850 OTU's to "spend" on his diving profiles to stay within the 1500 OTU recommended limit. Now let's examine the reality of an actual dive on EAN 32:

To illustrate the absurdity of singling out nitrox divers we will look at a typical exposure for Grand Cayman diving conditions. Dive operators on that island enforce a 100 foot maximum depth limit on their dives. This depth is well within the safe limits for a 32% O_2 mixture and yields only a 1.3 ATA exposure. This would allow a *three hour* single dive exposure before approaching CNS toxicity thresholds. But since these operators usually allow only a 20 minute dive plan at this depth, a grand total of approximately 30 OTU's could be accumulated. (1.3 ATA O_2 mix yields 1.48 OTU's per minute.)

Now let's assume that you could even find an operator that would let you do three dives on this profile in one day. If you could, then less than 100 OTU's would be earned. Since we know that divers can conservatively take up to 1500 OTU's per day and a typical treatment only has about 650 OTU's, any intelligent observer can readily see that the consequences of a diver breathing nitrox are virtually negligible! (By the way, the same dive profile on air would produce about 45 OTU's.)

To make the point even more effectively, let's assume that a regular compressed air diver displays DCS symptoms following a conventional dive. The boat operator properly puts him on oxygen via demand valve/ mask during the two hour transit to the chamber. Guess what? *That diver just got more of an oxygen dose (120 OTU's) than the nitrox diver who did three dives!* And I don't seriously expect that the chamber staff is going to refuse to treat him no matter what gonzo logic is used.

No one is served well when incorrect information is perpetuated. The popularity of nitrox diving continues to grow throughout the U.S. and Caribbean. It would behoove those responsible for the emergency health care of divers to be technically aware of all elements of therapy and not be drawn into an unfounded policy of discrimination that could unnecessarily threaten the care of anyone simply because he used nitrox or ate chili for lunch. Accurate information and common sense go a long way to promoting coherent policies. "Just the facts, m'am", would better serve the diving community when it comes to our medical facilities, not emotional breast beating from uninformed "experts".

PRODUCTION OF NITROX MIXTURES

This information is offered as an overview to the gas blending procedures currently in use to produce oxygen enriched air. SafeAir, Nitrox and EANx are all terms in wide use to describe these custom breathing mixtures of oxygen and nitrogen; in essence, they mean the same thing. Precise terminology should be dealt with, but not in the scope of this chapter.

The primary concern is pure, contaminant-free breathing gas as the final end-product. How that is achieved at the cylinder refill station is varied.

PRE-MIX

The simplest way to dispense a gas mixture other than air is to purchase professionally pre-blended gas from a gas supplier. For Nitrox blends used in recompression chamber facilities as a therapy gas, standard procedure is to order Nitrox pre-blended in this manner to typically yield a 50/50 or 60/40 nitrogen/oxygen mixture. These cylinders may then be plumbed into the therapy gas manifold just as medical oxygen cylinders are. A Nitrox refill station for use in open circuit scuba equipment could use this same system. It is still suggested that the end-user analyze the gas in each cylinder prior to hooking the storage cylinders into the cascade/bank connection. Connect the cylinders and dispense by using an oxygen clean, oxygen service booster pump. The gas quality of gas mixtures dispensed in this manner is high as no impurities or contaminates are likely to be present.

DYNAMIC GAS MIXING

This method is generally employed by commercial diving operations or facilities that will have need for high volumes of mixed gas. In most situations, this is beyond the budget or needs of most sport or scientific programs. In this system, the high pressure gases are supplied to a mixer, then analyzed and discharged to a special compressor for pumping to storage, or directly to the diver in surface supplied operations. (Butler, G. 1991)

PARTIAL PRESSURE BLENDING

Partial pressure, or "cascade" mixing is probably the best known and most common method of gas mixing. These systems can be as simple as a fill hose, adapter and oil free compressor (or standard compressor with special filtration) used to fill a single scuba tank at a time, or designed for the production of thousands of cubic feet per day of Nitrox, Heliox or Trimix. Based on Dalton's Law of Partial Pressures, this method employs several high pressure gas sources to produce a mixture based on the partial pressure of each component gas.

One method that is employed by some is to use the aforementioned method, but purchase U.S.P. grade air and U.S.P. grade oxygen. By having two "unmixed" gases, (of course, air is a mixture of gases) the operator may achieve any desired mixture of oxygen enriched air. By storing different mixtures in different banks, the refill station may immediately dispense several Nitrox mixtures. Air _is_ a Nitrox mixture with "impurities" from other trace gases present in the natural atmosphere.

Some operators use their oil-lubricated compressors to produce high pressure air and then filter it again (to grade E standards) to remove even more hydrocarbon contaminants. They then refill banks after adding pure oxygen to enrich the mixtures to the desired levels. This is the cheapest way to offer this service as only a separate bank and filter is required. There are numerous safeguards that could and should be added to this type of system. While this system can work with the proper safeguards in place, it does require vigilance and dedication to proper filtration to insure hydrocarbon free air. Using this method, there is a progression of lube oil and contamination aggregate. This amount is a function of relative volume/use to compressor wear, maintenance and filter quality. This system has been used with complete success and no sacrifice in air quality by facilities such as Dick Rutkowski's in Key Largo for over a decade.

The most hazardous procedure is partial pressure blending in individual scuba cylinders (commonly known as "home brew") by nonprofessional blenders. This is particularly dangerous when divers conspire to "sucker" an unknowing refill operator into completing the fill process for them. A small amount of oxygen is transferred from an oxygen storage cylinder to an empty scuba cylinder and then it is taken to an unsuspecting dive store to be topped off with air. This practice has been most prevalent in Florida. Even the casual observer can see the obvious serious potential for improper blends, fire/explosion risk etc. when an unwitting fill operator is duped in such a manner.

Although proper partial pressure blending has been practiced successfully and with reasonable safety in the field for years by many highly experienced, trained professionals, it is strongly discouraged for *all others* for several reasons:

1. The equipment is seldom properly oxygen cleaned.
2. This process requires handling of high pressure oxygen. This is dramatically different and potentially more hazardous than high pressure air.
3. The air used in the top-off fill generally comes from an oil lubricated compressor and may have too many hydrocarbon contaminants.
4. Even if the equipment starts out oxygen cleaned, after several refill cycles from an oil lubricated compressor, the equipment is usually contaminated with hydrocarbons increasing the risk of explosion or carbon monoxide transfer.
5. Pure oxygen should not be added to scuba cylinders that are not compatible with 100% oxygen.
6. Gas analysis with accurate analyzers is not always done. Remember, this is largely regarded as the <u>cheap way out.</u>
7. Unless the cylinder is totally empty and O_2 purged, this procedure yields even more inaccuracy.

8. Gas transferred must stand for considerable time to permit thorough mixing through molecular migration.
9. Gauges used to measure pressure are seldom accurate enough for this purpose. A gauge selected for this purpose should have an accuracy of +/- .25%. That's 1/4 of 1%!
10. Gas must be again analyzed prior to use. This rule should be applied to <u>any</u> gas mixtures.

ATMOSPHERIC ENTRAINMENT MIXING (CONTINUOUS BLEND)

The development of the NOAA Continuous Mixing System in 1987 by Dr. J. Morgan Wells, has revolutionized and greatly simplified enriched air techniques. This method incorporates an oil-free or oil-less lubricated compressor as the main component. By injecting low temperature/low pressure oxygen into the gas stream, the percentage of oxygen may be carefully controlled. This allows storage banks or individual cylinders to be effectively and safely refilled. By utilizing this system, low pressure or liquid oxygen (LOX) can be used. This is the preferred procedure and is approved by virtually all engineering experts as the currently accepted standard method. This eliminates many of the attendant hazards involving the transferring of high pressure oxygen.

However, *properly filtered* air from oil lubricated compressor systems to blend nitrox is equally acceptable and is in widespread use for facilities who wished to use existing compressor systems to get into nitrox. Several manufacturers now produce specialty after-filters that can be added to an existing air system to remove hydrocarbons and contaminates and allow responsible mixing protocols. This eliminates the necessity of purchasing an oil -free compressor simply to produce nitrox. Most facilities *would* opt for an oil-free compressor if making an initial purchase and nitrox dispensing was anticipated. But revisions to existing systems are acceptable.

Do not attempt to blend or mix gases on your own without formal training from a credentialed professional. Blending is a precise science that requires specialized training and equipment. The use of enriched air breathing mixtures have many safety and physiological advantages if used correctly. Production of the suitable blend is only one step in the process and most divers will obviously prefer to leave such procedures to professional operators.

USAGE

In many ways the introduction of nitrox into the sport diving community has stimulated opposition from conservatives along the same lines as multi-level diving computers did with their release a decade ago. Ironically, it may well be the next generation of dive computers incorporating nitrox in their decompression algorithm that assures the widespread acceptance of these alternative breathing mixtures by divers in the nineties.

The use of enriched air (or nitrox) breathing mixtures by sport divers first achieved major use levels in 1991. In spite of controversy, this alternate to compressed air begin to make inroads within traditional recreational user groups as well as the emerging "technical" fraternity. Since first being introduced to civilian divers by Dick Rutkowski in 1986 after two decades of use by scientific personnel in NOAA, the use of nitrox was initially limited and regionally centered in the southeast.

BACKGROUND

Sport divers essentially borrowed methodology developed and refined by NOAA's Dr. Morgan Wells and applied it to conventional recreational dives above 130 feet. Concerns and cautions as to the appropriateness of this more complicated technology in the hands of John Q. Public were expressed by some critics. At the other end of the discussion, some advocates of nitrox diminished their own credibility by feuding on safety issues and promising unrealistic benefits including increased sexual vigor.

Luckily much of the pro and con issues were afforded responsible debate by recognized experts in hyperbaric medicine, gas blending, and diving operations and workable consensus standards were adopted. Much of the over-enthusiastic hype, along with the unsubstantiated "gloom and doom" predictions, were thus effectively put to rest. Mike Menduno, publisher of the technical journal *AquaCorps*, reflects, "Though there still appears to be a few rumblings in some quarters, nitrox diving has become pretty much a non-issue in U.S. sport diving circles. In the aftermath, it appears that people from all walks of the industry are now seeking out more education. That can only be a good thing."

AGENCY POSITIONS

The traditional scuba training agencies remain divided on the nitrox question. NAUI and NASDS have had recognition programs in effect for some while that allow their members to issue nitrox certifications if they are instructors for IAND, TDI or ANDI. Both provide insurance coverage for such training. SSI's official position is that nitrox training is outside the realm of their curriculum and that such training should more appropriately be handled by the specialty agencies who can handle the responsibility and liability. SSI's Gary Clark says, "We're not against nitrox, it's just not something we do right now. Maybe in the future we will have a program as the popularity increases." PADI takes a similar stance. "We do not have an enriched air program at this time, nor plans for one," notes Karl Shreeves, PADI's Manager of Technical Development. "We feel that individuals should be free to engage in non recreational dive activities, including nitrox, but should be properly trained, equipped and willing to accept the associated risks".

That's fine with IAND, TDI and ANDI. Based upon the number of active instructors, the three specialty agencies have already become major players in the certification industry eclipsing all recreational agencies in the U.S. except for the "Big Three" (PADI, NAUI, SSI). The legitimacy of fully funded liability coverage for instructors has gone a long way to influence industry acceptance. Perhaps most important is the fact that ANDI, TDI and IAND have a perfect safety record for training. That's unequaled by any other agencies.

Although PADI does not actually have a nitrox training program they do provide insurance coverage for supervising such divers along with store coverage for nitrox fills and servicing nitrox equipment. In fact they are a sponsor of TEK'94, a three day conference devoted solely to technical diving. Shreeves notes, "By sharing information, various diver groups can learn ways to improve diver performance and safety. Also, today's cutting edge technology often becomes tomorrow's day-to-day equipment..." Clearly the door has been left open for future development.

CONSUMER USE

So how are divers actually using nitrox. Wells' interest for NOAA and scientific applications centered on maximizing a diver's allowable underwater time within safe operating parameters. Some divers like these benefits and use the NOAA Nitrox Tables or other derivatives to gain more bottom time or reduce time sitting in the boat between dives. Increasingly though, more sport divers are embracing nitrox as a safety hedge by using it for the "physiological advantage" in conjunction with air tables or conventional air dive computers. This can afford a significant reduction in the risk of decompression sickness (DCS). In this type of use, the only primary risk is observation of the maximum depth limit for the oxygen exposure. With 32% nitrox, by far the most common mixture, a depth limit of 130 feet is imposed. Since this dovetails nicely with the recommended sport diving limit anyway, it would seem that nitrox would be a ideal marriage for divers within these zones.

Several divers who used to have problems on compressed air dives made the switch to nitrox with dramatic results. Reports Steve Clemens, "I'm 43 years old and a full-time dive instructor here in the Northwest. My primary reason for using nitrox is to combat post-dive fatigue. When I use air, I'm wasted after a full day's diving. But using nitrox with my air computer really makes a difference. The headaches are gone and my energy level is way up."

George Power, owner of HI TECH Divers Inc. in New Jersey solved another type of problem. "One of my students was getting skin bends after nearly every air dive. After going to nitrox with her air tables, she's been completely clean and she's stayed in the sport. That saved me a valued customer and potential diving dropout."

Nitrox has developed a following faster on the East Coast where some shops now pump more nitrox fills than standard air. At New York's Enchanted Diver, owner Bob Raimo found a surprising interest. "During the summer season we average about 700 consumer fills a month. Over 60% are nitrox fills. Almost all of our customers use nitrox 32% with their air computers. We have never had an accident of any kind. Last year I noticed that the nitrox certified diver dove more than the air certified diver. It appears to me that nitrox divers are more educated and better divers overall. They tend to take their diving more seriously, spend more money on equipment, and then spend more time actually diving. They're great customers."

John Comly of Blue Abyss Dive Center in New Jersey reports that "we've seen a major increase in the demand for nitrox in the past two years. Right now it makes up about half of our business and next year we expect something in the range of 75% of our customers will be requesting nitrox instead of regular air."

In Washington state, Larry Elsevier of Bellingham Dive-N-Travel is one of the largest nitrox filling facilities in the U.S. "Marine harvesters make up a big chunk of our business. These divers went to nitrox for the increased safety factor and to counteract the wiped out feeling from a heavy day of hard work on repetitive dives in cold water. If you're only doing one or two dives in warm water, you really don't feel the change as much. But in our conditions, once you've switched, you'll never go back to air again. Now we have customers that drive up to 350 miles to fill cylinders.

"We've been pumping nitrox for four years now and have cranked out about 15,000 fills. Our demand is so high that during our heaviest months we have used four 4500 cubic foot liquid oxygen cylinders to keep up. Sport divers caught on pretty quick. We also fill for two stores in Vancouver, two in Seattle, and one in Portland. And our business is still growing."

Nitrox facilities are now in operation throughout the Caribbean and other resort destinations. Paul Christman of DIVE, DIVE, DIVE in the Bahamas found he had enough demand to dedicate an entire dive boat to nitrox users. They are able to do longer dives in a shorter time frame and get back in earlier. "This appeals to divers who have other interests they want to accommodate on vacation instead of tying up four or five hours for a half day trip. Before my regular dive boat gets back, they're showered, changed and at the fourth tee on the golf course. Others are attracted to nitrox for the peace of mind derived from the safety factor using it as air. All of our staff has gone to nitrox since they're doing four dives a day. It makes them feel better and they have more pep at the end of the day."

RISK

What do they experts say? Used properly, most medical and scientific experts agree that nitrox has about the same potential risk as conventional air diving when used to maximize bottom time or shorten surface intervals. Of primary concern is whether the average sport diver has the discipline to not exceed the depth limit for a particular mixture thus placing himself at risk for oxygen toxicity induced seizures. That hazard is real enough and would almost certainly be fatal. But the core of every nitrox training course is centered on exactly this risk and the imperative to observe depth limits. Unquestionably, the untrained user could quickly get himself in trouble by going too deep. The key then would seem to be encouraging diver education, not suppressing it.

A plethora of misinformation was loosed on the diving public in the past that tended to obscure the valid safety concerns of legitimate professionals. Warnings that nitrox divers could not be treated in standard recompression chambers were not only incorrect but dangerously so. Imagine the consequences if a chamber had refused a patient simply because he was a nitrox diver.

DAN's Joel Dovenbarger puts that issue to bed. "Our DAN diver insurance policy covers nitrox diving. Nitrox diving within recreational limits does not compromise any recompression treatments. We will treat any diver who needs care regardless of what he was breathing."

Another concern is control over the gas blending process. Since divers rarely mix their own nitrox any more than they pump their own compressed air, this concern falls squarely in the laps of the facilities dispensing the fills. The training for blending and mixing technicians has also been standardized. Enforced analysis of each nitrox mix is accompanied by a signed log for the recipient diver to ensure each fill is exactly the oxygen percentage desired. Again, the nitrox filling stations for ANDI, TDI and IAND enjoy an unblemished safety record.

Dr. Dick Vann, Director of Research for DAN, is cautiously neutral. "It's all a matter of acceptable risk. And there are some things which we just don't have enough data on yet to really offer a solid opinion. Theoretically, nitrox diving should carry the same risk as air diving. But there is some suggestion from individual case studies that oxygen toxicity thresholds are less forgiving in mixed gas. I'd like to see the depth limits made a little more conservative, maybe a recommendation to use 32% nitrox down to only 110 feet instead of 130 feet. But using that mix as 'air' with air tables or dive computers has obvious value to reduce decompression sickness risk. I'd just be happier with a slightly lesser depth."

Dovenbarger notes, "Most of our bends cases are from diving between 80 and 130 feet. If divers used standard 32% nitrox with air tables or computers, they would probably realize an increased safety factor for DCS. But they would have to strictly observe the depth limit of the mixture to avoid problems of oxygen toxicity."

COMPUTERS

Nitrox, once dismissed as a passing fad with only a limited market, has emerged as a growth industry. It probably will not reach its ultimate popularity until a wide selection of nitrox computers are available at affordable prices. A certain segment of nitrox users will immediately embrace such devices that will allow them to discard nitrox tables in favor of the convenience and increased bottom times of computer controlled profiles. Indeed, for some divers that is the only thing holding them back from making the switch.

Lynn Hendrickson explains, "I do a lot of professional underwater modeling and using tables is just inconvenient and cumbersome. And we're always working a variety of depths on any single dive. I'd love the extra no-decom time with nitrox but I'd want a full function computer to maximize the benefit. On some jobs now we're faced with literally hours of decompression on the last dive that nitrox would virtually eliminate with a computer."

Dive Rite Manufacturing introduced its programmable nitrox computer in early 1994. Known as The Bridge, this unit allows the diver to pre-select his oxygen percentage from 21% (standard air) to 50% nitrox mixes. By allowing a flexible option, the diver can now switch mixes on each dive to match his planned depth. Armed with such tools, some divers would go into hypothermia before they ever went into decompression.

Another new player in the computer field is Cochran Consulting with both air and nitrox versions of their Nemesis models. The Nemesis is making fresh tracks in an industry segment that continues to boldly improve every year. In addition to being able to track up to an incredible 350 dives in its memory for full downloaded analysis in a PC, it will also track oxygen toxicity exposures, is fully integrated for cylinder pressures and diver breathing rate, is variable in O_2 percentage like The Bridge, and has a menu of separate information functions displays that reads like a menu in a Chinese restaurant.

The Nemesis employs a first stage mounted powerful processor and the diver wears a wireless compact wrist mounted display. Another revolutionary option is the Nemesis Divemaster which can interface and display the dive information from up to ten other users on one wrist display. Imagine being able to instantly monitor the breathing rate, depth, tank pressure and decompression status of a dive team or students at a single glance.

Now the cost/benefit decision for divers will be moot. Currently, nitrox fills average about twice the price of conventional air fills. But when nitrox can be used with variable mixes in tandem with automatic multi-level profiling, it's likely that an avalanche of popularity will ensue.

NEW DEVELOPMENTS

The last obstacle to nitrox will be the cost of purchasing oxygen in bulky, heavy storage cylinders that are needed for the blending process. At land based facilities this is simply an added expense and minor inconvenience. However, to the liveaboard operator who must run his vessel in remote areas and Third World countries, obtaining oxygen and storing it is a logistical and financial nightmare.

But that all may change soon. Rutkowski and Wells (remember them?) are close to perfecting a device that may eliminate the need for an outside source of oxygen at all. Wells notes, "Both nitrogen and oxygen can be obtained in a wide range of concentrations from atmospheric air by the use of molecular sieve based 'oxygen concentrators' or differential permeability membrane technology, basically air separation systems in layman's terms. Membrane separators can also produce useful oxygen 'rich' and 'poor' nitrox mixtures over a wide range. Typical separated gases can contain from 5-30% oxygen with the balance being nitrogen, argon and trace gases. We're working on producing an oxygen concentrator as a replacement for high pressure bottled oxygen. These molecular sieve based units will produce 90-95% oxygen. Our experimental unit developed at NOAA will produce nitrox mixtures of 25-40% oxygen with high efficiency."

With a smile Rutkowski concludes, "This means you can produce nitrox anywhere with any compressor and you never have to lug another oxygen tank. With one of our units mounted on a bulkhead on the dive boat, you could make all the nitrox for 20 divers doing six dives a day for a week... for free!"

Will all liveaboard operators beat a path to their door? "Safer, but not necessarily longer bottom times are an obvious advantage on any liveaboard as they have a tendency to be some distance off shore," says Peter Hughes, owner of the popular *Wave Dancer* and *Sea Dancer* vessels in the Caribbean.

That removal from easy access to evacuation of bends victims makes nitrox attractive but with some understandable cautions.

"No matter how many times we offer our recommendations or advice to divers in reference to depth, particularly when these divers are making four or five dives a day for at least five consecutive days, many divers ignore us and continually push the limits well beyond the safe and reasonable. This fact is my one great fear in the use of nitrox," he continues. "It is my opinion that, with exception of the aforementioned, nitrox on offshore liveaboard offers a plus from a safety point of view as long as divers use it as air and commit themselves to an absolute depth limit of 130 feet. Can you be sure they will do this? I regret to say, I can't."

Hughes' concerns are valid. If nitrox is to come of age, it is imperative that all divers complete proper training and follow the few simple rules that apply.

Andrew Mrozinski, hyperbaric technician at St. Mary's Hospital in West Palm Beach, observes, "We are now going through a period of technological discovery where educated, responsible divers have access to the tools to make their diving safer. Realizing that zero risk does not exist, many divers are employing more conservative tables, slowing ascent rates, adding safety stops, and using computers with new caution to avoid problems. These are all very valuable practices, however, we have treated many divers who have observed all of them and still gotten bent. Current DAN statistics and corroborated chamber experience suggests that half of all diving accidents occur within supposed safe limits.

"It is important to point out that our facility has not treated *any* nitrox divers who followed the basic rules as outlined in the training programs or manuals. This should suggest a real value to adding nitrox to our list of responsible choices to increasing diving safety and enjoyment."

CONCLUSION

Noted diving professional Bill High, ex-President of NAUI and veteran of over four decades of scientific diving, has this response to the critics who have raised various arguments, "I hear a lot lately about recreational and technical divers being somehow greatly different. It looks as though all good, serious divers are being reclassified as technical divers. Certainly recreational divers, regardless of how technical they have become, *can* and *do* safely dive Nitrox. They require no more complex training than was given for basic air scuba." High has a private bet with an associate that by the year 2000 all divers will be using Nitrox. At its current rate of growth, his vision of the future may well be attained ahead of schedule.

CHAPTER 11

An Overview to Mixed Gas

"Our original investigation into mixed gas protocol and operational physiology left me fairly convinced of one thing, at least... there has to be a better way of doing this."

Hannes Keller

LAYING THE GROUNDWORK

Until recently, the great majority of sport diving was conducted with compressed air, the same gas that is available free from our surrounding atmosphere. Technically, of course, air is a mixed gas since it is composed of approximately 21% oxygen, 78% nitrogen and 1% other gases (including argon, helium, hydrogen, krypton, and carbon dioxide). Air as it naturally occurs has served us pretty well: it readily supports life at the surface, requires no special preparation, and is economically viable for compressing into scuba tanks. So why bother altering its normal composition to produce alternative "mixed gases" for diving?

The answer is that both of the major components of air can cause problems when breathed at depth under elevated partial pressures. Nitrogen, which serves as the natural diluent inert gas, poses problems due to its inherent narcotic impairment at deeper depths. This phenomena of "nitrogen narcosis" varies widely in individuals but its symptoms will generally manifest at depths approaching 130-150 fsw or deeper. Oxygen is the basis of all life support but too much of a good thing can be dangerous as well. At high partial pressures, oxygen can invoke convulsions and other lesser symptoms in a diver after certain exposures and times. This is known as central nervous system (CNS) oxygen toxicity and is a genuine physiological hazard. Its complexities are such that most divers lack a complete understanding of this insidious risk. Control of these two effects has prompted sport divers to borrow technological advances from the military/commercial sectors to make their diving safer.

NITROX

Before jumping off into a discussion of the pros and cons of mixed gas in deeper diving applications, it should be noted that Enriched Air Nitrox (EANx), widely used in depths above 130 fsw, is also a variety of mixed gas. Divers employing EANx mixtures increase, or enrich, the oxygen percentage of the gas. As the oxygen percentage is increased, typically to 32% over the standard 21%, the corresponding nitrogen percentage is decreased. This allows the diver to gain two distinct advantages over air:

1. By diving standard air tables or air dive computers in conjunction with EANx, a significant physiological benefit is realized. The extra oxygen percentage (and corresponding reduced nitrogen) provides an increased safety edge that is attractive to many divers especially those who may be getting older or may be losing some fitness. In this application, no special dive planning or equipment changes are necessary except to observe the depth limit of the EANx mixture imposed by CNS oxygen limits. In the case of this standard 32% EANx mix, the depth limit is 132 fsw. This fits nicely into standard parameters for traditional recreational divers.

2. Some divers opt to use the mixture to obtain extra bottom time with no decompression. This is possible since the percentage of the inert gas, nitrogen, has been reduced with the addition of an extra 11% of oxygen. Therefore, less nitrogen is taken up by the tissues during dive exposures. Within certain depth ranges, this can quadruple no-decompression limits over a matching air dive. Even down to depths of 130 fsw, EANx has double the allowable no-decompression time. This also translates to shorter surface intervals between dives.

If your goal is to reduce your risk of decompression sickness (DCS) or more safely extend your dive time, and you do not intend to dive deeper than 130 fsw, then EANx may be the mixed gas for you. Other EANx mixes are available along with special tables and EANx compatible dive computers. Seek out a qualified professional EANx instructor for prior training and never attempt to "mix" your own gas.

EANx use to obtain the physiological advantage (used with air tables or computers) is a fairly simple course that can be taught in one day. It is not "technical diving". Those who wish to maximize bottom times or use varying mixtures should take the more intensive advanced or "technical" EANx programs. This distinction needs to be made since entry level EANx use is a fairly benign science that requires little more than open water certification skills and knowledge on behalf of the user.

DEEP DIVING MIXED GASES

The primary use of other mixed gases is found in divers exploring deeper depths. This is technical diving by any definition and requires considerable training and experience before use. By manipulating the component gases, precise control over the negative factors of narcosis and oxygen toxicity can be attained. Let's look first at the problems of narcosis.

Almost every diver knows that nitrogen becomes a narcotic influence at deeper depths. By replacing this inert gas with helium, narcosis can be virtually eliminated. This mixture is commonly referred to as

Photo by Bret Gilliam

Trimix divers get ready to explore a deep wreck.

"heliox" since it is comprised of helium and oxygen. Heliox has a proven track record in navy diving and with various commercial companies. For technical divers using open circuit scuba equipment, heliox proved to be excessively expensive for several reasons. Primarily this was influenced by the cost of obtaining helium in bulk cylinders and then transfilling into storage banks or scuba tanks. The mechanics of mixed gas preparation generally dictated the introduction of low pressure oxygen into the system first up to a certain pressure. Then the helium was added to yield the final working pressure. As the helium supply pressure was reduced, mechanical booster pumps had to be employed to raise the overall mixture to the desired pressure, sometimes as much as 4600 psi. Since helium is most commonly sold in cylinders rated at 2400 psi, this places the small, independent professional blending station at a marked disadvantage right from the start.

The answer, for this market segment, was a compromise that borrowed liberally from earlier commercial experiments: trimix. Essentially, this means three gases in the mixture. "But", you ask, "isn't this even more difficult to mix?" Surprisingly not. Trimix gained its first use when it was discovered that at extreme depths on heliox (generally in excess of 550 fsw), a peculiar shakes and instability phenomena called "high pressure nervous syndrome" (HPNS) manifested in divers during compression. The introduction of a small amount of nitrogen back into the mixture "buffered" the effects of HPNS. Trimix tables were developed and its popularity eventually eclipsed that of heliox. Among other advantages were its ability to provide a friendlier decompression schedule.

But the real selling point for technical divers was that it eliminated the need to use helium as the "top off" gas. Instead, helium could be transfilled first at low pressure, and then regular, natural air used to top off the mixture.

Since nitrogen occurs for free in air along with oxygen, it eliminated any requirement to deal with those gases individually. By controlling the amount of helium during the first phase of blending, an almost infinite number of trimix blends can be produced for a fraction of the cost of heliox.

Of course, you don't get something for nothing. By adding nitrogen back into the mix, some minor narcosis was brought back. This can be controlled to such an extent that a diver has the option of selecting an "equivalent narcosis depth" or END. Most divers have little if any problems with an END of 130 fsw or less. Some custom tables will opt for an END even more conservative. A sample mix for a dive to 250 fsw could reflect 12% oxygen, 40% helium, and 48% nitrogen. This provides an END of approximately 130 feet even though the diver is breathing at 250 fsw.

Preparation of this mix is relatively simple from a mechanical perspective. The dispenser only has to compute 40% of the desired cylinder's working pressure for the initial helium transfill, and then add the final 60% with compressed air from his regular compressor. The existing natural percentages of oxygen and nitrogen in air provide the proper final gas mixture. (For a set of doubles rated to 3000 psi, first put in 1200 psi of helium, then top off with 1800 psi of air. When the mixture is tested with an oxygen analyzer, it will read 12% O2. Since we know that 40% of the mixture has to be helium, the balance must be nitrogen.) Due to its economical advantages and ease of handling, this type of trimix has come to be known as "Poor Man's Mix".

TABLE 11-1

Physical Properties of Gas

	HYDROGEN	HELIUM	NEON	NITROGEN	OXYGEN	ARGON
Molecular weight	2.016	4.003	20.83	28.016	32.000	39.944
Density at 0° C, 1 atm (gm/liter)	0.0056 (lb./ft.3)	0.1784	0.9004	1.251	1.429	1.784
Viscosity at 0° C, 1 atm micropoise	89.2 (28.1° C)	194.1	311.1	175.0 (19.1° C)	201.8	221.7
Thermal conductivity at 0° C, 1 atm, cal/° C-cm²-sec	39.7×10^{-5}	34.0×10^{-5}	11.0×10^{-5}	5.66×10^{-5}	5.83×10^{-5}	3.92×10^{-5}
Specific Volume, 70° F, 1 atm, cu..ft./lb.	192	96.7	19.2	13.8	12.08	9.67
Specific Heat C_p cal/mole degree	3.39	4.968	4.968	6.95	6.97	4.968
Solubility in water at 38° C cc/1000gm	168.6	9.7	13	28.9 (25° C)	26	
Solubility in oil at 38° C cc/1000gm	50 (40° C)	15	19	61	120 (40° C)	140

THE OXYGEN FACTORS

OK, we've dealt with narcosis so our problems are licked. Now we can dive to 300 feet with a clear head. Not so fast! As we discussed earlier, oxygen exposures must be maintained within certain limits and this involves balancing two types of oxygen toxicity.

In CNS toxicity, we are primarily dealing with high partial pressures of oxygen for relatively short times (doses). Remember, in any discussion of oxygen we express the exposure in partial pressure (PO_2) atmospheres absolute (ATA). Both NOAA (National Oceanic and Atmospheric Administration) and the U.S. Navy set 1.6 ATA O_2 as the threshold of CNS toxicity. This can be tolerated for up to 45 minutes by a diver working in the water. Most technical diving experts recommend backing off this exposure to 1.5 or less for strenuous dive plans.

In the trimix of 12% O_2, 40% He, 48% N_2 as described above, a maximum operating depth (MOD) of 407 fsw would be accommodated.

But by using it at 250 fsw we have kept the oxygen exposure under 1.1 ATA for a *very conservative* safety edge. Using an understanding of O_2 limits, the diver can vary his trimix to yield exactly the exposure he wishes at any depth. In effect, he can balance his narcosis and oxygen risk by adjusting their percentages in the mixture. As depth increases, so does a gas's partial pressure. (Refer to the chapter on oxygen for detailed discussion and for exposure limits)

DISTINCTIONS

Although EANx, trimix and heliox are all varieties of mixed gases they can be distinguished easily by the operational goal in their preparation. EANx *increases* the oxygen percentage in the mixture to reduce inert gas uptake and provide a safety margin for DCS or extending bottom times etc. Trimix and heliox are prepared with *lesser* percentages of oxygen to manage the risks of oxygen toxicity. Additionally, the more narcotic gas nitrogen is reduced or eliminated to control narcosis impairment.

EANx is primarily used above 130 fsw and fits traditional sport diving quite well. It is easily taught and requires no skills beyond entry level certification if used with air tables or computers. For more advanced usage to extend dive duration or to aid in more efficient decompression (such as a 40% O2 60% N2 blend at 50 foot stops), additional training is required and this is considered "technical diving". Trimix and heliox are used in most applications as a deep diving gas. EANx, or nitrox as it is commonly called, is not for deep diving at all with its primary advantages found between about 50 fsw to 130 fsw. Don't get confused by jargon, it's important to understand what each mixture is designed to do for the diver.

CHOICES

0 TO 50 fsw: Unless you have a compelling need for extremely long bottom times, air is still probably the best choice. It's inexpensive and provides more than ample dive times. In fact, most divers will get cold or bored before they run out of dive time on air at these depths.

Fifty to 130 fsw: In these depth ranges, EANx is a clear favorite. Most bends accidents occur in this zone and use of EANx would significantly reduce DCS risk. In activities that require a safer way of extending bottom times and reducing surface intervals such as in scientific collecting, filming operations, cave penetrations, or frequent repetitive diving, EANx provides a proven NOAA track record of safety and reliable tables. However, it must be remembered that an oxygen dictated depth limit must be vigilantly observed. This seems to be a small trade-off for the benefit derived. There is no sound basis for arguments that an EANx diver cannot take standard hyperbaric treatment tables in the event of DCS.

130 to 190 fsw: This is a zone where compressed air becomes viable again for most divers. With proper programs, advanced divers can and have been trained for years to dive within these ranges with an acceptable risk. NOAA, AAUS (American Academy of Underwater Sciences), and U.S. Navy standards all allow dives to the 190 fsw level on air. They do require strict supervision and a high level of experience. Sport divers will have to seek out specialty training through technical dive centers as a thorough knowledge of dive planning, decompression techniques, equipment selection, fitness, physics, and physiology are required. This level of curriculum does not currently exist within the traditional national agencies such as NAUI, PADI, SSI etc. This depth range also stays within comfortable oxygen limits (less than 1.4 ATA).

190 fsw and deeper: This is where most people should simply stop. It requires discipline, experience and commitment to dive deeper. It also will get expensive. Trimix or heliox is the gas of choice and these require extensive training under the close supervision of trained professionals. It is not safe to experiment with mixed gas diving on your own.

If a diver has the motivation and operational need to pursue depths in excess of 190 fsw, mixed gas will take him there with a reasonable degree of safety. It will reduce or eliminate narcosis and allow him to effectively manage his oxygen exposure. This is definitely safer than diving on compressed air to these depths.

However, mixed gas will require longer decompression schedules, multiple gas switches, extra equipment in the form of various gas cylinders and redundant systems etc., and it will always carry the added risk of all scenarios associated with deep diving e.g. the deeper you are, the more likely a simple problem can escalate to a more complex and serious one.

Mixed gas is a tool to make diving safer and more efficient. It is not a fad. It is not a black science or "snake oil". It's efficacy has been proven over decades of diving internationally and, when properly used, can expand the horizons of underwater explorers in the technical diving community. The future is no longer a distant fantasy. The dreams of many of us are materializing today. The use of mixed gas rebreathers is emerging in the sport/technical diving population. Increased dive duration and safety are incorporated into these systems. Just as man pushes exploration into space, the whole frontier of innerspace, the ocean wilderness, is being opened to a new universe of underwater exploration.

THE DETAILS

The primary thrust of this text is aimed at divers using compressed air, but as we have already discussed, air divers involved in lengthy decompression schedules routinely utilize other gases to make decompression more efficient and faster. The use of NITROX and oxygen in these applications usually lays the groundwork for most divers' introduction to the complexities of mixed gas and its emerging wider use among the high-tech community.

As with NITROX, the diver needs special training in order to be a safe "user" of the gases selected. Under no circumstances should divers attempt any mixed gas diving without proper training. This training is becoming readily available and the reader is urged to consult with one of the training facilities listed in our reference section. Divers should not be intimidated by the science of mixed gas diving; if you have been comfortable with the subject materials presented thus far in this text you should be able to make a smooth transition to mixed gas under the responsible supervision of one these experts.

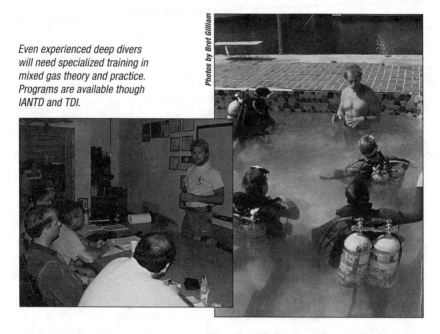

Even experienced deep divers will need specialized training in mixed gas theory and practice. Programs are available though IANTD and TDI.

Photos by Bret Gilliam

This chapter is concerned with the elements involved in the choice of breathing mixtures for diving. Two aspects are obligatory from the beginning: a diver's breathing gas must be supplied under pressure approximately equal to that of the diver's lungs, and all mixtures must contain appropriate amounts of oxygen.

Beyond this the trade offs begin, and the ideal choice of a gas mixture is a compromise of several factors. These factors, oxygen toxicity, metabolic requirements, inert gas narcosis, HPNS, density, voice, thermal properties, decompression, fire safety, cost and logistics... are covered in the second part of this chapter.

A summary of the various factors involved in the choice of a diving gas as they relate to certain gases is given in Table 11-1.

Current diving modes require the selection of optimal breathing mixtures for each of several operational situations. These include scuba, closed and semi-closed breathing systems, surface supplied gas, and the atmosphere of both submersible and deck chambers. In addition to the equipment used, the particular diving situation affects the choice of the gas mixture. Physiologic factors also are involved. These include duration of exposure, ambient water temperature, work load and whether the diver is immersed in a gas mixture or breathing it by mask or mouthpiece. We will discuss the typical gas mixes such as HELIOX and vari-

Trimix doubles and decompression cylinder properly labeled.

ous TRIMIX blends and take a look at some experimental mixes currently under evaluation.

The immediate future promises an affordable closed circuit rebreather with fully redundant safeguards offering up to 12 hours bottom time regardless of depth. Dr. Bill Stone of CIS-LUNAR Development Laboratories has gone beyond working prototypes with his Mark 2R unit and the implications of such a system for expanding the "envelope" in deep diving has veterans dizzy in expectation. Stone noted in 1990, "Metabolically, enough O_2 (if used with 100% efficiency) could be carried in one standard 2200 liter cylinder for a diver to remain underwater for more than two days at a depth of 95 meters!"

PROPERTIES OF GASES

The properties of the various gases are intimately involved in the choice of the best ones to use for diving. The pertinent gas properties are summarized in table 11-1. Detailed listings of properties of the gases and gas mixtures traditionally used in diving, as well as details of gas mixing and the use of breathing apparatus, are contained in the *U.S. Navy Diving Manual, Volume II*.

OXYGEN: Metabolic Needs and Toxicity

The fundamental requirement in a breathing gas is for oxygen to meet the metabolic needs of the body. These needs are met by supplying a breathing mixture containing an adequate partial pressure of oxygen.

The partial pressure of oxygen (PO_2) considered "normoxic" and to which man is adapted is 0.21 atmospheres inspired. A healthy person can maintain normal blood oxygenation at an inspired oxygen partial pressure of about 0.16 atmospheres; below this point a relative hypoxia (mistakenly called "anoxia" by some) will prevail. There was concern for a time early in the development of deep diving techniques that extremely dense mixtures (e.g., 80 atm of He-O_2, or 12 times the density of air at sea-level) would cause a diffusion limitation in the lung ("The Chouteau effect," Chouteau et al., 1967) and that this could render a PO_2 of 0.21 atm inadequate. Subsequent experiments, however, involving densities twice this great showed no evidence of this limitation (Strauss, et al. 1972).

The upper limit for oxygen breathing is discussed in great detail in section C of this chapter. In practical terms, oxygen limits can be set for in-water work, for chambers, and for habitats. Where decompression is to follow, it appears that an advantage lies in maintaining the highest possible PO_2 during the pressure exposure. For a lone diver in deep water and working hard, a limit of 1.2 to a maximum of 1.4 atm is a reasonable compromise between toxicity and optimal decompression. Under less strenuous conditions up to 2.0 atm may be tolerable. These are practical limits which consider such features as mixing variations and analytical errors. In-water work at higher PO_2 than this may be risky. Some experienced diving operators avoid the use of pure oxygen in the water at all. However, others embrace the utilization of pure oxygen in water during decompression.

For a habitat the same lower limits (0.16 atm) should prevail; 0.25 to 0.5 atm seem to be an optimal operational level for indefinite periods, while pressures up to 1.0 atm may be maintained safely for only a few hours. During treatment for decompression sickness using the U.S. Navy Oxygen Treatment Tables a diver is exposed to 2.8 ATA for several 20-minute periods. This has been found to be tolerable to most divers and hence operationally suitable, but a certain risk of convulsion is never the less present.

Another aspect of the oxygen requirement of a diver, in addition to a suitable partial pressure range, is the amount of oxygen needed to supply metabolic needs. In the diving situation where oxygen is usually supplied at tensions near the upper limit of tolerance and where CO_2 elimination is usually the predominant factor controlling breathing, metabolic needs are easily met. Semi-closed breathing rigs and conventional helmets, as well as all closed chambers, must be supplied with oxygen in accordance with the physiological demands of the diver. The

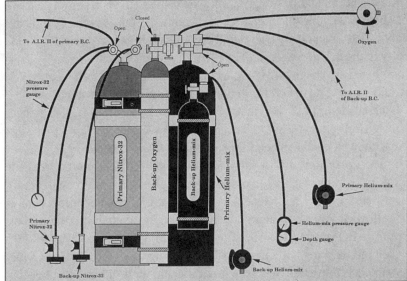

A custom TRIMIX setup by deep water fish researcher Richard Pyle in Hawaii.

oxygen actually consumed by the body varies from about 0.5 liter per minute at rest to about 1.0 liter per minute for moderate work to 3.0 or more liters per minute for very heavy work. The requirements for supplying the various types of gas with the appropriate oxygen flow are given in detail in the U.S. Navy Manual.

INERT GAS NARCOSIS

The cause of the narcotic effect of nitrogen seen during the course of dives performed using air at depths in excess of 100 fsw has remained obscure for more than a century. In the older literature dealing with caisson operations, the usual mood of workers in a compressed-air atmosphere was euphoria. In scuba diving the expansive feeling at pressure depths is euphemistically referred to as "rapture of the depths."

Damant (1930) and Hill (1932) observed that deep-sea divers at depths of 270 to 300 fsw (9 - 10 ATA) had difficulty in assimilating instructions and making decisions. Severe emotional disturbances, as well as loss of consciousness, were reported. In the Harvard pressure chamber at 4 ATA, it was apparent that even at this relatively low pressure, individuals experienced varying degrees of euphoria with tendency to fixation of ideas accompanied by some impairment of fine manipulative procedures. Behnke et al. (1935), in reporting reactions under seemingly favorable environmental conditions, attributed them to the narcotic effect of nitrogen in accord with the Myer-Overton hypothesis that inhaled gases, generally with high lipid-to-water solubility ratios, were narcotic/anesthetic in varying degrees.

The term, narcosis, designates general depressant phenomena produced by drugs and gases. Anesthesia is a special instance of the general phenomenon characterized by loss of consciousness, altered cortical electrical activity, loss of pain sensation, and other signs familiar to the medical practitioner. Narcosis is an apt term to denote many psychic reactions, including stupefaction and neuromuscular impairment associated with inhalation of inert gases under pressure, which may or may not be followed by loss of consciousness.

The gas of primary concern to the deep scuba diver is nitrogen, or in particular, air. There is no established upper limit for the safe breathing of nitrogen; a partial pressure of 15 atmospheres has been shown to cause severe narcosis and possibly nausea but is not incompatible with survival (Adolfson 1967; Hamilton 1972).

It is generally considered safe to dive to about 200 fsw breathing air, primarily due to the tolerable degree of impairment seen at these depths. However, dive conditions can vary this "safe depth." Cave diving and wreck penetrations can be assumed to mandate a greater degree of alertness than a comparable open water dive. Increasing hazards will thus set the acceptable depth limits to shallower depths. Dives utilizing air in these depths ranges produce a noticeable narcosis on the first exposure, but a great deal of accommodation is seen on the next few dives to the same depth if they follow no later than a day or two. A diver living in an undersea habitat acquires a resistance to narcosis related to the partial pressure of nitrogen in the habitat.

Nitrogen is believed to "interact" with high levels of both oxygen and carbon dioxide; these gases apparently increase the susceptibility of the diver to the narcotic effect of nitrogen. Thus, consideration must be made as to the performance of the breathing apparatus as it relates to carbon dioxide levels at depth. The leading cause of elevated carbon dioxide levels during scuba dives is the inability of many regulators to deliver adequate fresh gas flows to meet the physiologic requirements of the diver (maximum fresh gas flows delivered to the diver, and the work of inhalation and exhalation all can contribute to this problem).

Helium and neon are non-narcotic. Hydrogen apparently causes a narcosis at very high pressures that is balanced by the hydrostatic pressure effect. All other gases are more narcotic than nitrogen; this category theoretically includes oxygen, but the narcotic properties of oxygen are not manifest until well beyond the usual CNS toxicity limits. Argon has been used in diving; however, it is about twice as narcotic as nitrogen and its solubility presents severe problems in decompression.

HPNS AND HYPERBARIC ARTHRALGIA

The high pressure nervous syndrome (HPNS) is an increasingly important consideration as depths exceed about 600 fsw. It is invoked by gases with low lipid solubility, hence its early designation "helium tremors." Helium, and to a slightly lesser extent neon, is associated with HPNS because they allow high hydrostatic pressure to be applied without a compensating narcotic effect. In situations where HPNS is a problem, its effects may be counteracted by including in the breathing mixture a gas with sufficient lipid solubility to counterbalance the compression effect (presumably in the lipid component of cell membranes). The optimal "doses" are not yet established, but it has been shown that rapid compression to 1000 fsw cause far less tremor and other manifestations of the syndrome when 12-25% nitrogen is included in the inert component of the breathing mixture. Lessor percentages of gases which have higher anesthetic potency might also be used with the effect on decompression being the deciding factor.

Another direct pressure effect is hyperbaric arthralgia. The mechanism of this phenomenon is likely to be different from that of HPNS – perhaps due to osmosis – and the mitigation effect of narcotic gases has not been demonstrated. Slow rates of compression seem to be the best procedure for managing this problem, or for short jobs the opposite approach of a rapid compression and faster decompression. In any case, until hyperbaric arthralgia is better understood the choice of gas will most generally be determined by other operational considerations.

DENSITY AND VISCOSITY

As a diver's depth increases, the density of his breathing gas increases as an almost linear function of his absolute pressure. High gas densities act to limit the diver's ability to ventilate his lungs and to increase the work required; this effects acts on both the diver and his equipment. The viscosity of a gas, however, does not change appreciably with depth, and the viscosities of most respiratory gases are similar (Lamphier, 1969). Breathing a mixture of dense gases at sea-level has been shown experimentally to be essentially identical to breathing a lighter gas at increased pressure, provided the densities are equivalent (Maio and Fhori, 1967).

The salient facts are that during laminar flow the pressure required to cause gas to flow is a linear function of viscosity, but that during turbulent flow, pressure must increase approximately with the square of the flow. Turbulent versus laminar flow has an important role in both the breathing equipment and in the pulmonary system. Fittings and/or connectors that cause gases to make sharp changes in direction increase the degree of turbulence seen in breathing equipment. All efforts should be made to eliminate the inclusion of these types of fittings in regulators used at depth. Normal breathing at rest involves some turbulent flow and consequently the work of breathing is increased when denser gases are breathed. This effect is exaggerated during exercise, when respiratory flow rates are increased.

In diving the physiological effect of a limitation in breathing capability is slightly different from that at sea-level, in that oxygen partial pressures are usually more than adequate to meet the metabolic needs. Restrictions on lung ventilation, therefore, cause only a buildup in CO_2. The rate of removal of CO_2 is entirely a function of ventilation volume flow (VE) whereas adequate oxygen can be delivered at very low rates of ventilation.

Another important factor in respiratory mechanics is the concept of airway collapse. In a forced expiration there is a maximum possible rate of gas flow beyond which extra effort will not provide extra flow, but instead will force temporary constriction of the airways (intrathoracic airways). This situation is reached more easily with denser gases (with denser gases a higher intrathoracic pressure is required for the same flow rate), and although a person does not require these high flow rates under normal circumstances, at high densities the maximum flow capability and minimum ventilatory requirement tend to converge. The result is that a limit will be encountered at increasing pressures of the amount of work which a diver can do. Artificial respiratory assistance is not likely to be very helpful other than to do the extra work of overcoming the resistance of the breathing apparatus.

Gas densities as great as 25 times that of sea-level air have been breathed experimentally (Lambertsen, 1972); it was found that work was restricted to less than 3/4 the sea-level maximum for the individual, but that this amount of work could be accomplished at densities up to about 18 times normal. These experiments were conducted with equipment having low resistance and low dead space; with standard diving gear, problems will be encountered.

The same gas properties prevail in breathing equipment as in man, and both density and viscosity of the gases to be used must be considered in engineering design. It is worth mentioning that equipment must be designed to provide the maximum peak flow during a breathing cycle, rather than just the average minute volume.

Ordinarily, breathing gas density is not a limitation in the use of air or nitrogen-oxygen mixtures (or argon) since narcosis becomes a definite problem before density becomes limiting. This may not be the case where deeper depths can be tolerated as a result of adaptation to nitrogen in a hyperbaric habitat. Also, the density of air at 200-300 fsw is enough to be difficult to breathe through inadequate equipment or at inadequate supply pressures. One other difficulty with air is that with any CO_2 accumulation which might occur it can interact unfavorably with the effects of both the nitrogen and the oxygen of air.

One of the most desirable characteristics of helium is its low density and the consequent ease with which it is breathed. The same applies to hydrogen. Experiments at the University of Pennsylvania have shown that density equivalent to that of a helium-oxygen mixture at 5,000 fsw can be tolerated at light work levels (Lambertsen, 1972). Because narcosis does not limit the depth at which it can be used, neon mixtures can pose density limitations to both equipment and man. A good practical depth limit for Neon 75 (75% neon, 25% helium) using current equipment is 650 fsw.

VOICE

Voice distortion is encountered when light gases (e.g., helium and hydrogen) are breathed, and the distortion increases in severity with increasing depth. This is due to an increase in the speed of sound in the gas, and the effect of this increase in the phonetic properties of the resonant cavities used in speech (Sergeant, 1969). (Some distortion occurs when air is breathed at depth, but this is a minor problem at the depths man is limited to due to narcosis.) Helium speech involves a linear increase in the frequency of important formants (the frequency bands which make up the phonetic quality of vowel sounds) by a factor of about 2.25 (Gertsman

This deep diving submersible is equipped to handle up to ten divers and three crew with a depth rating of 1000 feet. The pilot and crew enter though the top main hatch and remain dry at normal pressure throughout the operation. Divers breathing mixed gas can "lock out" of the rear chamber and enter the water for exploration or research, and then return to complete decompression aboard in comfort. Such technology is available to anyone with the right budget.

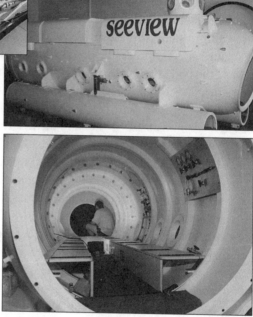

et al., 1966). Electronic devices (helium speech unscramblers) which restore these formants to their original frequency will restore the intelligibility of helium speech, although quality must necessarily be sacrificed if this is to be done in "real time." A practical aspect of the frequency shift is that many formants are shifted out of the range of ordinary communications gear, so that a really useful system requires suitable microphones and preamplifiers as well as an unscrambler.

Hydrogen causes slightly greater distortion than helium – but in one experiment at 200 fsw no greater loss in intelligibility than seen with helium at the same depth (Sergeant, 1972) – but is reasonably well translated by a good helium speech unscrambler. Neon causes much less distortion than helium, preserving a high level of intelligibility throughout the depth range of up to 600 fsw. Many diving operators add 10 or 15%

nitrogen to a helium-oxygen mixture in order to improve voice intelligibility (as well as to help keep the diver warm). The addition of small amounts of very dense gases such as SF6 or CF4 have also been suggested.

THERMAL PROPERTIES

Another gas property which has a prominent effect on the success of a gas used for deep diving is the way it influences the loss of heat from a diver's body. Divers lose heat by two routes, the skin and the respiratory tract. An unprotected diver in shallow water has most of his heat loss to the water through his skin, but even here the tremendous heat exchange capabilities of the lungs are significant. At greater pressures, especially where helium is used, the proportion of heat lost through the breathing system increases with the increase in density of the breathing gas, until at 20 atmospheres this may equal the metabolic heat production of the body (Webb and Annis, 1966). Exercise at depth to produce more heat is no help because respiratory gas exchange increases almost linearly with increased metabolism. Most deep diving experience is based on helium and it has been found that respiratory heat losses where helium-based mixtures are used as breathing gas is a considerable problem. It is practically impossible to carry out prolonged deep dives (beyond one hour) in cold water without heating the breathing gas (Webb, 1973). This problem is complicated by the pressure effect on insulation. Virtually all thermal insulation relies on vacuum or "dead" gas space; at pressure, conventional insulations are compressed to a fraction of their original dimensions and to make matters worse the little remaining space may become filled with a thermally conductive gas (e.g., helium). Insulation containing tiny non-compressible spheres is effective, or a new gas space can be created by addition of pressured gas as depth (but helium is not much help here; air, nitrogen, argon, freon, or carbon dioxide are more effective insulators).

As in the case of voice improvement, small proportions of a denser (hence less thermally conductive) gas added to a helium-oxygen breathing mixture may reduce heat loss enough to be worth the added density and decompression complications. Neon has been used in large proportions (up to 75%), and subjectively appears to help.

Another important situation concerning heat loss to a gaseous medium is that of the transfer bell of a SDC (submersible decompression chamber). The bell is a particularly difficult problem since a diver may be required to decompress in the bell for several hours after leaving the water, already in a chilled condition and without a chance to rewarm.

Heat loss is an important aspect of undersea habitats and saturation chambers. Divers in helium atmospheres are comfortable at about 30°C. Though they feel comfortable, there is an extra energy burden which may approach 2,000 kcal per day in helium habitat dwellers (Webb, 1973).

DECOMPRESSION CONSIDERATIONS AND COUNTER-DIFFUSION

A discussion on the relative merits of the different inert gases with regard to their effect on decompression will, if it sticks to experience with human divers, be almost entirely concerned with the relative merits of helium versus nitrogen. The properties which presumably govern the decompression characteristics of a gas are solubility in water, solubility in fat, diffusibility, thermodynamic properties and derived factors such as oil/water solubility ratio.

Helium was first suggested as a diving gas on the basis of its low solubility with regard to its low density and high diffusibility. In small animals the advantages of helium are substantial, resulting a reduction of safe decompression time as compared with nitrogen. These advantages prevail in humans, but to a lesser extent. Because it is taken up much faster than nitrogen (2.65 times as fast in diffusion limited compartments), there are situations where this advantage is lost (usually seen in dives of less than approximately 100 minutes).

A convenient way of comparing the decompression properties of these two gases is to look at the limiting half-times that are 2 to 3 times as long as those of helium.

It has been suggested, on the basis of the "independent" partial pressures of gases in a mixture, that a "porridge" of gases could be prepared which would permit immediate decompression. If seven different inert gases were used, each giving a partial pressure of one atmosphere, then a dive to 200 fsw would involve no more than one atmosphere of each gas, hence no supersaturation for any one gas. In practice this does not work; partial pressures are additive with respect to tendency to form a gas phase (Graves et al., 1972).

Whether or not all gases in solution act independently, there is evidence that changing the gases being breathed during decompression can substantially influence the decompression (Workman, 1969; Buhlmann, 1969, 1983, 1987). Standard practice in deep commercial helium-oxygen ("mixed gas") diving involves a shift to air as the breathing mixture during the later stages of decompression, with a final shift to 100% oxygen at the final stages.

Other gases which are considered here from a decompression point of view are oxygen, neon and hydrogen. Argon is appreciably more soluble than even nitrogen, and because of this must in any event be used sparingly. Neon has a low solubility in the same order as helium, both in fat and water, but resembles nitrogen more in diffusion. How each of these factors affects whether one gas is "better" than another depends on how each gas is used and in what manner a comparison is made. For example, though helium is "unloaded" about three times as fast as nitrogen (if diffusion only is considered), certain deep, short dive profiles result in a shorter decompression time with nitrogen than with helium (Workman, 1969).

The metabolic gases CO_2 and oxygen also play a role in decompression. Oxygen displaces inert gas, and if time is allowed for it to be consumed in the tissue it will not likely be involved in bubble formation; however, oxygen acts as a vasoconstrictor at high pressures and as such no doubt influences gas transport. On the other hand, carbon dioxide acts as a vasodilator, and likewise will affect gas transport. In tunnel work a high level of CO_2 has been observed to be associated with an increased bends incidence (End, 1938; Kindwall, 1973).

Different theorists in decompression computation treat the matter of different gases in different ways. The basic "Haldanean" approach was used for the development of the U.S. Navy Helium Tables. Here a 2.15:1 ratio was used, with the longest half-time 75 minutes; by contrast, the exceptional exposure air tables used a longest half-time of 240 minutes and a 2:1 ratio (Workman, 1969).

The same approach, essentially, is used by Buhlmann in a slightly different way; he sums the nitrogen and helium partial pressures in equivalent compartments (240 minutes for helium and 635 minutes for nitrogen) and uses a Haldane ratio which varies for the two gases (and is averaged based on the percentage of each inert gas present) and is reduced as a function of total pressure. Buhlmann basically considers that gas movement and transport is perfusion-limited (Buhlmann, 1969, 1983, 1987). Schreiner (1971) uses a further pragmatic yet physiologic modification of this method in which the half-times are determined for any gas on the basis of the oil-water solubility ratio and blood perfusion assumptions; all gases are summed in each compartment, and ascent is controlled via a matrix of M-values (Workman, 1965) which reflect total depth. Hempleman's single-tissue concept considers helium's properties, since it is based on the rate of linear diffusion into a "slab" of tissue. Hill's (1969) thermodynamic model regards gas transport as diffusion-limited, and consequently considers the diffusion properties of the gas in question.

Under certain conditions it is possible to evoke many aspects of the syndrome associated with decompression sickness without a change in pressure. This phenomenon, known as counter-diffusion, results when a diver is loaded with and immersed in one gas (e.g., helium) and breathes a denser, more slowly diffusing gas (e.g., nitrogen). The most apparent effect is intense itching of the exposed skin (skin covered with foil or blanketed in the gas being breathed does not itch), but symptoms similar to vestibular decompression sickness have been seen (Blenkarn et al., 1973; Idicula et al., 1972). For the helium-nitrogen system a "soak" of at least two hours in helium is needed at a pressure of at least several atmospheres before breathing the nitrogen; symptoms then appear in about 20 minutes. Lesions seen in animals are clearly bubbles of gas. An in-vitro model system has been devised with demonstrates that supersaturation can occur when two gases of different diffusiveness (and perhaps solubilities) are diffusing in opposite direction through a lipid layer (Graves, et al., 1972).

The most obvious relevance of this phenomenon to diving is in the laboratory, where such exposures have taken place and where a new tool is now available for the study of gas transport. The severity of the symptoms seen makes intentional human exposure not advisable. Whether the effects will appear when a diver immersed in nitrogen breathes helium is not apparent; even if skin lesions are not seen, disorders in the ear, for example, are possible. A diver saturated in a nitrogen habitat who wishes to make a deep excursion breathing helium-oxygen may be more susceptible to decompression sickness than he otherwise would be.

FIRE SAFETY

Fire safety is mainly of concern in habitats. The choice of a breathing gas mixture has significant effect on fire safety if it results in a chamber having an oxygen level which will support combustion readily. It is the percentage of oxygen more than the partial pressure which determines its flame propagating character, mixtures with less than 6% oxygen being safe. It is more difficult to heat materials to the ignition temperature in a helium-oxygen atmosphere than in an equivalent one with nitrogen, but once ignited things burn better.

Effects of other possible diving gases on flame propagation have not been determined, with the exception of hydrogen. Here, of course, the fire safety situation is of a different order of magnitude. Mixtures of hydrogen with less than 5 or 6% hydrogen will neither burn nor support combustion, but safely making these mixtures and coping with other general handling problems with hydrogen are formidable tasks (Edel, 1972).

COST AND LOGISTICS

This section is concerned with the question of obtaining, storing and delivering to a dive site the various gases. Air is, of course, the least expensive gas available, requiring only a clean compressor (with proper filtering) provided a pollution-free atmosphere is available. The components of air, nitrogen and oxygen, are likewise inexpensive, and handling, mixing, analyzing, storing, etc., makes up the bulk of the cost of using nitrogen-oxygen mixtures. These costs apply to some extent to any gas used except air.

Nitrogen-oxygen mixtures may have roles in diving which are as yet unexploited, in their use in habitats from which excursions are made to deeper work sites (Hamilton, et al., 1973). The narcosis which limits safe use of air or N_2/O_2 mixtures can be tolerated at greater depths on excursions from saturation than in bounce dives from the surface (Schmidt, et al., 1973). By using the normal oxygen consumption of the divers to "breathe down" the oxygen in a habitat to a tolerable range, such operations can be conducted entirely by means of compressors and gas available at the site.

The term "mixed gas" in its broadest interpretation as applied to diving refers to any gas being used for diving except air (and perhaps the rarely used pure oxygen case). In its general usage, however, the term refers specifically to helium-oxygen mixtures, which may or may not contain a little nitrogen.

Helium, although abundant in the universe, has been found in commercial quantities in only certain places on earth. It is usually found with natural gas in practical percentages of from 1 to as much as 8%. Until

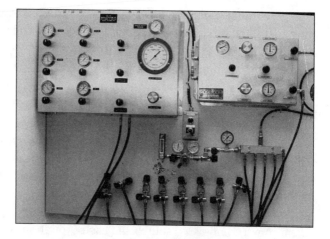

Mixed gas panel at John Comly's Blue Abyss Dive Center in New Jersey.

recent years the only helium production was in the U.S., but sources have now been found in Canada, Poland, and the Soviet Union. The U.S. has had laws controlling export and requiring conservation of helium — these were relaxed in 1969; helium stockpiling by the Bureau of Mines was also discontinued and the Helium Research Unit at Amarillo was closed.

In the U.S. helium is not particularly expensive, a typical bulk price (in 1972 dollars) being about $0.06 per cubic foot. This cost can appreciate by a factor of 2x to 4x the base cost per cubic foot for gas delivered to a North Sea diver on the sea floor. The expense of using helium in diving operations in remote locations is dictated by the cost of handling, which includes mixing, shipping and storing. The basic container is the conventional gas cylinder, varieties of which hold 200 to 300 standard cubic feet of gas at pressures of 2,000 to 3,000 psi. The empty weight may be 150-200 pounds. For easier shipboard handling these are often manifolded into "quads" of four or six cylinders. Larger quantities of gas are handled in trailers holding 10,000 to 150,000 cubic feet.

Much mixed-gas diving is done using gas mixtures prepared on shore and shipped to the dive site as mixtures. In addition to the bulk shipping problem, this practice involves other inefficiencies. Depth of use (hence optimum oxygen percentage in the mixture) must be anticipated well in advance of need, and not only must the "steel" be shipped back, but in deep diving operations a considerable amount of gas remains unusable in the quads when its pressure falls below the appropriate delivery pressure. However, this system has certain advantages, in that large initial capital investments can be replaced by distributed shipping costs, and there is less dependence on highly trained technicians at the dive site.

With the addition of compression, storage and analytical equipment, gases can be mixed to order, invoking the obvious advantages. Still another method of preparing diving gas mixtures is by means of on-line mixing devices. Using a system of appropriate regulators and flowmeters, mixtures can be "dialed" as needed from bulk storage of the pure component (Gilardi, 1972).

As the final step in mixed gas logistics it is relevant to consider the methods of gas conservation, recovery and reuse. The basic breathing apparatus is an open-circuit demand system, whereby each inspiration is taken from a compressed source and each expiration is lost "overboard." Some breathing systems use partial or total recirculation of the breathing gas, removing the accumulated CO_2 with a chemical absorber. A "push-pull" hookah system returns expired gas from the diver to the bell atmosphere, where it is scrubbed and recirculated to the diver. On decompression the gas from the bell can be used to pressurize the deck chamber, with the divers transferring after equalization has taken place. Simple buffering, scrubbing and recompression systems can be assembled to permit re-use of a large fraction of the mixture used in a deep dive (Schmidt, et al., 1973). More sophisticated systems have been developed which actually re-refine helium, separating pure helium from all other components and contaminants in a mixture. These systems are complex, expensive and require a supply of liquid nitrogen, but where usage is great and supply lines long they can be cost-effective (Slack, 1973).

Along with the development of devices and procedures for conserving helium there has been a continual push to develop alternatives to the use of helium for mixed-gas diving. This effort has been to circumvent the physiological, economical and operational disadvantages of helium as well as to avoid dependence on a politically-sensitive commodity. The two gases considered as serious alternatives to helium are neon and hydrogen.

Neon is a product of the distillation of atmospheric air, being present at about 18 parts per million (air also contains 5 ppm of helium). Purified neon is too expensive to consider for ordinary diving operations, but mixtures of neon and helium that are produced as by-products of air distillation (commercial production of oxygen is via air distillation) are usable (Schreiner, et al., 1972). From the uncondensed fraction in an air distillation column (normally discarded) a mixture of neon and helium can be obtained, in the proportion of 72-78% neon, 22-28% helium. It is called "first run" neon or Neon 75. This mixture is relatively inexpensive; it could be available at $0.10 -$0.20 per cubic foot if bought in large quantities. The significant fact about neon is that as a product of the atmosphere it is available anywhere there is sufficient industrialization to require an air reduction plant.

Neon has another logistic advantage; because of its thermodynamic properties it is the diving gas most easily transported and stored as a liquid.

Hydrogen is available by electrolysis of water, and as such rivals air in its worldwide availability and low cost. Hydrogen's high flammability and diffusibility add to its cost — perhaps substantially — by increasing the difficulty of handling and mixing it safely (Edel, 1972). Increasing interest in the use of hydrogen as a low pollution fuel should result in future improvements in handling methods and equivalents.

CONVENTIONAL BREATHING MIXTURES

This section considers the various breathing mixtures in general use, their history, uses and advantages and disadvantages.

AIR AND NITROGEN-OXYGEN MIXTURES

Until the introduction of helium to diving in the late 1930's the history of diving was the history of air diving. Although most early diving exploits were breath-holding or snorkel dives, Alexander the Great is reported to have descended in an air-filled bell, and a compressed-air bell was designed in 1690 by Edmund Halley (of comet fame). Preminet first used a bellows to pump air down to a diver in the 1770's, but diving as we know it began in 1819 with the invention of the diving suit by August Siebe (Larson, 1959). This suit, supplied with compressed air, had all the essential features of the classical diving gear still in use today (Goodman, 1962).

Air, because of its availability and suitability for shallow diving, is the gas of choice for nearly all diving to about 150 fsw. Beyond this depth narcosis becomes a factor which will limit safe and effective diving to divers adapted to nitrogen and well trained for the job at hand. If suitable support (e.g., a diving partner, life lines, air supply, communications), is available the safe depth can be extended to 250, perhaps 300 fsw for short times (less than 0.5 hours). For short dives (usually 1.0

Michael Menduno wearing the Mark 16 rebreather. System is lightweight and provides up to six hours dive time to approximately 500 feet.

The U.S. Navy Mark 16 mixed gas (heliox) rebreather diving system with back shroud removed showing internal components including oxygen and diluent helium gas cylinders.

hour bottom times or less) in the deeper air range decompression is actually easier with air than with helium-oxygen mixtures.

Air is the gas of choice for undersea habitats to a depth of at least 70 fsw – at some depth beyond this, oxygen toxicity may cause lung discomfort after a few days—an appropriate depth-duration trade-off for this limit has not yet been established (however, it is known that by keeping the inspired oxygen partial pressures less than 0.5 atm, unlimited durations are possible with no toxicity).

Nitrogen-oxygen mixtures (NITROX) having a greater oxygen fraction than air are being used with more frequency in the last few years. The added oxygen being for the purpose of displacing inert gas and hence of reducing decompression. Nitrox is not an answer to diving deeper, but allows longer bottom times at appropriate depth with less decompression than required with a comparable dive utilizing air.

HELIUM

The record shows that C.J. Cooke applied in 1919 for a patent on the use of helium-oxygen mixtures to be supplied to men under pressure, but apparently never tried it (Edel, 1939). Credit for development of helium should go to the eminent chemist Dr. Joel H. Hildebrand, who with R. R. Sayers and W. P. Yant of the U.S. Bureau of Mines, tried helium decompressions with small animals (Sayers, Hildebrand & Yant, 1925). It was on the basis of its low solubility that these investigators proposed helium, and they reasoned correctly that this property would improve decompression time in comparison with nitrogen. It was not until End tried breathing helium, and, with Nohl actually tried helium on a 420 fsw dive (End, 1937; End, 1938) that the real advantage of helium was noted — its lack of narcotic properties. Shortly thereafter Momsen, with Behnke and Yarborough, at the U.S. Naval Experimental Diving Unit explored the use of helium to the pressure equivalent of 500 fsw (Ellsberg, 1939) and in 1941 it was successfully used in dives to 440 fsw (Behnke, 1942). The salvage of the submarine *Squalus* could not have been accomplished safely without helium.

The use of helium in diving has exceeded the expectations of its early proponents, with the 1,000 fsw mark surpassed at sea and depths twice that deep reached in the laboratory. These dives have not been without problems, however. Serious HPNS symptoms may result if compression is rapid, and long exposure to hyperbaric arthralgia and extended decompression are consequences of slow compression rates. Helium is presently the diluent gas of choice for virtually all commercial and military diving beyond 150 fsw. Where immediate decompression is to follow, oxygen is kept as high as possible in the mixture, so as to produce a bottom gas oxygen partial pressure of 1.2 - 2.0 atmospheres; the higher the oxygen in the breathing mixture the lower will be the exposure to inert gas during the dive. For saturation, oxygen is kept between 0.2 and 0.6 atm, but it should be raised during decompression.

Nitrogen is sometimes added to helium-oxygen mixtures for the purpose of improving voice communication and mitigating slightly the chilling effect. The range used for this purpose is 5-15%; higher doses might be used, but even 15% is enough to have a detrimental effect on decompression. Another purpose for adding nitrogen is to counteract the effects of the HPNS. Here 12-25% might be used; with the exact concentration required still to be precisely determined. Use of larger percentages of nitrogen of diving in the 200-300 (as used in the "Sullivan Connection" dives in 1988) fsw range has been suggested, where conservation of helium (and economy) is more important than hasty decompression.

To summarize the properties of helium as they affect its use as a diving gas: Helium is light and very easy to breathe; it has a low solubility and high diffusibility, which properties cause it to be easy to eliminate during most decompressions. The same low solubility gives it no narcotic properties (as predicted by the Myer-Overton hypothesis of narcosis), but allows the HPNS to become manifest in rapid compressions. Although not expensive, helium can only be obtained in certain locations. When kept under pressure helium has a high leak rate, and it can leak into devices stored in it, such as a TV tube or a diver's watch. And one of the most disturbing factors about helium is its sonic velocity, which when helium is being breathed makes speech difficult to understand.

NITROGEN-HELIUM-OXYGEN Mixtures (TRIMIX)

Recently, the use of helium-nitrogen-oxygen mixtures (TRIMIX) has received widespread publicity in the cave diving community, with the utilization of TRIMIX during the Sullivan Connection expedition demonstrating the feasibility of TRIMIX in the exploration of deep cave systems. TRIMIX was also utilized to some degree during the Wakulla Project, and has been used with great success during the recent re-exploration and mapping of Eagles Nest Sink in Hernando County, Florida (King, 1990).

TRIMIX has two advantages for the deep scuba diver over the use of HELIOX.

1) TRIMIX can be significantly less expensive in both gas and equipment when compared to a comparable heliox dive.

2) TRIMIX can also offer significant decompression saving when compared to a comparable heliox dive, especially when you consider the usual bottom times most of the high tech diving community are encountering.

Utilizing the same decompression calculation model, for short bottom times the order of total decompression required is:

Air < TRIMIX < HELIOX

This relationship holds true for bottom times less than 90 minutes, with total decompression times converging at approximately 125 minutes bottom. After that point, the order reverses with:

HELIOX < TRIMIX < Air.

OXYGEN

With the advent of fully-closed mixed gas rebreathing systems which produce no bubbles and allow a long bottom time on a single charge of gas, the incentive to use pure oxygen underwater has disappeared. The main use of pure-oxygen rebreathing systems was for clandestine operations where the presence of bubbles is unacceptable. The Italian Navy used closed-circuit oxygen rebreathing early in WWII, and the LARU (Lambertsen Amphibious Respiration Unit) was introduced in the U.S. Navy shortly thereafter (Larson, 1959).

Because of the possibility of CNS toxicity (convulsions) the use of such units is restricted to a maximum depth of about 25 fsw (partial pressures of 1.6 or less in the working diver are allowed).

EXPERIMENTAL BREATHING MIXTURES

This section deals with the more unusual diving gas mixtures – those which are not in routine use but on which some experience has been accumulated. A qualitative approach is used in this discussion, with attention directed primarily at the components of a mixture, not the proportions.

HYDROGEN

Although highly explosive when mixed with air in the proper proportions, hydrogen can be used in diving because at increased pressures enough oxygen to meet physiologic needs can be added and the mixture can still remain below the lower flammability limits (Dorr & Schreiner, 1969). Physiologically it appears to be inert.

Hydrogen was used in experimental dives with animals as far back as 1914, before helium had been discovered in enough abundance to merit consideration of its use in diving (Gaertner, 1920). More recently Zetterstrom made successful dives with hydrogen-oxygen mixtures, but unfortunately died in a diving accident (Zetterstrom, 1948; Bjurstedt & Severin, 1948). His death, although unrelated to the use of hydrogen, had the effect of setting back work with this gas.

In addition to its low cost and ready availability – advantages partially offset by its explosive properties – hydrogen has a physiological advantage which might make it the gas of choice for deep diving; the narcotic properties of hydrogen apparently counteract the neurological disturbances due to high hydrostatic pressures (Brauer & Wav, 1970). Hydrogen is about one-fourth as potent as nitrogen in causing narcosis. Further, its low density makes hydrogen mixtures the easiest ones to breathe at great depths.

The thermal properties of hydrogen seem comparable to those of helium, and it causes a voice distortion of equal proportions. Helium unscramblers, however, seem to work with hydrogen too.

Short diving exposures to hydrogen conducted by Edel have revealed no contradictory indications against the eventual use of hydrogen in diving (Edel et al., 1972). Decompression times appear to be generally comparable to helium, perhaps slower. Hydrogen offers an intriguing possibility for exploring the question of whether perfusion or diffusion plays the limiting role in decompression; it has a diffusion comparable to helium and oil/water solubility ratio like nitrogen. In practice, hydrogen appears to fall between helium and nitrogen in its decompression efficiency.

Not all reports on the use of hydrogen are favorable. Experiments conducted with rabbits at pressure of 280M (917 fsw) showed reduction in peculiar thermal susceptibility (LeBoucher, 1970).

Currently most of the work being done with hydrogen is being done in France by COMEX. They have reported successful manned dives (in the laboratory) to approximately 2,000 fsw

NEON

The high cost of neon has limited the study to this gas for use in diving. Numerous experiments with animals and other biological models have shown no detrimental effects (Schreiner et al., 1962; Miller et al., 1967; Hamilton et al, 1972); human exposures have verified this and also have shown that neon has virtually no tendency to produce narcosis to at least 1200 fsw (Hamilton, 1972).

Because of the expense of pure neon, most experiments have concentrated on the use of a mixture of neon and helium, Neon 75, which is obtained by distillation of air. Neon, therefore has worldwide availability in this form.

Experiments designed to evaluate neon as a diving gas in side-by-side comparison with nitrogen and helium (Schreiner et al., 1972) have shown it to be equivalent to helium in its effects on mental and psycho-

Recent evolutions of private sector development include the triple redundant CIS-LUNAR rebreather developed by Bill Stone for extended cave exploration.

motor processes, and that it presents no particular problems in decompression. Voice is less distorted by neon than by helium or hydrogen, and the lower thermal conductivity of neon might prove to be advantageous when diving in cold water. Divers who have used neon at sea report some subjective reduction in heat loss but definitive measurements of this factor remain to be made.

It appears that the optimal use of neon will be in the range 150-600 fsw. Deeper depths result in enough of an increase in gas density that Neon 75 mixtures may be hard to breathe by a diver doing heavy work and who is limited by breathing equipment designed for helium.

ARGON

The properties of argon are not beneficial with respect to its use as a diving gas. It has a high lipid solubility and is consequently narcotic and a problem in decompression. Further, its density makes it difficult to breathe at pressures, but it does allow effective voice communications and also acts as a fair insulator against heat loss.

Argon has been used as a decompression gas, with the purpose of reducing the inspired partial pressures of both helium and nitrogen (Keller and Buhlmann, 1965; Keller, 1967). The real benefits of argon in this situation have not been systematically explored, but its use seems to be effective (Schreiner, 1969).

Argon is about twice as narcotic as nitrogen, causing an equivalent decrement in performance test at about half as much pressure (Ackles & Fowler, 1971).

OTHER GASES

Few other biologically inert gases exist which seem to be practical as the major component of a diving gas mixture, and scant data exists on the ones that do exist. Heavier gases exhibit the same deficiencies as argon, having high lipid solubilities which result in both narcosis and difficult decompression, and high densities which cause increased breathing resistance.

Of the light gases, deuterium is not available in sufficient quantities to be considered; it should have properties similar to hydrogen and helium, and offers no particular advantage. Methane is sufficiently inert and lighter than most other gases, but its lipid solubility should make it reasonably narcotic. Like hydrogen it is not flammable if the oxygen percentage is kept low (below about 4%).

Certain gases have some value when added as only a small fraction of a breathing mixture. Gases known to be narcotic may reduce symptoms of HPNS. A heavy gas having a relatively low solubility may improve voice communication; such a gas is CF4, tetrafluoromethane (Airco; patent No. 3,676,563; July 11, 1972). Other fluorinated hydrocarbons (freons) are used as fire extinguishing agents. These freons are apparently not completely "inert," in that they exhibit certain toxic characteristics (see Freon references).

One additional use of gases in diving is to simulate other conditions in the laboratory. Examples are the use of nitrous oxide to cause narcosis similar to that of hyperbaric nitrogen (Brauer & Way, 1971; Hamilton, 1973). Nitrous oxide is 30 to 40 times more narcotic than nitrogen. Sulfur hexafluoride has a molecular weight of 146, making it about five times as dense as air. This property has been used to study breathing resistance as a function of density (Uhl et al.,1972; Antoneisen et al., 1971).

CONCLUSION

Only a few short years ago, a discussion of noncommercial divers using mixed gas technology would have been preposterous to many industry professionals content within the confines of traditional scuba. To suggest the use of affordable, safely engineered closed-circuit units would be as foreign as "man on the moon" predictions in the 1950's. But here we are, none the less, and poised on new technological breakthroughs every day.

Diving evolved historically from military applications and systems that were adopted by commercial interests and ultimately by sport divers. If you were to plot a line graph for the three segments an interesting shift would occur in the mid-seventies when commercial companies broke away from naval influences and began to chart their own course in innovative table research, saturation systems and specialized equipment. In the nineties, it appears that private sector development springing from the technical diving community may well provide the impetus and leadership in a bold new technology reaching for the twenty-first century.

CHAPTER 12

Dive Tables

"The reliability of a decompression table or procedure is not determined by any mathematical process, but by what works in practice. What works... is what works!"

John Crea III

"Any passive decompression device can only inform the diver of his or her decompression status. How that information is used is the responsibility of the diver."

Karl Huggins

DIVE TABLE EVOLUTION

The first research work in decompression physiology was not directed at scuba divers. It was noticed that people working at elevated pressures in either caissons (a caisson is a watertight box inside which men can do construction work underwater), or construction tunnels beneath rivers would succumb to symptoms of pain and paralysis. These symptoms were first witnessed in 1841 and by the 1880's were popularly called "the bends" because of the positions the workers took to alleviate the pain. Soon this high pressure disease was referred to as caisson disease. Later, in cases from hard hat divers, decompression sickness was termed "diver's palsy".

The DCS research conducted in the 1800's eventually gave rise to a series of principles as well as a set of decompression tables that were published in 1908 by Boycott, Damant and Haldane. The principles eventually came to be known as Haldane's Principles of Decompression and, in combination with the decompression tables, formed the basis for current decompression theory including the development of the original U.S Navy Decompression Tables.

For all practical purposes, there are four principles involved:

1) "The progress of saturation follows in general the line of a logarithmic curve... The curve of desaturation after decompression is the same as that of saturation, provided no bubbles have formed ."

2) "The time in which an animal or man exposed to compressed air becomes saturated with nitrogen varies in different parts of the body from a few minutes to several hours."

3) "In decompressing men or animals from high pressure the first part should consist in rapidly halving the absolute pressure: subsequently, the rate of decompression must become slower and slower so that the nitrogen pressure in no part of the body ever becomes more than twice that of air."

4) "Decompression is not safe if the pressure of nitrogen inside the body becomes much more than twice that of the atmospheric pressure."

The reader should note that although these four principles provided the earliest basis for decompression table theory, the latter two principles have been proven flawed and have since been extensively modified.

DIVE TABLES: A COMPARISON

Most divers accept the U.S. Navy diving tables as gospel and rarely question the validation of the model. Some interesting facts need to be considered, however, when we apply those tables in sport diving applications. Such as: the Navy tables were designed originally for single dives only. Further, the divers using them were to be closely supervised by a Navy divemaster who dictated their dive profiles and controlled their decompression, if any, by in-water stages. Most diving operations were supported by on-site recompression chambers and access to a diving medical officer. Even then, an incidence rate of decompression sickness around three to five percent was considered acceptable (facilities being available for treatment).

Now consider that the Navy made a grand total of approximately 120 test dives (!!!) with human subjects before accepting the repetitive dive tables for use. These tables still enjoy the widest use by sport divers, in spite of their apparent drawbacks when considered in the perspective of the average diver's age and physical condition.

None the less, these tables have proved to be valid and with some forty years of field use and perhaps millions of dives on them by sport divers, their worth must be accepted. Recently though, a plethora of new tables have undergone research and testing with an eye to producing tables more appropriate for actual sport diving needs.

In 1908, Haldane conducted extensive studies of decompression on goats while formulating his original "decompression model". Based on his work with goats in various hyperbaric chambers he derived what he concluded to be logical extrapolations to human physiological responses to pressure and subsequent decompression schedules. Some of his assumptions, of course, were later proved to be not entirely correct. But given the tools of research for his era and the primitive monitoring equipment at his disposal, his pioneering experiments and recommendations would provide the "seed" from which the "oak tree" of decompression science and diving tables would grow.

Originally, he felt that his animal studies had confirmed his hypothesis that if no symptoms of DCS where present post-decompression, then no bubbles were formed in the blood systems. Obviously, with the benefit of today's technology and Doppler monitors, we know that bubbles do occur in a statistically large percentage of dives made that were previously thought to be "safe" from such development. In assessing the saturation exposure for goats, he applied a time factor of three hours to assume full inert gas loading and later postulated that humans would reach saturation in five hours.

In designating his half-times for his five "tissue" groups (now generally referred to as "compartments"), he selected his slowest group to be the 75-minute tissue. This was selected since it would be 95% saturated after five hours in keeping with his hypothesis on maximum time for humans to reach theoretical saturation loading. Certainly he was on the right track, but most table model experts now allow as much as 24 hours for such saturation to fully take place and current custom table models employ slow "compartments" rated up to 1,200 minutes!

Haldane produced three table schedules for air diving:

Schedule One: for all dives requiring less than 30 minutes of de compression time.

Schedule Two: for all dives requiring more than 30 minutes of decompression time.

Schedule Three: for deep air diving to 330 fsw using oxygen de compression.

These schedules were typified by a relatively rapid ascent from depth to the initial decompression stop depths, then followed by markedly slower ascents to the surface. The British Royal Navy adopted these in 1908 and continued to use them with revisions well into the late 1950's. It should be noted that it was discovered that Schedule One proved to be too conservative for practical use and Schedule Two proved to be too "liberal" with the percentage of DCS hits unacceptable. In 1915, the first tables for the U.S. Navy were produced called the C and R tables (Bureau of Construction and Repair); these were used with success in the salvage operation on the submarine F-4 at a depth of 306 fsw.

In 1912, Sir Leonard Hill offered his "Critical Pressure Hypothesis" wherein he questioned Haldane's theory of staged decompression. Hill advocated the use of continuous uniform decompression and offered both experimental and theoretical evidence to support his position. Although the validity of his decompression schedules were not substantively disputed, the widespread use of staged decom stops remained in practice.

Other development included the works of Hawkins, Shilling and Hansen in the early 1930's in which they determined that the allowable supersaturation ratio was a function of the tissue half-time and depth and duration of the dive. Yarborough expanded on their work by recomputing a set of tables for the U.S. Navy based only on the 20, 40 and 75 minute half-time groups. These were adopted by the Navy in 1937 and used until the modified U.S. Navy Standard Air Decompression Tables came into use in 1957. These tables remain in widespread use today although continued research is being conducted by the Naval Experimental Diving Unit (NEDU) including recent work with the Navy E-L Algorithm which assumes that nitrogen is absorbed by tissues at an exponential rate (as in other Haldanean models) but is discharged or "out-gassed" at a slower linear rate. This predicts slower elimination during surface intervals and resultant higher residual nitrogen levels on repetitive dives.

The British Navy branched off slightly in 1958 to follow the theories of U.K. physiologist Hempleman. "He had observed that over a particular depth range, the first symptom of DCS to appear was usually pain at or near a joint... and assumed that the tissue involved (e.g. tendon) was, therefore, the tissue with the greatest overpressure of nitrogen for that depth range, and that gas elimination from that tissue must control the decompression. He pictured the body as a single tissue and believed that the quantity of gas absorbed in the body could be calculated by a simple formula which related depth and time. Unlike Haldane, who believed that gas uptake and elimination took identical times, Hempleman assumed that gas elimination was one and a half times slower than uptake. Utilizing the theory that the tissues could tolerate an overpressure of 30 fsw, [he] constructed a new set of decompression schedules... that are the current Royal Navy schedules." (Deeper Into Diving, Lippman 1990)

Workman, in 1965, introduced the concept of "delta P" for gas partial pressures which was easier to handle than ratios and fitted the data better. He introduced the concept of "M values": that each "tissue" or theoretical compartment would have a maximum nitrogen tension that can be safely tolerated at the surface without bubble formation. M is short for maximum and the M-value is the maximum allowable tissue tension at a specific depth.

Attempting to improve the safety of his original tables, Hempleman revised them in 1968 to include using a variable ratio of tissue nitrogen tension to ambient pressure to predict safe decompression. However, the Navy was not happy with the newly restrictive results and refused to implement them. Following more trials and revisions with Hempleman more closely attentive to the Navy's suggestions for practical work needs, the tables were modified, reproduced metrically, and adopted in 1972.

Schreiner changed the accounting from "per gas" to "per compartment" in 1971, thus making it possible to handle different gases and gas mixtures. Table computation then is largely "bookkeeping": keeping track of the gases in the compartments and comparing them with the "matrix" of M-values. Diving practitioners speak of "half-times" and "M-values" as if they were real entities, but it must not be forgotten that this is only a mathematical model. In fact, it is not really a "model" as that term is normally used, but rather a computational method.

In summation, we note that Haldane's calculations are inadequate:

1) Long, deep dives require more decompression than originally provided.

2) Fixing these tables messes up the short, shallow dives which are working fine.

3) Various tricks can be used to make the tables match the data using Haldanean calculations.

4) Other ways to calculate tables have been proposed and any model will work if there are enough variables to adjust and a data base in making the adjustments.

Currently, divers are faced with a diversity of tables and decompression models incorporated into diving computers. Some are simple reconfigurations of the basic U.S. Navy tables and others are distinctly different in their approach to decompression management. For the purposes of advanced deep diving, the tables available through the national scuba training agencies will prove excessively limiting to most readers of this book due their tendency to end around 140 fsw and to offer only minimal decompression information.

New developments in bubble detection equipment prompted Dr. Merril Spencer to suggest re-evaluation of recommended no-decompression limits with the goal of minimizing bubble development after a dive. His 1976 revisions where extensively tested by Dr. Andrew Pilmanis and Dr. Bruce Bassett and found to significantly decrease detectable bubble formation. In 1981, Karl Huggins, an assistant in Research at the University of Michigan generated a new set of decompression tables based on Spencer's recommendations. These became known variously as the "Huggins Tables", "Huggins/Spencer Tables", "Michigan Sea Grant Tables", etc., and were to be the basic algorithm used in the diving industry's first practical electronic dive computer produced by Orca Industries and known as the Edge.

Significantly, the Defence and Civil Institute of Environmental Medicine (DCIEM) in Canada has continued on-going revision to their tables based on ultrasonic Doppler studies. These tables have gained wide popularity due their unique criteria for development geared to minimal bubble formation. John Crea, a professional consultant in custom table generation and a practicing anesthesiologist, specifically recommends the DCIEM Tables for deep divers if a "stock" table reference is acceptable.

Other models include the conservative Buhlmann Swiss Tables based on the work of Dr. Albert Buhlmann of the Laboratory of Hyperbaric Physiology of the University of Zurich. His algorithms have been extensively integrated into popular diving computers such as Dacor's Micro Brain Pro Plus and Beuchat'S Aladdin Pro as well as use in the form of custom tables.

A group of researchers at the University of Hawaii have come to be known as the "Tiny Bubble Group" after their theory of physical properties of bubble nucleation in aqueous media. Their Varying-Permeability Model indicates that cavication nuclei, that are thought to "seed" bubble formation are "spherical gas phases that are small enough to remain in solution yet strong enough to resist collapse, their stability being provided by elastic skins or membranes consisting of surface-active molecules" (Hoffman 1985). In comparison of table models, Huggins observes (1987), "the ascent criteria for this model is based on the volume of bubbles that are formed upon decompression. Growth in size and number of gas bubbles is computer based on the physical properties of the 'skins' and the surrounding environment. If the total volume of gas in the bubbles is less than a 'critical volume', then the diver is within the safe limits of the model". Although tables have been produced based on this model, not enough actual human testing has been conducted to be considered statistically relevant. On square profile comparisons with the U.S. Navy tables, the "Tiny Bubble" model is more conservative down to the 140 fsw level.

Further projects in table models include the Maximum Likelihood Statistical Method developed by the Naval Medical Research Institute (NMRI). In consideration of a diver's exposure to depth/time "doses", they have produced a statistical model that reflects probabilities of DCS occurrence and are expressed as 1% and 5% tables. The diving supervisor would have the option of selecting his risk factor based upon the priority of work to be accomplished.

What tables, then should deep divers use? It's really too broad a question to pin down to a single answer as to "this table is the best". Many experienced deep diving professionals prefer to work with custom or proprietary tables specifically designed for their application (see next section of this chapter). Crea (1991) makes this observation:

"Computations can compare different tables or practices, but cannot determine what is best. As stated before, what works... is what works. Good tables are at the current state of knowledge empirical. The algorithms are good, however, to use yesterday's experience to predict tomorrow's dive."

In the process of table development and validation, several basic and separate steps are employed with feedback on field use:

1) *Concept or "algorithm" for a table, usually based on some experience. Laboratory trials, with feedback and revision as needed. Move to provisional operational use at some point. Provisional use "at sea". Acceptance as "operational". Results fed back, revisions as necessary.*

2) *Judgment needed as to when to take the next step; this should be a responsible body of the developing organization; this body decides how many trial dives under what conditions, etc.*

3) *This process, laid out in a workshop by the Undersea and Hyperbaric Society, is more or less what is currently practiced, but there is no set protocol for making the formal judgments.*

The following table will contrast nine of the current models for the reader's comparison. Extrapolated depth/times are available for deeper exposures.

Comparison of No-Decompression Limits

DEPTH (fsw)	NO-DECOMPRESSION LIMITS (in minutes)								
	U.S. Navy	Buhlman*	Spencer	Navy E-L**	British *	DCIEM	Tiny Bubble	NMRI 1%	NMRI 5%
30	None	300	225	296	232	380	323	170	240
40	200	120	135	142	137	175	108	100	170
50	100	75	75	81	72	75	63	70	120
60	60	53	50	57	46	50	39	40	80
70	50	35	40	44	38	35	30	25	80
80	40	25	30	37	27	25	23	15	60
90	30	22	25	31	23	20	18	10	50
100	25	20	20	27	18	15	15	8	50
120	20	17	15	24	16	12	12	7	40
130	15	15	10	20	12	10	11	5	40
140	10	12	5	17	11	8	10	5	30

* Metric conversion to next greater depth   ** Approximate calculations from Thalmann, 1984

For a more detailed history of tables and model evolutions the authors recommend reading "Development of Dive Tables" by Karl Huggins as contained in *Microprocessor Applications to Multi-level Air Decompression Problems* (Michigan Sea Grant publication 1987) and *Deeper Into Diving* by John Lippman (Aqua Quest Publications 1990).

Divers on particularly cold or strenuous dives should modify their plan to make more conservative allowances in dive table planning.

Dr. R.W. "Bill" Hamilton of Hamilton Research Ltd., the industry's decompression and custom table expert. Hamilton's experience includes work with commercial. Scientific, and military projects and he is Vice President of Technical Diving International (TDI).

CUSTOM OR PROPRIETARY TABLES

It is common practice in the international commercial diving industry to modify or build from "scratch" proprietary tables for use within their private companies. Historically, these tables have been religiously guarded and controlled for the company's own use for two reasons: 1. They are expensive to produce and validate. 2. Fear of potential liability if injury should occur if used by others.

Proprietary tables came into being in hopes of improving on the U.S. Navy Tables and making the working commercial diver safer and more efficient. Pioneering work in such tables was done by individuals like Bill Hamilton of Hamilton Research Ltd. (see Reference Materials) who consulted with various diving contractors and even foreign navies such as Japan, Sweden and Finland to create air and mixed gas tables for bounce diving, saturation work and treatment schedules.

Although the diving contractors still remain competitive with each other, much of the secretive nature of proprietary tables was relaxed in the late 1980's to reflect a more open exchange of information for safety purposes. And, realistically, the security of private tables was shaky at best. If a diver switched employers and had been happy with the set of tables generated by his old contractors, they had a mysterious habit of accompanying him to his new workplace.

The business of custom tables has seen new growth not only in the commercial industry but in the scientific and emerging high-tech sport diver communities. Our section entitled Reference Materials cites several sources for custom table production, but Hamilton remains preeminent among this small and esoteric professional group. His capable expertise has been applied to computer technology to design a program that allows the field user to produce custom tables essentially on his own. Hamilton's program is called DCAP and DCAP Plus (Decompression Computation and Analysis Program) and has been the basis for much of the field custom table generation.

In correspondence with Gilliam (1991), Hamilton notes, "About the matter of preparation of custom tables, this is somewhat of a sensitive issue and one about which I have mixed feelings. I think it would be worthwhile to discuss it a bit. One issue relates to whether professional diving physiologists should support the extreme environment diving that some folks want to do. Another is whether a 'calculated' table will be reliable enough to keep the user out of trouble. When I started in this business, 'they' told me what they were going to do. And it appeared that they would make up the tables themselves if I did not provide them. Thus blackmailed, and lacking humility enough to realize that some of the more experienced high-tech divers could easily construct a special table as well as I could, I went ahead with it. With some trepidation, I might add. It has worked out well, and because of the excellent feedback and sufficient repetition of the process, I am now relatively comfortable with it."

Hamilton is particularly concerned with the validation of the special tables and encourages precise record keeping of his tables in field use. He assigns a specific "Base case" identification to each set and provides up to 20 pages of generic instructions in their use with additional guidelines for special applications. He prohibits the resale of his tables as they are intended for the specialty end-user only.

Gilliam's Proprietary Tables

FIRST EDITION: Randy Bohrer to Bret Gilliam's specifications to 500 fsw. Produced in 1989.

Notes: Descent rate can be up to 100 fpm; descent time plus time at depth is equal to ten minutes. For example, the 500 fsw table is calculated for 100 fpm or five minute descent time, then five minutes at 500 fsw. This ten minutes ends upon beginning ascent. This technique adds a bit of conservatism, gives credit for the descent time, but does not bind Gilliam to a particular descent rate. Ascent rate is 60 fpm for the first 100 ft., then 30 fpm thereafter. Ascent rate between stops is instantaneous, so the stop should be left at a time such that the decompression time for that stop expires just as the next stop is reached. Diving gas is air, but if oxygen is used in any combination of the 30 through 10 ft. stops, each minute of breathing O_2 can be considered to two minutes breathing air.

Depth (fsw) **Decompression Stop** (ft. / min.)

	120	110	100	90	80	70	60	50	40	30	20	10	Total
300							1	3	4	8	13		29
350						1	3	4	7	10	20		45
400					2	3	3	7	8	14	29		66
450				2	3	3	6	7	11	19	42		93
500			1	2	3	3	6	5	10	15	26	57	128

SECOND EDITION: Modified to assume entire 10 minutes was spent at depth (no credit for descent time), 30 fpm ascent rate.

Depth (fsw) **Decompression Stop** (ft. / min.)

	120	110	100	90	80	70	60	50	40	30	20	10	Total
300						1	3	4	7	10	21		46
350					2	3	4	7	8	16	32		72
400				1	2	3	5	6	8	12	23	47	107
450			2	2	3	5	5	8	10	17	32	68	152
500	1	2	3	3	5	5	7	9	16	23	42	98	214

Note: Bret Gilliam significantly further modified the table before his record dive to 452 fsw on Feb.14, 1990; this table is presented as an exemplar of custom tables and under no circumstances should be used by other divers.

John Crea of Submariner Research and Randy Bohrer of Underwater Applications (see Reference Section) will also generate a set of custom tables for specific diving needs upon demand. The cost is not cheap; figure between $300 and $500 to set up a basic custom table. And, like Hamilton, they will probably extensively interview the applicant to insure his proper experience, equipment, training and reasons for the dive. Hamilton estimates in May of 1991 that 10-15% of his business was devoted to exceptional exposure applications.

Crea, an anesthesiologist, enjoys an exalted reputation in the high-tech circle since he is an active cave diver who actually dives his own tables. This is the ultimate in validation confidence. His program is called DECOM and is currently in its 9th generation.

The cave diving community is a prime example of a group benefiting from custom tables. Since cavers are faced with extremely long and deep penetrations (now approaching 400 fsw/121.2 m threshold) that require extensive penetration into the cave system, they pose a unique scenario in mixed gas table models. Modification to shorten their extreme decompression obligations with use of 100% O_2 is common and a new practice of constructing dry underwater "stages" is gaining favor. Likewise, extreme exposure tables for air can be generated as Bohrer did for Gilliam's 1990 assault on the depth record.

THE FUTURE

Hamilton is pursuing grant funding to develop a variety of "generic" custom tables to address several typical models to accommodate current requested profiles. Undoubtedly, we will see a continuing trend away from the "old standard" U.S. Navy Tables as technology pushes forward and as increasing data shows that Navy tables do not have an acceptable DCS rate with deeper/longer dives (Thalman 1985).

Perhaps we will begin to see the efficacy of shallow water saturation habitats emerge for special projects. Early scientific habitats such as NOAA's *Hydrolab* and *TEKTITE* proved the worth of sat diving in research and observation studies. *Hydrolab*, now enshrined in the Smithsonian, would be considered primitive by today's standards. Little larger than the interior of a recreational vehicle, it was able to support four aquanauts in saturation for a week or more and allowed deeper "excursions" from "storage depth" to 200 fsw (60.6 m) for up to two hours with only minor stage stops back to the habitat.

Saturation habitats similar to Hydrolab may be used in the future for cave and wreck exploration.

The high-tech community might consider *Hydrolab* or something similar a luxury for extended exploration of deep shipwrecks or extensive cave systems. By going to NITROX (any N_2/O_2 mixture other than air; the FO_2 may be reduced) as the chamber breathing gas instead of standard air, and relocating deeper to 80 fsw (24.2 m), an entire new galaxy of excursion dives opens up. Imagine two-hour bottom times at 300 fsw (90.9 m) on rebreathers or short excursions to 500 fsw (151.5 m) and beyond. It's all possible and the technology is available to implement such systems.

It's a quantum leap to saturation dives from a habitat for "sport divers" when only forty years ago we did not have repetitive diving tables for our Navy divers, but here we are staring down the face of the 21st century limited still only by our imaginations.

CONCLUSION

Much debate still centers on what is the "best" table to use, and there clearly is no pat answer to that question. The authors' opinion is that the best possible scenario for safe deep diving would include the use of a custom table matched to the individual and the dive application but obviously many divers will not utilize this level of technical support. But we urge our readers to make an informed choice in table selection. Don't

Controversy still divides experts on the intensive diving from liveaboards. Although in limited use in the early 1970's, these vessels have shown unrestrained growth into the 1990's. This photo taken in 1976 aboard the Virgin Diver shows Bill Walker, Geri Murphy, Paul Tzimoulis, and Bret Gilliam preparing for their sixth dive of the day; earlier dives had been as deep as 200 fsw. Tzimoulis, then editor of Skin Diver magazine, was an active supporter of the liveaboard concept and commonly practiced deep diving.

just grab the first thing that's handy and expect it to suit a myriad of dive situations. And in all cases, do not push a model to the edge of its limits.

Another area of continuing controversy is the question of multi-day repetitive diving. Until 1991, many experts have suggested limiting dives to no more than two a day and then taking a day off following the fourth day of diving. This was postulated to allow a safety edge and to lessen the chance of DCS. The recommendation actually had little basis in documented sport diving statistics upon close examination. Grossly, it would appear that some sport diver DCS incidence rates could be linked to multi-day repetitive diving but with a finer eye toward the "broad" view it seems that the real culprit is poor diving technique. Less experienced divers are the primary victim of DCS and this is due to a variety factors.

At the 1991 American Academy of Underwater Sciences Workshop on Multi-day Repetitive Diving held at Duke University, the recommendation for the "mid-week lay-off" was dropped from the guidelines basically because there was no lab or field data to justify the practice.

Gilliam was a speaker at that program and presented data obtained from a one year study of intensive four day repetitive diving by sport divers from age 7 to 72. In 77,680 dives during that period, he recorded only 7 DCS hits; all on relatively inexperienced divers. Interestingly, 5 of the 7 hits were within table limits and reflected diving averaging two dives a day usually to depths less than 100 fsw.

The more experienced diver population that made far more aggressive dive profiles typified by as many as five dives per day for up to four straight days had no cases of DCS. Gilliam's conclusions as to DCS occurrence centered more on the divers' watermanship than on their dive profiles. The more experienced group dived more and dived deeper than the less experienced group but they also were far more observant of ascent rates, hydration, safety and/or decompression stops, and displayed far better dive planning disciplines either through the use of tables or dive computers. It would seem that attention to these good diving skills played a far greater role in their safety than frequency of diving or depths. More research and particularly, more field data of actual diving practices needs to be accumulated to accurately make recommendations.

It is common practice on liveaboard dive vessels for guests to make from four to six dives per day. It is not uncommon for the serious photographers and "hard core" divers to do many more dives. Veteran dive travel specialist Carl Roessler of Sea & See Travel in San Francisco regularly did as many as 12 dives per day dating back to the early 1970's; his dives were "controlled" by the SOS/Scubapro decom meter popular during that era and still in use today. In 1976, Paul Tzimoulis, then editor of *Skin Diver* Magazine, averaged 6-8 dives per day with several Caribbean liveaboards. Many of his dives were repetitive 200+ fsw exposures and all were governed by the SOS meter. Gilliam, Mount, Tzimoulis, Roessler and a wide variety of other diving professionals have engaged in deep repetitive diving dating back to the 1960's and have progressed through profile planning dictated by Tables, the SOS meter and now modern dive computers. The point to be made is that aggressive repetitive diving even in deeper depths may not specifically suggest a statistically higher incidence of DCS; there are simply too many divers following such plans without any problems and the practice has been going on for decades.

In all cases, caution and prudence are recommended but the overly conservative "prohibitions" still offered by some academicians may not necessarily be proven in the field.

As has been noted several times in this chapter, "what works is what works". Tables and determination of "safe" dive profiles are very much an experimental science. Hopefully, we shall see more substantive objective research and data sampling emerge.

CHAPTER 13

Decompression Sickness, Theory, and Treatment

"Bends is a statistical inevitability..."
Bret Gilliam

"Decompression accidents are unique in that, with few exceptions, it is the layman who is responsible for patient assessment, diagnosis, early therapeutic intervention and, in some cases, even definitive care."
Dick Clarke

DECOMPRESSION SICKNESS

The "bends" is an occupational hazard of diving. It matters little whether the stricken diver was engaged in commercial, military or simply recreational pursuits. He's just as bent and same rules apply. The mixed gas diver and other high tech participants have to deal with another anomaly of diving: the fact that if you in trouble, it's generally your responsibility to get out of it without standard medical assistance.

That's right folks, if you get bent on a dive trip the chances of having immediate medical help are slim to none. It is vital that divers, especially those involved in mixed gas diving activities have a clear and thorough understanding of decompression sickness (DCS) symptoms and predisposing conditions. Early recognition of DCS signs and symptoms and appropriate first responder care are key to the stricken diver's successful recovery. DCS is a statistical inevitability and must be accepted as an assumed risk of any diver. You can do everything exactly by the book and still get bent; hopefully, this is not news to anyone. In Gilliam's study (1989-90) of sport divers covering the customers of a large liveaboard dive/cruise ship, 71.4% of DCS cases he treated in the vessel's recompression chamber were diving within the limits of their diving tables. There is no guarantee that any table or computer is infallible.

CAUSES OF DCS

In a nutshell, improper decompression resulting in occlusive inert gas bubble formation is probably our major our culprit in decompression sickness. Although some would argue to the contrary, most experts generally agree that ALL dives are decompression dives. Even ones without stage decompression obligations have ascent rates factored into their model as a means of decompression. Hopefully, divers are now routinely practicing slow ascents in the last two atmospheres (66 fsw to the surface) in conjunction with a recommended 5 minute "safety stop" around the 10-15 fsw level.

TABLE: 13-1

Contributory Factors to DCS

Primary Direct Effects of Physics: Depth, time, rate of release (dive profile)

Secondary Effects, Inherent: Physical fitness and overall health condition, age, body fat level (obesity or extreme lean condition), height, muscular makeup, old injuries that may affect circulation etc. , theories of male versus female susceptibility.

Secondary Effects, External: Thermal conditions (cold water or excessively hot conditions), physical exertion during and after dive (elevated CO_2 levels), constrictive equipment factors (tight wet suit, binding straps etc.), improper hydration, smoking, alcohol use, drugs.

Equipment factors: Breathing regulators with excessive resistance, inaccuracies of depth gauges or watch, failure of dive computers.

Decompression Models: Use of unvalidated tables, improper manipulation of tables for averaging or extrapolation etc., failure to compute repetitive dives correctly, improper decompression stops, compromised model or table through improper ascent rates, high altitude diving, use of extreme exposure tables, flying after diving.

Stress: Time pressure and task-loading.

There are many excellent reference texts cited in our bibliography that can provide a detailed subject treatment of the pathophysiology of decompression sickness and so only a brief review is offered in this section. We are more concerned with divers being able to recognize symptomotology effectively and react accordingly. Divers with a desire to delve deeper into the mechanisms of DCS are encouraged to access these separate materials.

At the surface, we are basically saturated with nitrogen at one atmosphere. As we descend breathing air or mixed gas in our scuba systems, pressure increases and the inert gas (nitrogen or helium) is dissolved and absorbed by the body's tissues and blood. The deeper we go, the more inert gas is "loaded". Theoretically, after a period of time (based upon the longest half-time utilized in the model) at any given depth, be it 60 fsw (18.2 m) or 600 fsw (181.8 m), we are saturated with all the inert gas we can hold and no further decompression obligation would be incurred no matter how long we stayed down. This is the basis of "saturation diving" theory where aquanauts are placed underwater in a bell or habitat to work for as much as a week or more and then decompressed when the project is finished.

As untethered free swimming-divers we do not have the luxury of saturation support equipment and we must come back to the surface. Herein lies the problem with the pesky inert gas we have absorbed (ingassed or loaded) during our brief, by comparison, sojourn into the deep.

Remembering our diving history, we will recall that Haldane originally postulated his theory that our body could tolerate inert gas pressure up to twice that found normally at the surface. This 2:1 ratio became the basis of the earliest dive tables and accounted for the presumption that we could have unlimited bottom times at 33 fsw (10 m). However, as more research study was accomplished it became evident that his ratio theory was flawed and has since been modified to be expressed as approximately 1.5:1, a significant difference. In fact, authenticated DCS cases have been observed in divers at 18 fsw (5.5 m) after extended time periods.

Haldane offered other valuable principles of decompression that included the theory of exponential inert gas uptake that provided the basis of tissue half-times and compartment M values. We are now overwhelmed with new decompression models or algorithms that stem from Haldane's early work and go considerably farther in scope. U.S. Navy tables were developed assuming a 120 minute tissue/compartment as the slowest; we now see use of models that incorporate compartments with 689 minute half-times in dive computers and far longer in custom tables!

But all this was to serve the purpose of preventing bubble formation in the blood as pressure was decreased upon ascent. Haldane and other pioneers in DCS originally thought that no bubbles would form if their decompression models were followed. Through the use of modern Doppler devices it is now known that bubbles may exist on every dive. Such scanning is frequently employed to monitor divers during test criteria for new table development and as a benchmark of decompression stress. "Bubble trouble" as a term was first popularized by Rutkowski as a convenient catchall for DCS and embolism manifestations. In our discussion, we are concerned with inert gas bubbles, of course, not air bubbles as would be the problem in lung overexpansion accidents typical of breath holding ascents.

Where these bubbles are located and their size will dictate the presentation of DCS symptoms.

SIGNS AND SYMPTOMS

Many texts distinguish DCS symptomotology into type I (pain only) or type II (serious symptoms, central nervous system involvement). To the layman or diver in the field, this distinction is not of great importance and requires special training in many instances to classify presentations. Most importantly we want our readers to be able to recognize any symptoms or signs of DCS and leave diagnosis and treatment selection to trained chamber staff or medical consultants. But what you do for the patient and the observations you can record and pass along to treatment personnel will be of significant aid to his ultimate hope of recovery.

TYPE I (Pain only, mild symptoms):

- "Skin bends"- skin blotching or mottling of the skin producing a red or purplish-blue tinge.
- Itching similar to fiberglass irritation.
- Fatigue
- Indifference, personality or mood swings, irritable behavior, diver unaware of surroundings.
- Pain usually associated in or near a joint such as shoulder or knee. Onset may be gradual and may be transient (niggle).

TYPE II (CNS involvement):

- CNS spinal and cranial abnormalities usually gradual in onset with initial subtle symptoms often masked by pain distractions.
- Cardiopulmonary symptoms are typically manifested by "chokes", a dry persistent nonproductive cough. Cerebral symptoms may follow; all effects in this group should be considered life-threatening.
- Unusual fatigue
- Dizziness or "staggers", vertigo
- Numbness, paralysis, progressive loss of feeling in skin patches.
- Shortness of breath
- Unconsciousness, collapse, syncope
- Loss of bladder and bowel control, inability to urinate.
- Muscular weakness, poor grip, poor resistance to restraint of motion.
- Visual disturbances, inability to hear fingers rubbed close to ears etc.
- Headache
- Abdominal encircling pain or lower back pain precursor of overt spinal symptoms. Frequently this presentation is misdiagnosed as less serious Type I DCS.
- Convulsions
- Any symptoms developing while still underwater.

The alert diver will recognize that many of these symptoms are nearly identical to those of embolism event presentations. Since treatment and first aid are essentially the same, don't worry about the distinction. This table illustrates symptoms as categorized by Type I and Type II but consider all symptoms serious in the field.

One of the most frustrating aspects of sport divers and DCS is their stubborn denial of symptoms and failure to accept early treatment. This has historically led to the majority of sport diver accidents being unnecessarily delayed for treatment. Even divers that knew beyond a doubt that they were at risk from their profile and were presenting early symptoms have refused oxygen when readily available due to some perceived ego threat or for fear that fellow divers would think less of them. Others refuse to accept the possibility that DCS could be involved since "I can't be bent, I was within the limits of the tables."

Early recognition, reporting and treatment of DCS problems dramatically improves patient resolution prognosis. Bends can happen to anyone, it is no one's fault and should involve no "loss of face". Indeed, the prudent diver and his dive group should overtly encourage prompt relation of any ailment that even remotely resembles the symptoms list.

Many divers may mistake DCS symptoms as muscle strains or limb numbness to sitting on it etc. **ALWAYS ERR ON THE SIDE OF CAUTION**. If you are suffering from DCS it is only going to get worse as symptoms are progressive. Don't wait to seek qualified help!

FIRST AID IN THE FIELD

Immediately give the patient oxygen for surface breathing. Many divers do not realize the importance of 100% O_2 administration and this can only be accomplished via a system incorporating a demand valve/ mask (or by use of an oxygen-clean scuba system regulator connected to an oxygen cylinder). This seal should be tight fitting to insure the maximum level of O_2 delivered to the patient. Air leaks around the mask will dilute the percentage of O_2 (FO_2) inspired. Care must be taken to insure the integrity of the mask seal especially in male patients with beards or mustaches or any patient with facial wrinkles etc. As a rule of thumb, you want the mask seal to be good enough for the patient to breathe on his back underwater. Free flow oxygen systems, although still widely in use, are not recommended. Most free flow devices usually will not deliver 100% O_2 and are extremely wasteful of the gas.

Oxygen is administered primarily to help eliminate inert gas and reduce bubble size to some extent. By breathing pure O_2 at the surface, the blood's oxygen partial pressure is elevated dramatically. This provides a breathing media totally absent of the harmful inert gas, and establishes a steeper gradient across the tissue-bubble interface. This allows more efficient outgassing of the occlusive nitrogen or helium, and also contributes to better oxygenation of the tissues where the bubble insult has occurred. Key to the outcome of this therapy is sufficient PO_2 (best accomplished by a 100% O_2 demand valve system) and adequate flow for delivery.

Many patients will relieve of symptoms simply by proper and immediate oxygen first aid techniques. Davis was a leading advocate of O_2 role's in field resolution and Gilliam's experience (1989-90) recorded 12 cases of symptomatic DCS that were completely relieved by 100% O_2 administration during transit of the patient to his chamber facility.

Training is available widely in oxygen administration. One of the first programs implemented was developed by EMT/dive instructor Jim Corry for NAUI and recently the Diver's Alert Network (DAN) has offered a similar course. Both programs are excellent and require between

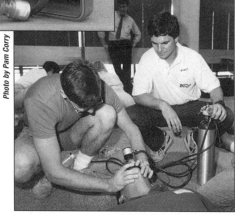

EMT/dive instructor Jim Corry (on right) developed one of the first training programs in oxygen administration. Derivatives of his original course are now taught by DAN, NAUI etc. worldwide. Shown is the DAN oxygen unit featuring demand valve mask and regulator.

six and eight hours of hands on training in equipment, patient scenarios and theory. Most diving conferences and trade shows will usually offer such courses as a seminar and the benefits to divers are invaluable.

Until recently patient management included positioning the diver in either Trendelenberg (head down, legs bent at knees, left side tilted down) or Scoltetus (head down, legs straight). Recommendations from DAN in 1990 have modified this traditional advice to suggest use of simple supine positioning (patient lays flat on his back). Trendelenberg proved to be of little benefit except in the first 10-15 minutes of surfacing primarily in arterial gas embolism (AGE) cases, and the difficulty of maintaining this posture was not felt to be significantly beneficial.

Removal of the diver's wet suit etc. is desirable but insure that he is kept warm and comfortable. Cover with blankets, towels or dry clothing. Observe for any "skin bends" symptoms. Continue administration of oxygen until delivered to medical care or supply is exhausted.

Oral fluids should be given if the patient is conscious. Regular drinking water or unsweetened apple juice in amounts of 12 to 16 ounces every 30 minutes will help keep the patient properly hydrated. This amount may require urination if transit is prolonged. This is a good sign and should be accommodated in the supine position. Inability to urinate may indicate more serious Type II manifestation. Such urinary retention will ultimately become quite painful. If the patient is unable to pass water within a reasonable time period, back off on continued administration of fluids.

Do not administer pain drugs other than two aspirin initially (aspirin has been shown to effect a decrease in platelet aggregation in the blood). Pain killers may mask other symptom development.

Be prepared to initiate CPR and rescue breathing if patient condition deteriorates. Mixed gas diving should automatically infer that the dive team as well as the surface support crew is well trained and well experienced in CPR techniques.

TRANSPORTATION

If you are shore diving, insure initial patient care and make sure victim is attended at all times. Hopefully, a properly planned dive will include a contingency list of medical professionals and the nearest recompression chamber facility. Call the chamber or hospital and advise them of the incoming patient. If they direct you to wait for an ambulance team, do so. Otherwise transport patient to the facility they designate and by their proscribed method, either vehicle or aircraft.

If at sea, call the Coast Guard via VHF radio or cellular phone. It may be necessary to relay messages through another vessel if sufficiently offshore that your radio cannot reach the mainland. Make certain that the Coast Guard knows that this emergency involves a diving accident victim and requires transportation to a recompression facility. At this point, they may direct you to proceed with your vessel to a designated port where assistance can meet you or they may decide to send an evacuation helicopter to intercept your vessel and extract the diver for faster transport (see **Table13-2**).

It is incumbent upon divers to know what facilities are available to them in an emergency. This becomes particularly important if your trip

TABLE 13.2

Helicopter Procedures

1. Post lookout to watch for chopper's arrival on scene.
2. Attempt to establish radio communication via VHF ch. 16
3. Maintain vessel speed at 10 to 15 knots if possible. Pilot will count on your constant speed for his approach. Do not slow down or stop.
4. Assume a course that places your vessel with the prevailing wind approximately 20 degrees on port bow. If wind is calm or insignificant, maintain course to shore.

5. Lower antennas, masts, flag staffs etc. that could interfere with chopper's deployment of uplifting device.
6. Secure all loose objects and equipment on decks. Prop wash from rotor blades can be severe.
7. Do not touch the lift device or cable until it has touched the deck of your vessel and grounded. Electric shock can result otherwise.
8. Have patient wear life jacket. If available, also give him smoke flare for day or night flare if dark. This will help find the patient if he falls out of the basket or if it is dropped. Have lookout watch patient until secure inside chopper. If patient goes into sea, follow man-overboard drill immediately. Have crew member ready to go overboard to rescue patient and establish buoyancy. Swift action and anticipation of contingencies are vital to insure patient's survival.
9. Secure patient in basket (stretcher) via provided harness or tie in with seizing line; ideally with quick release knots that patient can access if necessary.
10. If patient cannot communicate or is unconscious, fasten (duct tape, safety pin etc.) as much information about his condition, dive profile, name, age, address, next of kin, emergency phone numbers etc. as possible. If he was diving on a computer send it with him. Make note of tables utilized to acquire profile etc.
11. Advise or reconfirm that patient is diving victim and requires evacuation to recompression facility.
12. If patient dies while chopper is enroute, inform flight crew or Coast Guard operator. This may prevent a needless heroic effort at rescue by the flight crew if bad weather was a factor.

is remotely located or out of the United States. Prior to leaving on that long-awaited dive vacation to the south Pacific or Caribbean inquire as to the availability of medical staff, chamber locations and medivac flights if required. You should also determine if the resort or liveaboard has 100% demand mask O_2 available on their boats; insist on it. If enough divers demand proper equipment it will finally be made standard practice. Most mixed gas divers will already have made facilities for both surface and underwater oxygen delivery systems. Always plan for a surplus of O_2 in case decompression needs to be extended or for post-dive therapy.

Call DAN to confirm chamber locations and readiness with listings of local addresses and phone numbers. Now is an excellent time to join DAN's diving insurance program which can cover your costs if treatment or medivac "life flight" is required. Costs of air ambulance, chamber time and medical staff can easily exceed $30,000 from a remote location. DAN's insurance is an inexpensive hedge against such a financial burden. Although not widely known by most divers in the high tech community, DAN insurance has no exclusions for either depth or breathing gases. Therefore, if you do get a DCS hit while breathing trimix or heliox at, say 400 fsw, your treatment is covered by their current policy as long as you are engaged in recreational diving. The key word here is "recreational". If you stray into the realm of "commercial" diving by definition, you are excluded. It is not considered commercial diving if a sport diving instructor is being paid professionally as will be the case in many mixed gas high tech operations conducted for training or simply for the personal satisfaction of exploration.

Many of the editorial commentary and published articles by DAN senior officials might appear to be "anti" high tech and mixed gas diving. In the authors' opinion, the role of these professionals is to present a conservative posture that reflects their deep concern for diving safety as a whole. It's true that DAN has specifically recommended against the use of nitrox/EANx and mixed gases, but it's also nice to know that these same medical professionals are providing the best insurance available and are standing by 24 hours a day to assist in treatment should the need arise. DAN insurance should be a functional part of every diver's "equipment". If you don't have it already, sign up today. Call 919-684-8111. You simply cannot afford to be without this coverage.

Large clinical treatment facility with seating for up to a dozen patients at once. Technicians and supervisor control treatment from main control station.

RECOMPRESSION CHAMBERS

Many divers have seen a chamber either in photographs or in real life, but very few have ever had occasion to be in one unless they were being treated. As a result a certain "mystique has developed about chambers and many divers regard them as hostile and menacing environments. Briefly, we would like to acquaint our readers with the realities of these important devices.

Generally, chambers are divided into two categories: **recompression chambers** (used for the treatment of diving related injuries and other ailments) and **decompression chambers** (used for surface or deck decompression facilities so the working diver can be removed from the water and complete decom obligation in a dry and controlled situation)

Both of these units are also properly referred to as "hyperbaric chambers", meaning that the pressure inside will be higher than normal atmospheric pressure. These elevated pressures are usually expressed in feet of sea water (fsw) just as if we were diving in the ocean. Air pressure is introduced to the chamber to raise its internal pressure and begin the "dive". We can then use these chambers to treat DCS or AGE cases, conduct "dry" surface decompression schedules, or simulate dives for research purposes.

In Hospital situations, the role of hyperbaric medicine has been recognized as a specialty wherein victims of such injuries as crush wounds, burns, skin grafts, gangrene and carbon monoxide poisoning are treated with oxygen in large climate- controlled chambers. These typically are able to accommodate as many as 18 patients at once, have hatches shaped and sized like conventional doors, are equipped with air conditioning and humidity controls and even piped in music.

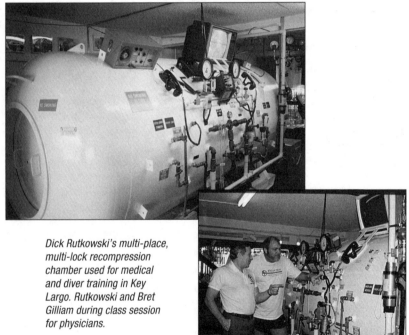

Dick Rutkowski's multi-place, multi-lock recompression chamber used for medical and diver training in Key Largo. Rutkowski and Bret Gilliam during class session for physicians.

In the field, things are just a little bit different. Forget the creature comforts and get prepared for close quarters. Although a well set up field chamber can provide the same therapeutic benefits to a stricken diver, they are substantially smaller in most cases.

Field chambers range in size typically from 48 inches in diameter to 72 inches and are usually made of steel. In the past, monoplace chambers were in common use in commercial diving theaters and were designed to pressurize one patient in a single cylinder. This did not allow an inside tender to attend the patient and therefore he was pretty much on his own once treatment was initiated. Rarely will these chambers be encountered today. Most will be variations on the multi-place (more than one patient or tender) multi-lock (two or more pressure compartments with sealing hatches). These allow several divers to be treated at once with an inside tender to monitor their condition. Medical equipment or relief staff can be "locked" into or out of the chamber by use of the outer lock which can be pressurized to equal the treatment inner lock and subsequently depressurized to travel back to the surface pressure.

From the outside of the chamber, the supervisor can control the depth of the dive or treatment schedule and choose what gases will be supplied to the occupants. Pressurization is accomplished with standard AIR but most modern treatments call for oxygen therapy beginning at 60 fsw (18.2 m and 2.8 ATA). NITROX mixes of 50/50 (N_2/O_2) or 60/40 (N_2/O_2) are commonly used deeper than 60 fsw instead of AIR to lesson narcosis and safely keep the O_2 partial pressures within tolerance ranges. Both O_2 and NITROX therapy gases are delivered to the patient or tender via BIBS (built-in-breathing-system) masks similar to aviator oxygen masks.

The chamber supervisor monitors his gauges that are calibrated to display pressure in fsw graduations. He also has an oxygen analyzer plumbed into the chamber to monitor the inside environment's O_2 percentage. Due to fire hazards, this percentage of O_2 (FO_2) will not be allowed to exceed 25%. Most BIBS are set up with "overboard dumps" that exhaust the expired oxygen outside the chamber to prevent the rapid rise of the FO_2. However, it is common to have some leakage of masks due to improper fit etc. and O_2 will be leaking into the chamber from this source. As the supervisor sees the FO_2 approach the 25% level he will institute a chamber "vent" where the inner lock is flushed with AIR by inputting pressure and simultaneously exhausting the incoming air from an outflow valve. This scrubs the chamber of excess O_2 and also cools and refreshes the atmosphere.

The supervisor is assisted by an outside operator and a record/time keeper who logs all stages of the treatment. They can communicate with the inner occupants via a low voltage radio or sound-powered phone handset to discuss patient status or to confer on treatment procedures.

Inside the chamber, the patient will either lie in a supine position or sit up with the legs outstretched while leaning back against the chamber wall. A fire retardant mattress is usually provided or bunks may be hung from the chamber sides. Medical equipment, or fluids etc. may be passed inside via a medical lock (small hatch door compartment usually about 12 inches in diameter) or through the same outer lock that accommodates staff transfers.

A patient is cleaned of all oils such as sun tan lotions or chap sticks and he is given fire retardant clothing to wear. This further reduces the chance of fire.

CHAMBER DIVES

As the chamber is pressurized with AIR, the occupants will immediately sense the pressure change in their ears and the equalization techniques will be necessary. Usually the outside operator will observe through signal from the inside tender that all occupants are clearing comfortably. If problems occur and someone is slow to clear, descent is stopped until rectified. Remember that our patient needs to get down to 60 fsw as quickly as possible to begin treatment so in many cases the dive is conducted as fast as the occupants can equalize. In cases where severe DCS symptoms are present and the patient cannot clear, the ear drum may be punctured by the inside tender to allow the dive to continue, (a ruptured ear drum will heal, DCS may not).

During the dive it gets quite noisy inside as air pressure is introduced and protective ear muffs are provided for occupants. It also gets hot! Compression of the air atmosphere rapidly raises the temperature inside the inner lock to nearly 100+ degrees F. in tropical locations. Newcomers will be surprised to notice the high pitched speech caused by the increased air density. This becomes more pronounced and distracting as depth increases. In deep treatments, as in Table 6A at 165 fsw, speech even between staff members is discouraged if the chamber environment is AIR. The altered voice effects can stimulate narcosis in less experienced tenders or ones with less adaptive time at chamber depths. Once reaching treatment depth the chamber will be aggressively vented to flush out the stale, hot, humid air and replace it with fresh. The patient will be breathing O_2 via BIBS mask in 20 minute intervals with five minute "air breaks" where the mask is removed and chamber AIR is breathed.

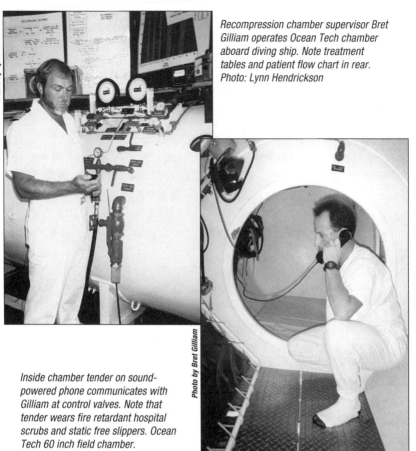

Recompression chamber supervisor Bret Gilliam operates Ocean Tech chamber aboard diving ship. Note treatment tables and patient flow chart in rear.
Photo: Lynn Hendrickson

Photo by Lynn Hendrickson

Photo by Bret Gilliam

Inside chamber tender on sound-powered phone communicates with Gilliam at control valves. Note that tender wears fire retardant hospital scrubs and static free slippers. Ocean Tech 60 inch field chamber.

Air breaks are provided for the patient's comfort and to allow him recovery time from breathing pure oxygen for prolonged periods. At any time during treatment if symptoms of chronic (whole body) or CNS O_2 toxicity are noted, the tender will suspend BIBS mask breathing and provide a 15 minute air break. This time is not counted as part of the treatment table. After this rest, the schedule is resumed on BIBS O_2. Standard treatment Table 5 is two hours and 15 minutes long and Table 6 is four hours and 45 minutes long. Extensions may be added to Tables at the supervisor's discretion.

Table 5 is reserved for the less serious, pain-only bends while **Table 6** is used for more serious DCS involvement and pain-only bends that is not relieved in the first ten minutes of O_2 breathing at 60 fsw. Most chamber supervisors will now go directly to Table 6 in treating sport divers. This is due to the fact that upon close neurological examination of patients it has been found that pain only symptoms frequently masked or distracted from the more severe but less compelling (in the patient's mind) Type II symptoms of numbness etc.

The more immediate treatment is instituted, the better the chances of complete recovery.

During treatment, the ascent phases will be marked by the chamber dramatically cooling as the pressure is reduced. In many instances, the air will become so humid that a dense mist is formed, almost like being in a cloud. The mist can be irritating to the throat if inhaled and cause coughing or choking so breathing is always done through the nose. If coughing etc. develops, the ascent will be stopped to avoid the hazard of embolism.

Training is available in chamber operations and medical support from several sources (see appendix). Some facilities offer seminars designed for sport divers to learn more about chambers and afford the opportunities to make actual chamber dives. The Catalina chamber sponsors such programs and Gilliam (1989-90) developed a PADI/NAUI certification program in Accident Management/Recompression Chambers that included patient handling and first aid, O_2 administration, symptom recognition and two chamber dives. Almost two thousand sport divers went through this training during that period aboard the dive/cruise ship Ocean Spirit. Similar programs will be offered in new dive ship operations.

QUALIFICATION OF DCS

When a patient is presented to a chamber facility, the diver medical technician (DMT) or chamber supervisor will want to perform a gross physical and neurological examination to list the diver victim's symptoms. There is a protocol for rapid neurological exams that can be done in five minutes (see **appendix 3**). In severe cases, the exam will be done in the chamber if the patient's condition precludes further delay. The DMT will note the patient's deficits and observe that many of them may fall in our symptom list. However, that alone does not qualify our patient as a confirmed DCS case.

Confirmation or qualification of DCS is accomplished by a Test of Pressure. The patient is recompressed to a depth of 60 fsw (2.8 ATA) and put on O_2 via BIBS mask for a twenty minute breathing period. If

TABLE 6 - MINIMAL RECOMPRESSION, OXYGEN BREATHING METHOD FOR TREATMENT OF DECOMPRESSION SICKNESS AND GAS EMBOLISM

1. Use - treatment of decompression sickness when oxygen can be used and symptoms are not relieved within 10 minutes at 60 feet. Patient breathes oxygen from the surface.
2. Descent rate - 25 ft/min.
3. Ascent rate - 1 ft/min. Do not compensate for slower ascent rates. Compensate for faster rates by halting the ascent.
4. Time at 60 feet - begins on arrival at 60 feet.
5. If oxygen breathing must be interrupted, allow 15 minutes after the reaction has entirely subsided and resume schedule at point of interruption.
6. Tender breathes air throughout. If treatment is a repetitive dive for the tender or tables are lengthened, tender should breathe oxygen during the last 30 minutes of ascent to the surface.

Depth (feet)	Time (minutes)	Breathing Media	Total Elapsed Time (minutes)
60	20	Oxygen	20
60	5	Air	25
60	20	Oxygen	45
60	5	Air	50
60	20	Oxygen	70
60	5	Air	75
60 to 30	30	Oxygen	105
30	15	Air	120
30	60	Oxygen	180
30	15	Air	195
30	60	Oxygen	255
30 to 0	30	Oxygen	285

TABLE 6 DEPTH/TIME PROFILE

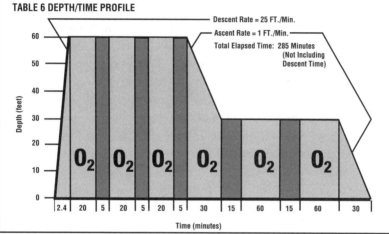

Descent Rate = 25 FT./Min.
Ascent Rate = 1 FT./Min.
Total Elapsed Time: 285 Minutes (Not Including Descent Time)

Table 5 is reproduced graphically below for information only.

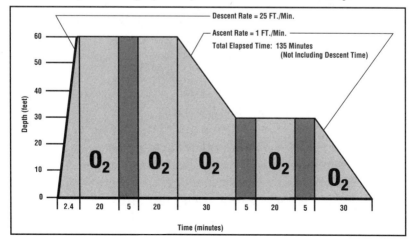

Descent Rate = 25 FT./Min.
Ascent Rate = 1 FT./Min.
Total Elapsed Time: 135 Minutes (Not Including Descent Time)

pain, paralysis, weakness etc. is relieved or improved during this test of pressure breathing period it is presumed that DCS exists and is the source of the patient's problems. Similarly, if no relief is noted then DCS is not considered a factor in the patient's ailment.

This distinction is important since divers can manifest symptoms that would be very similar to DCS from other problems including muscle strains from lifting gear or an idiosyncratic reaction to medication. This test of pressure confirms whether further recompression therapy would benefit the patient. Applying this test has proven to be nearly 100% reliable.

During the period of the test of pressure a determination will be made as to what the appropriate Treatment Table applies. This is determined by the time factor involved for the relief of symptoms and the seriousness of symptom presentation. Patients resolving in ten minutes or less have historically been treated on Table 5. If resolution takes longer or if any Type II symptoms were initially presented, a Table 6 is chosen. This is a judgment call and the current trend is more towards committing to a Table 6 regardless of time factor resolution. Experienced field chamber supervisors such as Rutkowski, Gilliam and Mount (1991) all suggest application of Table 6 if DCS diagnosis is made.

You may then ask: what about the patient who manifests symptoms, reports promptly and relieves after O_2 administration during transit? Opinion is divided on this issue. If the patient is asymptomatic and a test of pressure does not confirm DCS at that time, can they be considered a bends case?

Unquestionably, patients have had DCS and been relieved by O_2 breathing. This only confirms the importance and validity of aggressive O_2 use in first aid. If transportation from a remote site involving significant financial cost is a consideration, we recommend close observation and suspension of diving activities. However, if a field chamber is readily available and the diver's profile would seem to have put them at risk, we recommend treatment to be administered at least to the extent of Table 5. It can't hurt the patient, and may provide a safety net for recurrent symptoms.

An interesting observation is offered here for the reader's consideration. Can you get bent free-diving (breath hold diving) ? Most divers would answer no. But there is no requirement that you breathe compressed air from a scuba tank to manifest DCS. The malady is dependent on time and depth primarily and therefore expert breath hold divers can, in exceptional diving circumstances, place themselves within a window of vulnerability.

Competitive spear fishermen, South Pacific native working free-divers and Japanese Ama divers are most at risk. Typically, these divers can attain relatively deep depths (80 to 130 fsw) for up to three minutes bottom time. Their profiles reflect an average to rapid ascent followed by a "working" period at depth. Ascents are rapid, sometimes assisted by buoyant apparatus. Considerable exertion may be expended on the dive if the diver must struggle to land a large fish or to swim objects off the bottom.

Originally, little serious consideration was given to the prospects of free-divers falling victim to bends hits, but with Bob Croft's dramatic 240 fsw breath hold dive in 1968 some discussions were prompted. Dives exceeding four minutes had already been recorded and anecdotal accounts of longer breath hold dives were in circulation. A 1962 National Geographic article recounts the diving style of a South Pacific diver: "A man from the Tuamotos who at 59 years old went to 100 feet as many as 50 times a day summed up his attitude toward this skill, 'It is nothing... I have big lungs and a strong body. It is my work.' Two minutes, three, four... a long time if your are holding your breath, but what if you are trying to follow a fish?"

Surprisingly, no correlation between deep breath hold dives and symptomatic DCS was made in many cases. In National Geographic's 1980 book **Exploring the Deep Frontier** the authors relate rather naively, "Oxygen deprivation much longer (than four minutes)... can be damaging or fatal. In the Tuamotos, those who make successive, lengthy dives to great depths, risk a condition they call *taravana* , a sickness that includes vertigo, nausea, partial or complete paralysis, and unconsciousness." Don't these symptoms have something of familiar ring to them? A quick glance through the DCS symptom list should provide some easy match-ups.

Competitive free-diving spear fishermen in the Virgin Islands in the early seventies experimented with wearing the old SCUBAPRO/SOS decom meter during prolonged diving days with interesting results.

Many were able to advance the analog needle almost into the "red zone", indicating required decompression, while diving in 100+ fsw depths. During this same era, in St. Croix commercial lobster diver Sam Espinosa presented himself to Bret Gilliam for evaluation after suffering from numbness, exceptional fatigue and joint stiffness following his diving day. "I did a neurological examination on him and confirmed that his symptoms were progressively worsening. I was convinced he was bent. He told me that he had been diving since sun rise between 90 and 110 feet deep and stopped just before dark. It was only after I started to record his actual dive profiles and surface intervals, that I realized he was free-diving!" Espinosa responded well to a thirty minute breathing period on pure oxygen from a demand regulator and declined recompression treatment. When questioned further by Gilliam, he said several of his fellow lobster divers had similar episodes.

Admittedly, it takes an exceptional diver to get bent holding his breath but it obviously does happen. Readers are cautioned about deep breath hold diving following aggressive scuba diving activities. Dive instructor Scott Valerga of Virgin Gorda had made repetitive scuba dives in 1978 while taking tourist divers on scuba tours. When he was unable to free his anchor following the last dive, he made several dives to 90 feet holding his breath to break out the anchor. Within minutes after getting back on board, he was symptomatic of DCS. His previous diving schedule was within the limits of the U.S. Navy tables but with little safety margin. He was treated in the St. Croix recompression chamber operated by NOAA's *Hydrolab* facility with full recovery.

PORTABLE CHAMBERS

Recent advances in light weight low pressure designs have resulted in a practical portable field chamber that can actually be transported in two hand carried cases easily stowed in a van or dive vessel. Weighing around 160 pounds for the pressure tube and control panel, this unique package allows for a patient to be placed under pressure immediately in the field, blown down to 60 fsw with a patient O_2 BIBS mask including overboard dump, and then the entire unit evacuated to a full size field chamber of hospital based unit. Procedure for patient transfer without decompression is simple: put the portable chamber inside the treatment chamber and remove the patient after pressures are equalized.

This unit was first introduced in 1989 by SOS Ltd. of England and is called the HYPERLITE. The chamber is constructed of a remarkable seamless, flexible tube of Kevlar encapsulated in a silicone rubber matrix. Dimensions are seven feet long, 23 inches wide and weighs 88 pounds, approximately. Obviously, it was designed for one occupant but its value as a method of patient stabilization during transport is unquestionable.

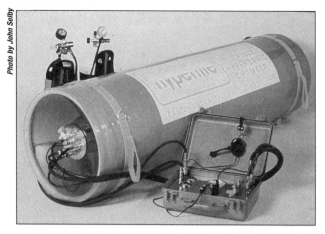

Photo by John Selby

The SOS Hyperlite portable field chamber showing control panel in case and scuba tank/ oxygen cylinders for pressurization and therapy gas.

End panels are placed in the tube with control pressure hoses equipped with non-return valves in the patient's foot end. Pressurization is accomplished by scuba tanks while O_2 is supplied from an included oxygen cylinder. Options include a portable O_2 analyzer and CO_2 monitor. Working chamber depth is slightly in excess of 60 fsw so it is compatible with standard Treatment Table depths.

If a formal treatment facility is accessible, the unit can be transported via land conveyance or by boat, or even winched aboard a helicopter. If in a remote site, the HYPERLITE can effectively conduct a full Treatment Table 6 on its own assuming enough O_2 is on hand for therapy gas and enough scuba tanks are available for pressurization and venting.

This innovative product would seem to be an affordable option for remote diving in exotic locations or carried as emergency aboard a liveaboard dive vessel. Dive clubs or expedition groups should contact the manufacturer at the address below; price in mid-1991 was approximately $28,000.

SOS LTD.
Box 328
London NW7 3JS
England (phone: 081-959-4517)

IN WATER RECOMPRESSION

Now we enter an area of major controversy. Ask any hyperbaric expert or chamber supervisor their feelings on in-the-water recompression and you will get an almost universal recommendation against such a practice. The logistics of attempting to manage equipment for sufficient gas supply, thermal protection for the patient, marine life considerations etc. not to mention the hazards of patient management all basically add up to a grim scenario. Most divers will not be equipped to handle even the compressed air requirements for an air Treatment Table which can last over six hours. And air is the *least* effective recompression gas; in fact such efforts could lead to worsening the patient's condition by loading him up further with nitrogen and subjecting him to debilitating cold even in tropical conditions.

A shade of gray is introduced if the dive team has access to surface supplied oxygen in adequate quantity. Rutkowski (1991) recommends that oxygen not be used deeper than 45 fsw (13.6 m) and only then in an extreme emergency. He would prefer a long "soak" at 30 fsw (9.1 m) on O_2 in 20 minute cycles with 5 minute air breaks. Ideally, O_2 should be delivered via a full face mask. The author emphasizes that this is not a blueprint for divers to follow, but represents a discussion of worst case scenarios where evacuation is not a practical or realistic possibility.

There are protocols for in-water recompression therapy in existence primarily with tables developed by the Australians. Missionary EMT Jack Thompson had surprisingly good results with custom therapy in-water tables in Roatan before a chamber was available and both Mount and Gilliam have successfully conducted in-water proprietary oxygen tables on patients with full resolution.

The decision must, of course, ultimately made based upon personal circumstances and training. However, when faced with no alternative such extreme practices may present a choice. The author does not sanction or endorse in-water techniques and they are presented here for discussion purposes only. The following table outlines the procedures for in-water decompression following the Australian method.

AUSTRALIAN IN-WATER TREATMENT TABLES

(from Diving and Subaquatic Medicine)

Notes: This technique may be useful in treating cases of decompression sickness in localities remote from recompression facilities. It may also be of use while suitable transport to such a center is being arranged. In planning, it should be realized that the therapy may take up to 3 hours. The risks of cold, immersion and other environmental factors should be balanced against the beneficial effects. The diver must be accompanied by an attendant.

EQUIPMENT

1. Full face mask with demand valve and surface supply system OR helmet with free flow.
2. Adequate supply of 100% oxygen for the patient and air for the attendant.
3. Wet suit or dry suit for thermal protection.
4. Shot with at least ten meters of rope (a seat or harness may be rigged to the shot.
5. Some form of communication system between patient, attendant and surface.

METHOD

1. The patient is lowered on the shot rope to nine meters breathing 100% oxygen.
2. Ascent is commenced after 30 minutes in mild cases, 60 minutes in severe cases, if improvement has occurred. These times may be extended to 60 minutes and 90 minutes respectively if there is no improvement.
3. Ascent is at the rate of one meter every 12 minutes.
4. If symptoms recur, remain at depth a further 30 minutes before continuing ascent.
5. If oxygen supply is exhausted, return to the surface rather have the patient breathe air.
6. After surfacing, the patient should be given one hour on oxygen, one hour off, for a further 12 hours.

U.S. NAVY METHOD

The U.S. Navy has another alternative protocol as detailed below:
"If the command has 100% oxygen-rebreathers available and individuals at the dive site trained in their use, the following in-water recompression procedure may be used instead of Table 1A:

1. Put the stricken diver on the rebreather and have him purge the apparatus at least three times with oxygen.
2. Descend to a depth of 30 feet with a standby diver.
3. Remain at 30 feet, at rest, for 60 minutes for Type I symptoms and 90 minutes for Type II symptoms. Ascend to 20 feet after 90 minutes even if symptoms are still present.
4. Decompress to the surface by taking 60 minute stops at 20 feet and 10 feet. (continued, next page...)

Short Oxygen Table

DEPTH	ELAPSED TIME in Min.		
(meters)	Mild	Serious	
9	030-060	060-090	
8	042-072	072-102	
7	054-084	084-114	
6	066-096	096-126	*12 Minutes*
5	078-108	108-138	*Per Meter (4 min./ft)*
4	090-120	120-150	
3	102-132	132-162	
2	114-144	144-174	
1	126-156	156-186	

Total Table time is 126 minutes to 156 minutes for mild cases 156 minutes to 186 minutes for serious cases.

5. After surfacing, continue breathing 100% oxygen for an additional three hours."

(U.S.Navy Diving Manual, Vol. One, Section 8.11.2, D)

This method can be easily adapted to full face mask diving systems or surface supplied oxygen. However, it requires a substantial amount of oxygen to be available, both for the in-water treatment and subsequent surface breathing period. If either the Australian or U.S.Navy method is considered as a "last resort" procedure, take care to provide the diver with appropriate thermal protection (dry suit preferred, wet suit with hot water hose etc.), safety diver in attendance at all times, and track the OTU/UPTD count from the prior dives and treatment period. Seek protected water location before beginning treatment. Diver should be supplied regular drinking water for hydration during treatment; this may be accommodated simply by flexible containers with integral "straws" with removable stoppers.

Air in-water recompression treatment tables are not discussed in this text for two reasons: the very strong possibility that a diver's condition could be worsened, and the requirements for available gas to conduct such treatments is probably beyond the operational and logistical planning capabilities of the dive team.

SUMMARY

With good diving practices and some luck you may never need to see the inside of a recompression chamber. But it is more than likely that you will encounter a DCS incident during your career for another diver. Remember, prompt treatment is vital. Administer oxygen by demand valve mask, if conscious provide oral fluids, do not give pain killing drugs and transport victim by fastest available method to a recompression chamber facility.

We strongly encourage signing up for the DAN diver insurance program as well.

Help promote recognition of DCS symptoms and prompt reporting. Denial of DCS problems is not macho, it is stupid.

REFERENCES

Waite, Charles; *Case Histories of Diving and Hyperbaric Accidents*, UHMS

DAN Underwater Diving Accident Manual, Divers Alert Network (1985)

Gilliam, Bret; *Diving Accident Management Field Guide: O2 Administration and Recompression Therapy*, Ocean Tech Publications

Bove & Davis; *Diving Medicine*, Grove and Stratton, Inc.

Edmonds, Lowery, Pennegather; *Diving and Subaquactic Medicine*, Best Publishing, Co.

Corry, James; *Emergency Oxygen Administration and Field Management of Scuba Diving Accidents*, NAUI Publications

Daugherty, Gordon C.; *Field Guide For the Diver Medic*, Best Publishing, Co.

Rutkowski, Richard; *Recompression Chamber Life Support Manual,* Hyperbarics Int'l.

Shilling, Carlston, and Mathias; *The Physician's Guide to Diving Medicine*, Plenum Press

Gilliam, Bret; *Evaluation of Decompression Sickness Incidence in Multi-day Repetitive Diving for 77,680 Sport Dives*, Proceedings of the 1991 Repetitive Diving Conference, American Academy of Underwater Sciences

U.S.Navy Diving Manual, Volume One, revision 1, June 1985, NAVSEA 0994-LP-001-9010

CHAPTER 14

Parting Shots

"Illiterate? Write now for free help"
Alabama bumper sticker

Do you ever get the feeling that the guys making up some of the rules for diving are the same guys that got fired from the M&M factory because they threw away all the "W"s? If that makes sense to you, then we have a cabinet post for you in the Ministry of Silly Diver Practices.

Here's a classic. In the early 1970's I was staffing an instructor training program and was evaluating several candidates who were demonstrating mask clearing technique. One guy launched into this discourse, "Roll over and blow air from your nose to allow the water to drain out the side of the mask."

"But," I queried, "wouldn't it be easier to look up and drain the mask from the bottom where the water will be more naturally channeled?"

"No," he quickly shot back. "I was trained to do it that way."

"Well, why? Does it make any sense?", I countered in my best Socratic teaching style.

A funny look came over his face and he admitted he had never really thought about it since his own instructor was an ex-UDT diver who knew everything. It turns out that his well meaning mentor had taught him that way because he learned to dive on a double hose regulator and in order to clear the mouthpiece if it flooded you had to roll on your side and get the exhaust hose to the lowest point. He was taught to clear his mask in that position since his instructor figured if your regulator had fallen out then your mask might have gotten dislodged as well. The technique made sense in its era. But with the adoption of the single hose regulator, equipment had evolved beyond what worked in the 1960's.

Inquiring minds might have some fun with a look at some of the more popular "Ten Commandments" in use today:

"Always be back on board the dive boat with a minimum of 750 psi" Why? Can you cash in that for credit at the air fill Bank & Trust? Since we all now should know the significant benefit of safety stops, wouldn't it make more sense to suggest arriving at the *decom bar* or the *anchor line at about 15 feet* with 750 psi remaining? Then use the air for a nice 5-7 minute safety stop. As long as you don't completely drain the cylinder there is no chance of getting water in it and that's more than enough reserve for a good hang and then to comfortably surface. Why waste 25% of your air? Use it underwater.

"Always put your weight belt on last" This is a holdover from when most horse collar style BC's had crotch straps, or tank harnesses were so complex that you had to be the "Lord of the D-Rings" to get adjusted. Most modern BC's have no crotch straps to potentially foul the weight belt and the waist/chest strap is secured with a buckle riding well above the hips. I put my weights on first and it makes donning the other gear far easier.

"Never put your mask on your forehead" Why do divers feel compelled to apologize for this benign and common sense act? Sure, there are some circumstances when it's not appropriate like in surf entries, but in most situations it is a logical place to put the mask while resting on the surface or swimming on your back. An easy one-handed motion restores it on the face quickly and you're back in business. Try that when your mask is pulled down over your neck. If you're a no-neck ex-football player like me that's an exercise in self-strangulation. Who cares where you place your mask as long as you remain in control of it. Lighten up, please.

"You are properly weighted if you float with a full breath and sink slowly when you exhale at the beginning of a dive" Hey, anybody here ever heard of safety and/or decom stops? You want to be able to hover or maintain neutral buoyancy at the end of a dive to perform stops in the 15 foot depth zone. Your aluminum cylinder may gain as much as six pounds of buoyancy as the air is depleted. If you do your weight test with a full tank you'll end up hopelessly positive by the end of the dive. Make adjustments for neutral buoyancy with a nearly empty tank.

"Blow some air from your tank on your regulator first stage dust cap" It's a mystery to me how this practice ever got started. Why not just dunk the whole thing in the ocean since it has the same effect? When you crack the tank valve following a dive there is a fairly good amount of salt water trapped in the o-ring groove which you immediately atomize into a wonderful salty grit forcibly coating the dust cap and then sealing that corrosive cocktail on your first stage. If you're really concerned about cleaning, dip it in fresh water or lick it off before replacing. That also saves a lot of needless noise from sudden tank blasts that the harried boat crew thinks was a burst disc or blown o-ring.

"Always wear a snorkel on scuba dives" If you want to carry one in a pocket or on your leg OK, but why would you want one attached to your head where it can distract you? Some snorkels these days are the size of nuclear exhaust chimneys and have sufficient drag to make you swim in a nice tight circle to the left. For a lot of divers attached snorkels don't allow the mask to seal comfortably, tangle the hair, and several accidents have manifested when the snorkel was placed in the mouth instead of the regulator in an emergency. And remember, most modern BC's are designed for surface swimming on your back rendering a snorkel useless.

"You can't dive if you have a beer with lunch" This is a real beauty of twisted logic. This is not aimed at abusive drinkers whom we all agree should not be allowed to dive impaired. No, the scuba police want to save you from the hazards of dehydration that might make you more likely to get bent. All well and good, but consider for a moment that alcohol has the same effect on anti-diuretic hormone (ADH) suppression as does the caffeine in soft drinks, coffee and iced tea. And the effect of moderate consumption of these beverages is of little consequence anyway. So until the storm troops want to curtail the diving of everyone having a cup of Colombia's finest over breakfast or the guy who knocks back a six pack of Coke routinely, I suggest that this may win the Medal for Pious Absurdity with Barley Hops Clusters.

"The best entry is a giant stride with an inflated BC" I guess it might make sense if you planned on bobbing around on the surface, but if your intent was to go diving *under the water*, why not just do a simple feet-first entry and continue right on with your descent. Most accidents manifest at the surface, it can be rough up there, and any surface wind or current tends to swiftly carry you away from the entry point. Say your good-byes before stepping off and get on with diving.

"Decompression diving is more dangerous than no-decompression diving" Sorry to burst the bubble (no pun intended), but this doesn't measure up for several reasons. First of all, *all dives* are decompression dives since the ascent rate is factored in as part of the decompression even on no-stop profiles. Secondly, divers can employ a wide variety of table or computer physiological models than will have different no-stop limits as a matter of proprietary design. The Navy tables use 60 feet for 60 minutes as a no-stop model while the Buhlmann based Micro Brain Pro Plus computer uses only a 44 minute exposure for the same depth. If the computer dictates a stop based on a square profile can anyone seriously argue that diver is more at risk given his conservative exposure by comparison?

Finally, if you run any decompression model up to its limit but stay just outside the required decom zone and ascend directly to the surface... you will find, in most cases, that this diver will have more sub-clinical decompression stress (detectable by Doppler) than the diver who went ahead and planned a dive that required stops but allowed a more complete and thorough outgassing.

"You can't get bent on one tank" With single cylinders now available boasting volumes in excess of 200 cubic feet, you can now have the luxury of bending yourself several times on one tank if you like. Even with single 50 cubic foot cylinders, I know dive guides who can get a couple wall dives out of one and still have enough left over to blow up the flat tires in their rusted out jeeps.

We can see that a few sacred cows continue to moo long after their milk ran dry. A healthy dose of common sense goes a long way. If the Emperor wears no clothes or your dive guide seems to have neglected to don his intellectual wet suit, then say so. We all benefit from a lively discussion.

Bret Gilliam

TRAINING AGENCIES

We encourage all divers to seek to seek out professional training before pursuing diving beyond the scope of traditional sport limits. The three agencies listed below have established curricula and standards along with a large number of experienced instructors.

AMERICAN NITROX DIVERS INC. (ANDI)

74 Woodcleft Avenue
Freeport, NY 11520
516-546-2026
Principals: Ed Betts, President
Doug Pettit, Vice President

ANDI's main concentration is on nitrox programs, called SafeAir in their system. They provide both student and instructor manuals along with support materials such as cylinder ID wraps, stickers, logs, tee shirts etc. An excellent gas blending course is available for store and resort operators. Although their name would suggest solely U.S. operations, ANDI has grown to have representation worldwide. Their staff can also consult on oil-free compressor systems. Liability insurance for instructors is available up to one million dollars in coverage.

INTERNATIONAL ASSOCIATION OF NITROX & TECHNICAL DIVERS (IANTD)

9628 NE 2nd Avenue
Suite D
Miami Shores, FL 33138
305-751-3958, fax 305-751-3958
Principals: Tom Mount, President
Dick Rutkowski
Bill Deans

IANTD was the first technical training agency formed in 1985 by Dick Rutkowski to promote nitrox within sport diving circles. He later cofounded ANDI with Ed Betts but is no longer involved with that agency. In 1991, Rutkowski brought in Mount, Deans and Bret Gilliam to concentrate on expanding the programs to include more technical programs and mixed gas training. (Gilliam left the company in 1994 to pursue other interests). A variety of course support materials are available including manuals and the usual peripherals such as stickers, tee shirts etc. A selection of custom submersible tables is also offered. Operations sphere is worldwide. Liability insurance for instructors is available up to one million dollars in coverage.

TECHNICAL DIVING INTERNATIONAL (TDI)

9 Coastal Plaza, Suite 300
Bath, ME 04530
207-442-8391, fax: 207-442-9042
Principals: Bret Gilliam, President
Dr. Bill Hamilton, Vice President
Mitch Skaggs, Vice President
Rob Palmer, Director TDI Europe
John Crea
Steve Pearson
John Comly
David Sipperly
John Jordan

Gilliam departed IANTD as an equity partner and launched TDI in early 1994 with a core group of investors already actively involved in all aspects of technical diving training. Their emphasis has been on six core programs including entry level nitrox, advanced nitrox, technical diver (air based deep training with decom gas switches), advanced wreck, rebreathers, and mixed gas diving. TDI also offers specific programs for store facilities in setting up nitrox and gas blending systems, integrating technical training into an overall store profit center, and specific consulting on equipment. Growth has been swift and TDI is now offered worldwide. Liability insurance for instructors is available up to one million dollars in coverage.

APPENDIX A

DEALING WITH DENIAL:
GETTING THE BENDS OUT OF THE CLOSET

by Bret C. Gilliam

Decompression sickness (DCS) or "bends" is a statistical inevitability in diving. It has no conscience and rarely abides by any set rules. Although we can identify certain predisposing factors to DCS in divers generically, it is still impossible to explain the exact mechanisms of physiology that allows one diver to be bent while his partner escapes unscathed. It is best that divers, particularly those in the high-tech community, accept that DCS hits will eventually occur and take steps to deal with treatment responsibly.

What concerns many of us in the business of treating divers is the unfortunate mindset that somehow has developed with the sport diving population that consistently denies the possibility of DCS. Indeed, a certain stigma to reporting symptoms has developed and this trend flies in the face of all common sense and logic. Why would any intelligent adult ignore symptoms with the knowledge that DCS manifestations are progressive in nature... they get worse with time. Further, any delays in reporting symptoms and seeking treatment only contribute to a poorer prognosis for recovery.

Historically, denial of symptoms and treatment delays are the rule in sport diver DCS injuries rather than the exception. The emerging high-tech diver community hopefully will be pivotal in reversing this "head in the sand" mentality. We have to remove the stigma of "blame" so improperly associated with DCS reporting. It is no one's fault that they got bent; a diver can play everything in his dive plan precisely by the book and still get hit. Likewise, a deliberately high risk dive profile may not produce symptoms. The point here is diving leaders have to stop pointing fingers and using antiquated analogies ("he screwed up and he got bent, the idiot!") or continued reluctance to report symptoms will prevail.

Almost all of us know individuals who have surfaced after a dive and variously exhibited DCS symptoms but steadfastly refused further evaluation or even basic first aid such as surface oxygen by demand valve/mask. It's not macho to attempt to "tough-out" shoulder pain or progressive numbness: it's just plain stupid.

In the working and commercial diver ranks an entirely different attitude prevails. Divers are trained to report symptoms as soon as possible and the attitude of diving supervisors is one of accident "containment" not accident "crisis" as in many sport diving situations. Bends is regarded as an occupational hazard that will occasionally take place and commercial operators and the more progressive sport diving facilities regard DCS as a manageable scenario. For the best outcome, divers and chamber supervisors work in a partnership of honest reporting of even slight symptoms with prompt evaluation and treatment.

Until recently, there were few operational recompression chambers in remote resort sites and divers who manifested DCS symptoms were faced with expensive medivac transportation and significant delays even in the best of circumstances. Possibly as a result of this, many so-called "experts" were prone to overly broad condemnations of sport divers who got bent and this attitude only contributed to diver denial. Negative peer pressure and professional loss of face proved to be powerful influences on divers to ignore DCS symptoms in the mistaken hope that they would somehow get better without treatment. Rarely was this the case, however.

Most chamber supervisors that I have known in my career feel that if DCS is promptly reported and evaluated with ensuing on-site treatment, then the prognosis for complete resolution is excellent. The attitude of many commercial diver medics and chamber operators is "No matter what the problem, if reported and treated quickly, we can clean the diver up". Type I DCS (mild symptoms, pain only) affords less risk than Type II DCS (serious symptoms, central nervous system involvement) but in either presentation aggressive oxygen therapy and prompt recompression has produced nearly a 98% success record. Many academicians find fault with the commercial operators' confidence in resolution of symptoms but their track record is enviable.

In March of 1991, I was an invited speaker at the joint DAN/AAUS/NOAA Multi-day Repetitive Diving Workshop held at Duke University. For the first time, this conference included representatives from the sport, commercial, scientific and "high tech" diving communities assembled to compare notes on actual DCS incidence rates in the field. Some interesting statistical patterns developed as the workshop unfolded. The overall incidence of DCS for commercial divers was (approximately) 1 in 1000 dives, for the sport divers it was 1 in 10,000 dives and the scientific diving community rated an extreme low of 1 in 100,000 dives. Sampling from the "high tech" segment was too low to be realistically tallied.

With this rather startling multiplier of 10 between groups, it would be tempting to draw the too obvious conclusion that the scientific diving group is 100 times safer than the commercial diving group. Actually, the incidence rates are interesting for discussion purposes but do not reflect much data to produce true comparisons of relative dive safety vis-a-vis DCS risk. Rather, a clearer pattern of diving "attitude" was defined. Discussion of what an acceptable rate of DCS would be provided the best indication of how several schools of thought can basically approach a complex problem from entirely different angles.

Most scientific diving projects are planned from inception at eliminating as much risk as possible in all phases of the diving operation. This is accomplished by strict supervision and training of divers and a markedly conservative discipline in dive profiling. In short, every possible precaution is taken to reduce the possibility of a DCS occurrence. At the other end of the spectrum, the commercial diving community must deal with a job performance/task completion goal motivated by economics. Therefore, the concept of "acceptable risk" comes into play for both groups but each deals with risk differently.

By extremes of discipline, supervision and training the scientific community hopes to prevent DCS incidence. With the use of highly trained supervisors, diver medical technicians and on-site recompression facilities, the commercial companies aim to effectively manage any accidents that may occur. It is difficult to quantifiably gauge the "end user" effectiveness of either group since DCS still occurs in scientific and commercial divers; the distinction being that if a commercial diver gets hit he is benefited by immediate and state-of-the-art medical treatment which may not be available to a science diver in a remote situation. Per capita DCS rates may or may not reflect the effectiveness of either approach to accident management, but the commercial operators are steadfast in their opinion that immediate evaluation and treatment are an acceptable alternative to a lesser statistical incidence rate.

All would agree that no bends hit is a good one, especially if you are on the receiving end. Terry Overland of Oceaneering International made this point at the conference: "While most sport and scientific dive operations would like to reach a goal of zero per cent DCS incidence, in commercial diving this is simply unrealistic. Ideally, we would like to reach a zero rate on Type II hits, but we still feel that our protocols allow us to treat DCS effectively enough that Type I hits are essentially manageable. I guess what I'm saying is that we accept the fact that if we give a worker a hammer, he will eventually hit his thumb and when he does we'll treat it. If we put a diver in the water to work, eventually he will get bent and we'll treat that as well. That's the simple facts. We have the technology to handle such hits and we feel that this is a more responsible outlook than attempting to unrealistically eliminate the malady. It's going to happen; we all know that. Let's be prepared to treat it. Importantly, our divers feel that our system works and it's their butts on the firing line, of course."

Further distinctions are sometimes made between "deserved" and "undeserved" DCS hits. Simply put, hits following a dive profile that would suggest the high-risk of DCS exposure such as clear Table limits violations or deep repetitive or reverse profile dives can be categorized as "deserved". Hits following dives that were within accepted limits are considered "undeserved". This is not to say that as chamber supervisors we sit back and blithely pass judgment on patients; categorizations of DCS hits using such terms merely allows a perspective on reasons for the presentation.

First and foremost, we have to encourage reporting of symptoms at the earliest observation. Second, the importance of surface oxygen by demand valve/mask cannot be overemphasized. Dr. Jefferson Davis was one of the earliest advocates of aggressive 100% O_2 delivery in the field and his pioneering work has resulted in the now accepted practice of oxygen therapy as a first line of treatment en route to the chamber. A significant percent of symptomatic DCS patients will relieve following a 30 to 45 minute oxygen breathing period if delivered by demand valve/mask. During a one year period while Vice President of Diving Operations for Ocean Quest International, I observed nearly a dozen cases of symptomatic DCS clear completely following demand system O_2 during transit to our chamber on the ship. Free-flow systems are far less effective and are wasteful of the gas.

I ran the Ocean Quest diving program along similar guidelines to a large commercial operation: expect the worst and be prepared to deal with it. We were very successful in encouraging divers to report any symptoms and had a 100% resolution rate on every one of the DCS cases we treated. Our overall incidence rate came out to be approximately 1 case in 12,000 dives; this is significant since we allowed an unlimited diving program with respect to depth and numbers of repetitive dives daily. In the space of one year we conducted almost 80,000 dives!

Thankfully, we are seeing more and more fully operable field chambers coming into use. Grand Cayman, Cozumel, Roatan and even some liveaboard vessels all feature state-of-the-art treatment facilities that would have been unthinkable only a decade ago. But remember, the chamber is only an effective tool if used (hopefully as soon as the diver notes a problem). It's incumbent on all divers to take responsibility for themselves and report any abnormality that could even be remotely linked to DCS. Use 100% O_2 at once and seek professional evaluation and a test of pressure if the possibility of DCS is suspected.

All divers should have a complete and detailed contingency plan for DCS management. For higher risk dive profiles, more attention to detail will be required and should include the provision for on-site recompression either in a properly staffed and setup field chamber or through use of an evacuation chamber such as SOS's Hyperlite.

With the advent of affordable medical insurance such as available through

DAN, the financial deterrent to admitting DCS and seeking help should be removed. There is nothing "macho" or "cool" about denial of DCS symptoms that could result in lasting injury such as paralysis or worse. It's time divers woke up to the fact that bends is an injury like any other and common sense dictates its treatment. Finally, the encouragement of prompt reporting with no associated peer or professional blame will vastly improve the safety of a sport infamous for symptom denial.

References:

Gilliam, Bret, *"Evaluation of DCS Incidence in Multi-day Repetitive Diving for 77,680 Sport Dives"*, Proceedings of the American Academy of Underwater Sciences Repetitive Diving Workshop 1991

Overland, Terry, *"Oceaneering International"*, Proceedings of the American Academy of Underwater Sciences Repetitive Diving Workshop 1991

Rutkowski, Richard, personal communication 11-91

Overland, Terry, personal communication 3-91

APPENDIX B

CARBON DIOXIDE RISK MANAGEMENT FOR DIVERS

by Bret C. Gilliam

For every liter of oxygen consumed, almost a liter of carbon dioxide is produced. This is, of course, specific to individuals and varies according to diet and can change dramatically when the diver is subjected to increased work loads or exercise. CO_2 is essentially a waste product of the metabolic process of energy production and is eliminated during the exhalation phase of respiration. Its molecular weight is 44.0103 and occurs in the natural atmosphere as approximately 0.03% of the total. In that concentration, CO_2 is colorless, odorless, tasteless and nontoxic. In greater percentages or under elevated partial pressures it has an acid taste and be dangerously toxic.

It is the primary stimulus to breathing in man. Remember the old "Ten and Ten Rule": if the percentage of either carbon dioxide or oxygen reaches 10% in the atmosphere, unconsciousness will usually result. Low oxygen levels (hypoxia) will trigger the peripheral chemoreceptors to send impulses to the respiratory center stimulating an increase in breathing rate. However, low PO_2 is far less of a stimulus than high PCO_2. This why the danger of excessive hyperventilation prior to extended or deep breath hold dives is so insidious.

Hyperventilation artificially blows off the normal equilibrating level of CO_2 and lowers it thus lessening the urge to breathe and extending the diver's bottom time. Upon ascent, the partial pressure of both CO_2 and O_2 is reduced as the diver rises in the water column. This results in the potential for latent hypoxia or "shallow water blackout". Our built-in warning system, carbon dioxide, has been altered through the hyperventilation process and is incapable or alerting the diver to his immediate hypoxic crisis. Several champion free divers have fallen victim to this phenomena and it is strongly advisable for divers to refrain from prolonged or excessive hyperventilation techniques.

Symptoms of carbon dioxide retention include headache, weakness, labored breathing, a feeling of air hunger, nausea, dizziness, and confusion. Observable signs are typified by clumsiness or foolish, incoherent actions and slowing or responses. At its higher plateau, CO_2 retention will manifest in unconsciousness.

Dr. Ed Lanphier published the first work and formal recognition of the CO_2 retention phenomenon in individuals in 1955. His early work specifically noted the relationship of retention to increased susceptibility to oxygen convulsions. He later noted (1959), that "perhaps CO_2 retainers are the *only* individuals who develop O_2 toxicity much more readily during exercise than at rest." The significance of this hypothesis might lead to speculation that continued cautions against working diver exposures to high PO_2 values could be re-evaluated with regard to ATA dose/time guidelines, but no definitive investigatory data has been pursued clinically.

Those individuals who are more susceptible to carbon dioxide may be categorized as "CO_2 retainers". Many diving physicians are sufficiently concerned about this abnormality in divers that they will recommend exclusion if a predisposition to CO_2 is detected.

Lanphier went on to observe (1975), "Whatever its etiology, the individual tendency to retain carbon dioxide during exertion appears to be the single most important factor in the problem of abnormal PA CO_2 and its potentially serious consequences." He noted other contributory elements such as increased work of breathing, higher percentage rates of CO_2 in the inspired gas, and excessive "dead space" in breathing apparatus (helmet air volume) as important, but "their effects appear to be greatly magnified in men who do not maintain normal carbon dioxide values, even under optimal conditions of work."

The difficulty in effectively identifying the "CO_2 retainer" from a working group of diver candidates remains a problem. Hashimoto et al. (1981) conducted studies on 19 healthy divers that indicated past predisposition to some CO_2 symptoms but was unable to distinguish these individuals specifically by use of such conventional testing. His conclusions, however tentative, suggested that "identification of retainers requires an exercise test and that tethered fin-swimming is particularly suitable." (Physiology and Medicine of Diving, 1982)

With regard to the role of elevated CO_2 in inert gas narcosis, both clinical and anecdotal field reports all clearly identify the serious effects of high PCO_2 with narcosis symptomatology. Case, Haldane, and later, Bennett all describe this effect and subjective professional reports from experienced divers in actual dive conditions appear to confirm all speculations. One diver who was working on a pipe construction project in 190 fsw on air had no noticeable impairment in his day to day exposures across a ten day period. However, when his routine was altered to include lifting several 60 pound boxes of pipe components onto the work stage area, he became sufficiently overcome with befuddlement that he was forced to terminate the dive. Upon reaching the surface, he was unable to remember beginning work or the circumstances that caused him to abort. His dive partner, not involved in the heavy work, was unaffected. However, he was unable to note any change in behavior by his dive buddy until he abruptly dropped his tools and swam away from the work site. (Temple, Gilliam 1972)

While conducting tests on diver performance in 1963, Lanphier "rediscovered" the effects of CO_2 under pressure dramatically in an "episode of terror that has had no equal in his life". While working in a dry hyperbaric chamber at approximately 224 fsw he began testing a new bicycle ergometer at moderate exertion levels. His breathing system was modified to supply him with only about 50% of his respiratory needs. Onset of narcosis was rapid and escalated to collapse in coma. "Dyspnoea, which was very prominent before loss of consciousness, turned into a formless threat of indescribable menace when exercise ceased and awareness began to return. Had such an experience occurred in open water, survival seems improbable." (Physiology and Medicine of Diving, 1982)

Lanphier describes the incident in his own words: "I'm the exact opposite of a CO_2 retainer; but I discovered that I wasn't immune to serious CO_2 effects. A student and I were testing a new bike at 7.8 ATA in the dry chamber in my lab in Buffalo. Nitrogen narcosis is very evident on air at that pressure, but we were doing OK until we started breathing on the measuring circuit. That, it turned out, gave us only about half the air we needed at that work rate set on the bike. Herb tried the bike first. He stopped pedaling after about three minutes, out cold with his eyes rolled back."

"As soon as I could get Herb out of the way, I took the bike. I knew I wasn't getting near enough air, but I was too narc'd to think straight and was determined to finish the 5-minute test no matter what. I pedaled myself right into oblivion, and coming around slowly afterward with a horrible feeling of suffocation was the worst experience of my entire life. Both of us surely would have drowned if such a thing had happened when we were alone underwater." (*AquaCorps* 1992)

In closed or semi-closed circuit systems, attention to proper CO_2 removal is essential. Absorbents such as lithium hydroxide, Sodasorb, or Baralyme are commonly used agents. Efficiency of such products is reduced in lowered temperatures so an awareness of thermal surroundings must be part of the diver's equation. In closed environments such as underwater saturation habitats, submersibles or submarines elaborate CO_2 "scrubbers" are employed. In recompression chambers, periodic aggressive venting of the vessel interior will provide a refreshed and comfortable atmosphere.

CONCLUSION

It is extremely important for divers to consider the effects or CO_2 in planning their diving activities. Aside from the obvious problems of CO_2 toxicity itself, elevated partial pressures of CO_2 contribute to the onset and severity of both nitrogen narcosis and oxygen toxicity. Matching a high performance regulator to his operational needs is vital. Breathing resistance *and* exhalation resistance must both be considered in selecting equipment. Increased gas density with depth can potentially overload the performance of many regulators in spite of glossy ad claims from manufacturers.

Proper breathing technique is equally important. Never engage in "skip breathing"; it will only contribute to CO_2 retention. Slow, deep ventilation cycles are recommended.

References

Bennett & Elliot, *The Physiology and Medicine of Diving*, (1982) Best Publishing, Co.

Bove & Davis, *Diving Medicine*, (1990), Grove and Stratton, Inc.

Shilling, Carlston & Matthias, *The Physician's Guide to Diving Medicine*, (1984) Plenum Press

Lanphier, Ed, *The Story of CO_2 Buildup*, Aquacorps Journal, 1992

PERCENT CO_2	EFFECT
0-4%	No CNS derangement
4-6%	Dyspnea, anxiety
6-10%	Impaired mental capabilities
10-15%	Severely impaired mental function
15-20%	Loss of consciousness
>20%	Uncoordinated muscular twitching and convulsions

APPENDIX C

FIVE MINUTE NEUROLOGICAL EXAM

Examination of a victim's central nervous system soon after an accident may provide valuable information to the physician or chamber supervisor responsible for treatment. The Five Minute Neuro Exam is easily learned and performed by individuals with no medical experience at all.

The examination can be done step-by-step while reading from this text. Perform the steps in order, and record the time and results.

1. ORIENTATION

Does the diver know name and age?

Does the diver know present location?

Does the diver know what time, day or year it is?

Even though a diver appears alert, the answers to these questions may reveal confusion.

Do not omit them!

2. EYES

Have the diver count the number of fingers you display using two or three different numbers. Check each eye separately and then together. Have the diver identify a distant object.

Tell the diver to hold head still, or you gently hold it still, while placing your other hand about 18 inches in front of the face. Ask the diver to follow you hand with his eyes. Then move your hand up and down, then side to side. The diver's eyes should smoothly follow your hand and should not jerk to one side and return. Check that pupils are equal in size.

3. FACE

Ask the diver to whistle. Look carefully to see that both sides of the face have the same expression while whistling. Ask the diver to grit the teeth. Feel the jaw muscles to confirm that they are contracted equally.

Instruct the diver to close the eyes while you lightly touch your fingertips across the forehead and face to be sure sensation is present and the same everywhere.

4. HEARING

Hearing can be evaluated by holding your hand about two feet from the diver's ear and rubbing your thumb and finger together. Check both ears, moving your hand closer until the diver hears it. Check several times and confirm with your own hearing. If the surroundings are noisy, the test is difficult to evaluate. Ask bystanders to be quiet and turn off unneeded machinery.

5. SWALLOWING REFLEX

Instruct the diver to swallow while you watch the "Adam's apple" to be sure that it moves up and down.

6. TONGUE

Instruct the diver to stick out the tongue. It should come out straight in the middle of the mouth without deviating to either side.

7. MUSCLE STRENGTH

Instruct the diver to shrug the shoulders while you bear down on them to observe for equal muscle strength.

Check the diver's arms by bringing the elbows up level with the shoulders, hands level with the arms, and touching the chest. Instruct the diver to resist while you pull the arms away, push them back, up and down. The strength should be approximately equal in both arms in each direction. Check leg strength be having the diver lie flat and raise and lower the legs while you gently resist the movement.

8. SENSORY PERCEPTION

Check on both sides by touching as done on the face. Start at the top of the body and compare sides while moving downwards to cover the entire body. The diver's eyes should be closed during this procedure. The diver should confirm the sensation in each area before you move to another area.

9. BALANCE AND COORDINATION

Be prepared to protect the diver from injury when performing this test. Have the diver stand up with feet together, close eyes and stretch out arms. The diver should be able to maintain balance if the platform is stable. Your arms should be around, but not touching the diver. Be prepared to catch the diver who starts to fall.

Check coordination by having the diver move and index finger back and forth rapidly between the diver's nose and your finger held approximately 18 inches from the diver's face. Instruct the diver to slide the heel of one foot down the shin of the other leg. The diver should be lying down when attempting this test.

Check these tests on both right and left sides and observe carefully for unusual clumsiness on either side.

SUMMARY

The diver's condition may prevent the performance of one or more of these tests. Record any omitted test and the reason. If any of the tests are not normal, injury to the nervous system should be suspected. The tests should be repeated at frequent intervals while awaiting assistance to determine if any change occurs. Report the results to the emergency medical personnel if attendance at the chamber or responding to your call.

Good diving safety habits would include practicing this examination on normal divers to become proficient in the test.

APPENDIX D

PRACTICAL USE OF DIVING COMPUTERS IN SPORT DIVING APPLICATIONS

by Bret C. Gilliam

Any discussion of dive computers should immediately identify the problems associated with current survey methodologies. What should be of interest to us as medical and diving professionals is not what we *think* divers should be doing, but rather what they are *actually* doing. That is the reality of sport diving and that is the market that most diving computers is aimed at. Do they meet the demands of providing an acceptable risk for exposures they can control? Let's talk about that. But first a little background.

One of the greatest obstacles that must be overcome by many divers in their acceptance of diving computers is their initial "comfort level" with the concept of multi-level diving theory. This is a foreign and alien concept for many divers whose dive planning has traditionally followed square profile planning paradigms. In fact, a certain "suspension of disbelief" is necessary to grasp the allowed multi-level exposure that deviates so radically from fixed norms such as "60 ft. for 60 minutes" etc. Like many new evolutions in equipment, dive computers were initially met with skepticism and outright condemnation by some members of the diving community. In retrospect, much of this hostile reception was undeserved. The most vocal critics tended to be the so-called experts who were never fully cognizant of the theory of multi-level diving that was widely applied as far back as the late sixties.

HISTORICAL PERSPECTIVE

For those who were already familiar and comfortable with multi-level diving through the use of various analog devices such as the SOS Decompression Meter, the switch to modern electronic computers was less traumatic. In spite of the obvious flaws in the "computational" method of the SOS device, once the field user was able to sort out a practical SOP, the units became virtually indispensable and were used with success by thousands of divers for over twenty years.

The SOS Decompression Meter was introduced in 1959 but did not gain widespread U.S. distribution until Scubapro gained import rights in 1963. Although not a "computer" by any stretch of the imagination, this relatively simple device provided the first basis of practical underwater calculation of multi-level diving and became immensely popular with professional photojournalists, film makers and divers who were tired of being boxed in to the confines of historical "square profile" table plans. Although many simply dismissed the "decom meter" as unvalidated and branded it the "Bend-O-Matic", thousands of divers used it without incident and only grudgingly parted with their well-worn units to make the switch to electronic computers.

Obviously, the old "meter" users were comfortable with multi-level profiling and the transition to modern computers was a natural progression. Some early computer models failed to live up to expectations or suffered from design failures that led to flooding, power failures, etc. These initial problems were almost completely eliminated and in 1993, today's diver has over two dozen highly accurate and reliable computers to choose from.

The introduction of electronic computers in the early 1980's was initially met with the same skepticism by critics who loudly trumpeted the perils of any device that could possibly allow a dive exposure of "100 feet for an hour and half". As anyone who has used computers in multi-level applications knows, such an exposure is not only attainable and routine, it is also relatively benign since the dive is typified by the initial deep phase and then followed by progressive ascending stays at shallower depths.

So why use a computer? Quite simply, they are more accurate in measuring depth and time, and virtually every model available incorporates a decompression algorithm *more conservative* than the standard U.S. Navy tables. Most divers use computers to gain more time underwater safely since the units are "active" devices that compute theoretical tissue/compartment inert gas loading and outgassing based upon actual depths and times. This provides an obvious benefit to "square profiles" where the diver's uptake and release are modeled on assuming that the entire dive was spent at the deepest depth for the total dive time.

But even if you have a problem accepting the theory of multi-level diving, then modern computers will give you a safety edge based upon their highly accurate depth measuring sensors and timing devices. Using them solely in this application can provide a safety buffer for the strict table user. Some models are significantly more conservative than the Navy tables. For instance, we can all remember that the U.S. Navy tables allow 60 minutes at 60 feet with no decompression. By comparison, the Dacor Micro Brain Pro Plus computer allows only 44 minutes for the same depth based on its Buhlmann model and program that presumes diving at slight altitude.

The acceptance of diving computers has literally swept through the industry in the nineties. Just a glance around any liveaboard vessel will confirm this, and more and more entry level divers are purchasing computers during or immediately after training. Although any piece of equipment can fail, modern dive computers are extraordinarily reliable. Additionally, the safety of their decompression models has been proven. In Gilliam's study (1989-90) of 77,680 dives by sport divers, he had zero cases of DCS among computer users (who made up over 50% of the data base).

Recent workshops and symposia have seen respected experts predict such a dominance by computers that dive tables as a primary dive planning protocol may well become obsolete. Although not willing to go on record officially, the majority of professional underwater photographers, resort guides, etc. have already abandoned tables and use computers exclusively.

TABLES VERSUS DIVE COMPUTERS

Are dive computers the answer to increased diver safety when considered in comparison to dive tables?

Fundamentally, it's a question of learning retention by students. Dive tables are a skill learned primarily to pass a test and whatever brief proficiency is acquired during training is quickly lost. The facts in this area are fairly indisputable. Dr. Kelly Hill sponsored a volunteer survey on elementary dive table problems in 1988 that had a failure rate of better than 50%. Even more alarming is that his survey divers included experience levels from basic open water ratings to instructors! So much for long term retention. Any resort divemaster can confirm the same problems daily.

Compounding the confusion for the student is the myriad variety of tables in use. Some students begin training in one agency system and progress in another. They are then expected to relearn either new tables, modified versions or altered configurations. In a 1986 trial during cross-examination of a prominent hyperbaric expert witness (who shall mercifully remain nameless), I gave him a set of PADI tables to work a simple two dive repetitive scenario. He failed three times in his attempt from the witness stand and totally discredited himself with the jury. And this was one of the country's foremost medical experts on diving treatments who worked with tables every day. He was used to the U.S.Navy tables. But switching the format on him was a curveball he couldn't hit. Why should we expect basic students to do any better?

Unfortunately, I don't think we can completely eliminate the teaching of tables to students unless they clearly indicate that are going to purchase a diving computer. A background in Table use is good and is an ideal introduction to computer theory. Computer training should be given the same level of importance though. Why? Because it is easier and more efficient for divers of all levels to dive with these instruments. Their automatic functions eliminate most of the record keeping responsibility that divers are so sloppy with and it also takes away any mathematical burden in computations. Also, when considered on direct comparison with Navy tables, virtually all computer algorithms are more conservative on normal square dive profiles.

I can assure you that if you handcuffed 50 entry level divers together and lowered them on a diving stage to a certain depth for a certain time and then brought them up at the same rate that when you asked for their dive profile you would get about 50 different answers.

Computers remove a significant amount of human error in the equation. Yeah, sure all things mechanical can fail... but you can also get hit by a bus crossing the street on your way to the dive store to buy a new set of tables. Modern dive computers are incredibly reliable and incorporate timing and depth measuring devices that are far more accurate than most other separate instruments. With the refinement of immersion switches over the last two years, a diver does not even have to be smart enough to turn the unit on. (Those with no sense of humor please note that my tongue is firmly in cheek.)

My perspective has always been to use the available technology to make diving safer and easier. Computers meet that criteria. Recent surveys (Gilliam 1989-90 and Halstead 1992) show that anywhere from 57% to 81% of active divers are using computers. On some liveaboard boats it is a rarity to find a conventional table diver at all. Those who continue to deny their validity are probably still griping about power inflated BC's, submersible pressure gauges, octopus second stages, and wet suits that aren't black.

The argument that some computers will "allow" a deliberately provocative dive exposure ignores the fact that dive tables will do exactly the same thing if used improperly. A healthy dose of common sense should be brought to the forefront in dive planning no matter what tools the diver uses to calculate his exposures.

USAGE

Some basic operating guidelines should be employed by all divers in using any dive computers. This includes observation of programmed ascent rates; refraining from reverse profile repetitive dives; selection of a model that is appropriate for the user's age, fitness, and planned diving environment; and adherence to the manufacturer's guidelines for maintenance and battery life. In repetitive situations, it would be prudent to recommend that such dives be limited to 2-4 a day separated by appropriate intervals of around one and half to two hours. But we also need to recognize the reality that active divers, especially in liveaboard situations, will typically conduct five or more dives per day and their incidence rate of DCS is remarkably low (reported at less than .02% in two large data surveys.) I also recommend that within the entry level diver market, say those with less than 75 dives, that computers be utilized exclusively within no-stop limits. This is what we recommend for sport divers anyway.

It is good practice for divers to familiarize themselves with the manufacturer's recommendation for computer failure. Each model applies different "Murphy's Law" procedures and are provided in the computer manual. There is a protocol for at least one computer (ORCA models) so that the diver may re-enter U.S. Navy tables. Michael Emmerman authored this suggested procedure and does offer the only viable return to tables scenario. Realistically, his method requires a certain applied discipline and record keeping ethic that may be lacking in most divers.

Computers, like any instrument, can fail but their track record is extremely good in retrospective. As it has been pointed out ad nauseam by some critics, it is theoretically possible for a computer to "allow" a potentially hazardous dive profile. However, even a mild grip on reality will suggest that computers be used conservatively much the same as safety buffers have been added to tables (next greater depth or time) for years by divers seeking a cushion. Don't run your computer to the edge (no pun intended) of its decompression model. Proper maintenance and care including battery changes well before they run out all part of the diver's responsibility. Please let's not blame the computer when the batteries crap out because you wanted to squeeze an extra few days out of them.

That pretty much constitutes the generic user guidelines that I feel are necessary to provide reasonable risk. Nothing in life is safe. But, as an active sport, diving is apparently far safer than many others. Indeed our risk has been equated with that of bowling. And when was the last time we read of another tragic bowling injury? Do we really have a problem? Arguably not. What works is what works. Taken as a user group there is no significant risk for computer divers as compared to table divers. Indeed, since our reporting systems including that of DAN and URI are only inputting *accidents* the entire question of accurate analysis is questionable since we do not know how many *safe* dives are conducted. To put it another way, we know the numerator in the fraction but have no idea what the denominator is.

SUMMARY

Dive computers have a valid role in diving if used correctly and within their model limitations. The author advocates redundant computers per diver if tables are not used. As divers involved in wreck and cave penetration become involved with more extensive bottom times, the potential of pushing the limits of the decompression model become greater and increase the attendant risk. Custom tables should then take precedence with computers primarily used as digital depth/time instruments and their decompression information used in a backup role.

Computers have increasingly altered traditional dive planning practices since the diver now has an effective means of calculating deviations from a fixed plan while underwater. Table divers are more regimented with a "plan your dive, dive your plan" discipline, but multi-level divers with computers can realistically "plan" their dive as it happens. It is recommended that divers have a working dive plan scenario prior to water entry, but deviation to take advantage of unexpected marine life appearances or dramatic coral formations discovered at deeper depths is reasonable and will not compromise safety. The computer (and backup) will allow far more flexibility and yet keep track of no-decompression or decompression obligations. The diver must, of course, manage his gas supply accordingly.

Use computers as the valuable tool they can be but don't expect any device to think for you. What we need is appropriate and realistic field surveys with user controls and continuity of dive computer equipment. Lab tests alone will not be sufficient. If you're going fishing, go where the fish are.

The illustrated extremes of theoretical computer dives that will predictably produce DCS are not necessarily realistic in practical use. I'd like to see a survey of a broad based diving user group employing computers of the exactly the same model and with the ability to download the profile for examination across the entire profile. This will require sampling in a thirty second time interval to provide for a true depiction of the dive profile.

Some critics have suggested that substantially more testing or controlled data base of use is required before unleashing dive computers on an unsuspecting public. The bottom line is simple. Are diving computers performing to a reasonable degree of safety? Yes, for the typical sport diving application. There is a decade of track record with existing units that suggest an incident rate of DCS equal to or less than that of table dives. The technology is here now. Let's use it and effect the modifications necessary as we identify them.

Likewise, let's not hold the manufacturers to an unreasonable standard of testing and/or built-in "safety factors". As Paul Heinmiller, Vice President of ORCA, has noted, "We gave up trying to make our products foolproof. The fools are simply too ingenious."

SUPPLEMENT

The following is excerpted from Bret Gilliam's original paper "EVALUATION OF DECOMPRESSION SICKNESS INCIDENCE IN MULTI-DAY REPETITIVE DIVING FOR 77,6800 SPORT DIVES" presented at the Repetitive Diving Workshop in March 1991 at Duke University. The paper is available in its complete form including sample DCS case histories in that workshop's Proceedings available through the American Academy of Underwater Sciences (AAUS) or from the author.

The results of our data keeping have been widely reported. Some critics have implied that the survey was an editorial designed to promote the use of dive computers. That is completely false. My records were kept as a corporate risk management tool not as a computer study. Our only concern was the incidence of DCS and the demands on our onboard chamber system and staff. They were reported after one year and nearly 80,000 dives because we felt there was a variety of information that was of interest to the diving community including habits of dive planning, ascent rates, hydration disciplines, and repetitive diving. It came as some surprise to myself and the staff that the computer divers enjoyed such an excellent safety record. But since we entered our data keeping with no preconceived hypothesis, it would be best for all reviewers to keep that simple fact in mind. We put a tremendous amount of sport divers into the ocean and were able to keep track of a few basic elements of their diving habits. We were not funded or supported by anyone. All the staff participating in the record keeping were volunteers who provided their help in spite of full time duties on a very busy ship. Our company purchased all the rental dive computers and were in no way financially supported by any manufacturer.

Whatever conclusions or interpretations that are drawn by the various readers are solely their own outside of the summaries that I have delineated. For those who lament that some computer manufacturers have pointed to the success of dive computers within this population, I have no control over that. An examination of the text will also show that we recommended regular drinking water and unsweetened apple juice as hydration consumptives. I have no apologies if the apple juice vendors adopt that as an implied endorsement.

PREFACE

The author conducted the log keeping data contained here as a private project in association with his contract position as Director of Diving Operations for OCEAN QUEST INTERNATIONAL. The majority of the data is from personal review of dive boat logs, passenger records, diver interviews, recompression chamber histories and interviews with member of the professional dive staff of the ship.

The author was responsible for the overall diving coordination of the ship including orientation of the sport divers each week, development of the computer diving program and certification course, supervision and operation of the recompression chamber facility, development of the treatment protocols, and captaining one of the ten 32 foot dive boats deployed from the ship. Additionally, as a USCG Merchant Marine Master, he served as a senior officer aboard the 457 foot cruise ship.

BACKGROUND NARRATIVE

In June of 1988, I was contacted through my consulting firm, OCEAN TECH, by representatives of OCEAN QUEST INTERNATIONAL who wished me to undertake a variety of technical projects on their behalf. This corporation wished to enter the sport diving market with a cruise ship converted in order to carry 160 sport divers on diving vacations in the western Caribbean. It was anticipated that these customers would be offered as many as 17 dives in a four day period during these one week cruises.

Initially, I was asked to design a high speed, high volume air filling system, design and build the custom dive boats and consult with the ship's engineering firm on a gantry crane to launch and recover them, hire the diving and medical staff, write the operations manuals, develop the training programs and refit a 60 inch multi-place, multi-lock recompression chamber for installation aboard the vessel.

One of my first concerns about the operation was the large number of dives to be offered in such as short period. This program called for four dives per day for four straight days with a night dive added in the same period. This meant that I would be facing as many a 2,720 dives by sport divers each week if the company was successful in realizing its market. To this figure would have to be added the diving schedules of the 28 professional staff members; approximately 500 additional dives. Looking at the possibility of handling over 3000 man dives per week posed obvious operational cautions. Putting it in perspective, <u>many top dive resorts do not conduct that much diving in a whole year!</u>

Addressing the issue of expected incidences of decompression sickness (DCS) left many unanswered questions. No one has ever seemed to be in agreement on the statistical incidence of DCS in sport divers. Several "experts" were polled on this issue and a wide spectrum of "qualified" responses were received. One respondent predicted 12.5 cases of DCS per week. This type of feedback was daunting to say the least.

After going forward with the design projects etc., I was asked to join the company under a consulting contract as an Executive Staff member with specific responsibilities as Director of Diving Operations. This paper will address the data compiled after one year of operation of the vessel in that market. Statistics presented were recorded March 4, 1989 through March 1990. 77,6800 man dives were logged during this period.

THE MULTI-LEVEL QUESTION

Traditional sport diving resort operations typically deal with far smaller numbers of divers and rarely conduct dive operation schedules that permit up to four dives per day. Virtually all resort diving in the summer period of 1988 was conducted by "divemaster log sheets" handwritten at the dive site Most diving was calculated using conventional Tables with the Haldane model U.S. Navy Tables seeing the widest use. Given the extraordinary number of dives that this company was committed to, I wanted to provide every possible safety edge and discipline of logging dives. The basic weakness of most sport diver profile logs has been two-fold:

1)   Sport divers are notoriously poor record keepers with regard to times, depths and surface intervals.

2)   Several surveys and volunteer test studies have proved evidence beyond doubt that the majority of sport divers cannot calculate repetitive dive planning correctly.

One issue that came up almost immediately was whether any meaningful dive profiles could be allowed if the divers exclusively used "square profile" computational methods. In most circumstances, it proved unworkable for a four dive schedule in the time parameters allowed for the ship's strict sailing routine. Therefore, the viability of "multi-level" profiling became interesting. We felt that this method was best accomplished through the use of diving computers and eventually our program showed almost 57% of sport divers utilizing these devices.

By the Fall of 1989, we made minor changes to the ship's itinerary and had modified the diving schedule to average 13 dives per week for the sport customers. However, the numbers of divers had increased dramatically during certain periods and we frequently handled in excess of 200 divers per week. We had actually gotten to the point where we considered 100 divers a week to be a slow period. One day in December of 1989, we did over 1000 dives!

THE SUMMARY NUMBERS

- Through the one year period March 4, 1989 to March 4, 1990, we conducted a total of 77,680 dives including customers and professional staff.
- During that period, we treated seven cases of DCS for customer sport divers and none for staff.
- Approximately 57% of our dives were done on computers, total: 44,277
- All of the DCS cases were on divers using Tables.
- There were no attributable hits on any divers using dive computers correctly.
- Of the 7 divers clearly symptomatic of DCS, all were successfully treated in the ship's recompression chamber with full resolution.
- Five of the seven divers with DCS hits were diving within the limits of their Tables and can be categorized as "undeserved hits".
- Diver age groups ranged from 9 years old to 72 years old. All DCS hits fell in the 26 to 45 year old range.
- Divers averaged three dives per day although a significant number (over 20%) of customers made over 5 dives in one day if weather circumstances permitted.
- Divers were instructed to limit their diving to a maximum of 130 FSW with a 30 minute ascent rate above 60 FSW; or to conform with their computer's ascent rate, whichever was more conservative.
- The great majority of diving was conducted with exposures of 100 feet or less.
- Reverse profiles were conducted by many divers with no adverse effects reported. Computer divers frequently admitted to reverse profiles in their personal dive scheduling.
- In conjunction with some other on-going research projects, members of the professional staff made over 600 dives to depths of 250 FSW. All were calculated by the computer (Buhlmann model) and repetitive dives were taken the same day. There were no incidences of DCS.

- No hits were recorded for the professional staff. Most members averaged 500 to 725 dives during the one year period. Age span was 21 to 43 years old with approximately a third of the staff being female. Dive staff members averaged between 11 and 15 dives per week.
- No hits were recorded during the first two days of diving.
- All seven patients who were treated for DCS had limited dive experience; usually less than 40 dives.
- Of the seven hits, 4 were women and 3 were men.
- Five of the seven cases had profiles of less than 100 FSW.
- In four of the seven cases, ascent rates in excess of 60 ft./min. were reported.
- In five of the seven cases, no "safety stop" at 15 FSW was taken.
- Although not sanctioned, we had knowledge of sport divers doing dives in excess of 130 FSW routinely while conducting their own dive plans. Over 40% of the computer owners questioned admitted to frequently diving below 130 FSW; several to depths in excess of 200 FSW. No hits were recorded.
- Water temperature ranged from 77° F to 85° F and cannot be considered a factor in any DCS hit.

INCIDENCE RATE OF DCS

With 77,680 dives in the total data base and seven DCS cases, the incidence rate is .00901% or approximately one in 10,000 dives.

If just the group using Tables is considered, the incidence rate is .02%, 2 in 10,000 dives.

The computer calculated group had a zero (0%) incidence rate.

DISCUSSION

Originally, this project was to keep records for a six month period. This was expanded as the diver population aboard ship increased. Of particular interest to this author was the lack of DCS incidence in computer users and in the more "aggressive" experienced diver population. Precisely the diver group that we suspected was most at risk to DCS proved to be the safest. Why?

Several factors may provide partial answers. We observed the computer diver/experienced aggressive diver groups to be far more disciplined in their regard for ascent rates, "safety" and/or decompression stops, and general watermanship skills. Most were also more attuned to proper hydration and generally refrained from alcohol consumption during the evening periods. The decompression algorithm employed by their computers were generally more conservative than the typical Haldane U.S. Navy models. The great majority of our sample group used the Buhlmann model which on direct comparison of "square profiles" is dramatically more restrictive than U.S. Navy Tables or any other Tables then in use.

Overall, the low incidence of DCS surprised all involved in the record keeping project. Taking the whole group into perspective with the benefit of hindsight lends the author to several observations which may further account for the excellent DCS safety record.

The ship's schedule had sport diving customers board the vessel on a Sunday and depart that afternoon. Monday was an orientation day with a safety lecture required for all divers. To insure their attendance, it was made clear that dive boat assignments would be conducted immediately following the conclusion of the one hour orientation. Fear of being left off the boat list or not being assigned to a favorite boat crew provided virtually 100% cooperation in attendance. Also, since the ship was at sea and no other diversions offered, it was relatively easy to lure divers.

We tried to get sport divers to regard their role in our operation as a mutually cooperative one with the professional staff. We avoided any domineering or "lecture" attitudes and endeavored to communicate safety and environmental protection information with a "we need your help to best serve you" approach that was generally well received and not resented. Many divers reported our orientation to be more instructive and less intimidating than typical resort "tirades", no matter how well intended.

Orientation served to acquaint the divers with our ship's diving operations but also had detailed general safety recommendations that we feel should be emphasized within all sport diving groups in resort settings. Of particular importance in our opinion was reinforcing disciplines of ascent rates and "safety stops" at the 15 FSW level for at least five minutes. By this author's observation, most sport divers initially have little concept of safe ascent rates even if given instruction during their entry level scuba training. Most seem to understand that slow ascents are important but fail dismally to execute proper ascents in the field.

If anything, we over stressed adherence to a 30 ft./min. ascent rate at least in the last 60 feet of the water column. The "safety stop" was further emphasized and we felt that even if ascent rates were compromised that instilling the "safety stop" ethic would at least slow the divers down approaching this ceiling. Many other resort operations stress returning to the dive boat with anywhere from 700 psi to 500 psi remaining in the diver's scuba tank. We departed from this conventional instruction and urged divers to arrive at the safety stop level with sufficient reserve for a 5 minute "hang" and then to use the remaining air for additional stop time saving only a small reserve for the easy return to the surface. Each boat was equipped with a weighted 20 foot PVC pipe bar hung from the dive boat's side at 15 FSW. This afforded an easy and comfortable platform for "safety stop" observance and the large size of the "Deco-bars" enabled as many as a dozen divers to be accommodated at once.

From observations, we found a significant number of divers did not realize that their ascent rates were excessively rapid. Typically, we would time divers in ascents ranging from 100 to 125 ft./min. and upon questioning, the diver would express surprise and voice the opinion that they thought they were conforming to 60 or even 30 ft./min. rates. Most divers simply find these recommended rates to be ridiculously slow (from their perspective) and only through continued education and patient explanation will the disciplines of proper ascents be applied. Most important however, is to establish a non-confrontational relationship with sport divers so a willingness to learn will evolve. Our staff was trained to emphasize all safety recommendations again daily on the dive boats and to observe divers in the water. Tactful suggestions and critique were to be offered in areas divers could improve technique. We had great success with these methods and felt reasonably confident that 90% of our customers were complying.

Due to the temptation of being aboard a cruise ship where the availability of alcohol were ever-present we felt obliged to remind divers that alcohol consumption the night before a heavy diving day was ill-advised. Surprisingly, we met with little problem from our diver populations in this regard. Most got their "partying" out of their systems on the Sunday night departure from the U.S. port and refrained or adopted modest alcohol attitudes until the four days of diving were completed. Staff example went a long way to promoting compliance. Our professional divers generally observed a voluntary curfew on evenings before diving of 11:00 PM. Since most diving would begin as early as 8:30 AM, we encouraged a good night's rest in customers and staff. For staff, it was a necessity due to their heavy diving and work schedule.

Another strong emphasis was placed on proper hydration of divers. We recommended consumption of noncarbonated beverages; but suggested staying away from orange, tomato and grapefruit juices due to their tendency to precipitate seasickness in many divers. Each boat was supplied with large containers of cold fresh water and unsweetened apple juice (the latter affectionately known as "EMMERMAN" due to this individual's advocacy in his many articles on hydration). Each boat crew pushed consumption of these fluids between dives during the course of the diving day.

We also included a detailed segment on recognition of DCS symptoms. Since we had a fully staffed and functional recompression chamber aboard we made our guests aware of its location and that we used it not only for training programs but that we expected to use it for treatments as they presented.

Denial of symptoms and subsequent delay of treatment has always been a major problem in sport divers. We tried to make it clear that DCS has a certain statistical inevitability and that no stigma or "blame" would be placed on an individual who reported problems. We let our divers know that each boat captain was trained in diver first aid and each boat was equipped with O_2 units equipped with demand regulators to insure delivery of 100% O_2 if needed. There was no charge for the O_2 or for evaluation by the author and diver medical technician. In fact, we did not charge for tests of pressure or treatments.

As a result of the orientations, we overcame the traditional reluctance to report symptoms and in many cases found ourselves burdened with evaluations of numerous non-DCS related muscle strains etc. But at least, our divers were enthusiastically coming forward to report even slight perceived symptoms. We would always prefer to err on the side of caution and the few cases of obvious non-DCS injury were welcomed in preference to denial attitudes so frequently prevalent in the past.

RECOMMENDED READING:

Divers Alert Network. DAN 1992 (and prior) report on diving accidents and fatalities.

Durham, NC: Divers Alert Network

Gilliam BC. 1992. Evaluation of Decompression Sickness Incidence in Multi-day Repetitive Diving for 77,680 Sport Dives.

In: Lang MA, Vann RD, eds. 1992 Proceedings of the American Academy of Underwater Sciences Repetitive Diving Workshop. AAUSDSP-RDW-02-92. Costa Mesa, CA: American Academy of Underwater Sciences

Halstead B. 1992. How Do Divers Dive? A Survey and Opinion

In: Sources. Sep/Oct 1992. Montclair, CA: National Association of Underwater Instructors

Lang MA, Hamilton RW, eds. 1989. Proceedings of the American Academy of Underwater Sciences Dive Computer Workshop. USCSG-TR-01-89. Costa Mesa, CA:

American Academy of Underwater Sciences

Loyst, Ken 1992. Dive Computers: A Consumer's Guide to History, Theory & Performance:

Watersport Publishing, Inc., La Mesa, CA.

BIBLIOGRAPHY

The following compilation of books, periodicals, newsletters, and organizations is provided as a source of reference that will hopefully prove to be a valuable addition to this text. All books, periodicals, and newsletters were selected for their relevance, in one way or another, to the material covered in the preceding 13 chapters. The authors cover several subject areas that would be useful to deep divers (or, for that matter, any divers) and would provide one with a good cross-section of diving-related information. The organizations/equipment suppliers listed were chosen for their overall importance to sport divers and their of the unique information/equipment provided.

BOOKS

A Medical Guide to Hazardous Marine Life, Auerbach, P.S. (1987), Progressive Printing Co.

A Pictorial History of Diving, Bachrach, Desiderati & Matzen (editors), Best Publishing Co.

Advanced Diving: Technology and Techniques, National Association of Underwater Instructors

Biology of Marine Life, Fourth Edition, Sumich, James L. (1988), Wm. C. Brown Publishers

Case Histories of Diving and Hyperbaric Accidents, Waite, Charles L. (1988), UHMS

Cave Diving: The Cave Diving Group Manual, Bedford, Bruce (editor), Mendip Publishing, England

Caving, A Blueprint For Survival, Exley, Sheck, NSS/CDS

Cold Weather and Under Ice Scuba Diving, NAUI/NDA Technical Publication Number 4, Somers, Lee H., Ph.D (1973), National Association of Underwater Instructors

DAN Underwater Diving Accident Manual, Divers Alert Network (1985), Duke University Medical Center

Deep Into Blue Holes, Palmer, Rob Unwin Hyman, England

Dive Computers: A Consumer's Guide to History, Theory and Performance, Loyst, Ken with Huggins, Karl and Steidley, Michael (1991), Watersport Publishing, Inc.

Dive Rescue Specialist Training Manual, Linton, Rust, Gilliam (1986), Dive Rescue, Inc./International

Diving Accident Management Field Guide: O_2 Administration and Recompression Therapy, Gilliam, Bret C., Ocean Tech

Diving Medicine, Second Edition, Bove & Davis (1990), Grove and Stratton, Inc.

Diving and Subaquatic Medicine, Edmonds, Lowery, Pennegather (1983), Best Publishing Co.

Emergency Oxygen Administration and Field Management of Scuba Diving Accidents, Corry, James A. (1989), NAUI Publications

Field Guide for the Diver Medic, Daugherty, Gordon C. (1985), Best Publishing, Co.

The Last of the Blue Water Hunters, Eyles, Carlos, Watersport Publishing, Inc.

Living And Working In The Sea, Miller, James W. and Koblick, Ian G., Van Nostrand Reinhold Co.

Medical Emergencies at Sea, Kessler, William (1986), Hearst Marine Books

Men Beneath the Sea, Hass, Hans, St. Martin's Press

NITROX Manual, Rutkowski, Dick (1991), Hyperbarics International, Inc.

NOAA Diving Manual: Diving for Science and Technology, Second Edition, Edited by Miller, James W., U.S. Government Printing Office

Physiology in Depth: The Proceedings of the Seminar, Edited by Graver, Dennis (1982), Professional Association of Diving Instructors

Recompression Chamber Life Support Manual, Rutkowski, Dick (1991), Hyperbarics International, Inc.

Safety in Diving, Dueker, C.W. (1985), Madison Publishing Associates

Search and Recovery, Erickson, Ralph D. (1983), Professional Association of Diving Instructors

Solo Diving: The Art of Underwater Self-Sufficiency, von Maier, Robert (1991), Watersport Publishing

Stress and Performance in Diving, Bachrach and Egstrom (1987), Best Publishing, Co.

The Adventurous Aquanaut, Hauser, Hillary, Best Publishing Co.

The Art of Safe Cave Diving, Gerrard, Steve, NACD

The DAN Emergency Handbook, Lippman and Buggs (1989), J.L. Publications

The New Practical Diving, Mount and Ikehara (1979), University of Miami Press

The Physician's Guide to Diving Medicine, Shilling, Carlston and Mathias (1984), Plenum Press

The Physiology and Medicine of Diving, Third Edition, Bennett and Elliott (1982), Best Publishing Co.

The University of Michigan Diving Manual, Volume I: Diving Theory, Somers, Lee H. (PhD) (1990), The University of Michigan

U.S. Navy Air Decompression Table Handbook and Decompression Chamber Operator's Handbook, NAVSEA (1985), Best Publishing, Co.

U.S. Navy Diving Manual, NAVSEA (1980), Best Publishing Co.

Your Offshore Doctor, Beilan, Michael (1985), Dodd, Mead and Co.

INDEX

King, Jim   **72, 73, 80**
Krasber   52
Krasberg, Alan   52
Kristovich, Dr. Ann   **6** 37, **39, 40, 42, 44,
82, 84**

L

La Pilita   **40**
Lago Maggiore dive   **60**
Lanphier, Dr. Ed   **321**
LARU (Lambertsen Amphibious
   Respiration Unit)   **261**
Leonard, Mark   **6, 217**
LIFE magazine   **25, 49, 53, 59**
Lift Bag   **143**
Line Reel   **143**
Link, Clay   **64**
Link, Ed   **64, 65, 66, 67**
Lippman, John   **274**
liquid oxygen (LOX)   **223**
Lockwood, Jim   **6, 26, 27, 28, 29, 71, 72,
73, 75, 76, 77, 79, 82, 109, 117, 173**
Lorraine Smith Effect   **130**
Lost Sink   **71**
Loyst, Ken   **6, 181, 182, 184**

M

M-values   **271**
Maas, Terry   **68**
Man-in-the-Sea II   **64**
Manion, Dr. Dan   **6, 35, 36, 84**
Mante   **45, 84**
Martini's Law   **109**
Martz, Frank   **71, 72, 74, 75, 84, 109**
Maximum Likelihood Statistical
   Method   **273**
Mayol, Jacques   **53, 69**
McKenney, Jack   **53, 54**
McLeish, Kenneth   **59, 84**
McNabb, Charles   **70**
Meek, Bob   **66**
Men Beneath The Sea   **60**
Menzies, Jock   **66**
Merchant, George   **50**
metabolic gases   **252**
Meyer-Overton hypothesis   **108, 260**
Michigan Sea Grant Tables   **272**
Micro Brain Pro Plus   **185**
Microprocessor Applications to Multi-level

Air Decompression   274
Milner, Dr. Gilbert   **118**
Mims, Jim   **6**
Monitor   **30**
Morrison Spring   **72**
Morse, Dennis   **50**
Mother   **54**
Mount, Tom   **6, 26, 27, 35, 71, 72, 74, 75,
76, 77, 78, 79, 81, 91, 93, 108, 109, 112, 125,
183, 204**
Mount-Milner Test   **118**
Mrozinski, Andrew   **231**
Mystery Sink   **84**

N

NACD   **77**
Nacimiento   **38**
Nacimiento del Rio Mante   **21**
Nacimiento Huichihuayan   **47**
Nacimiento Mante   **37, 47**
narcosis   **2, 25, 26, 27, 28, 29, 31, 32, 34,
42, 47, 75, 78, 107, 108, 109, 110, 111, 112,
113, 114, 115, 116, 117, 118, 119, 120, 124,
125, 127, 128, 136**
NASA   **9**
National Speleological Society   **24**
Naval Experimental Diving Unit
   (NEDU)   **270**
Navy E-L Algorithm   **270**
Nemesis   **229**
Neurological Exam   **324**
Nevada's Devil's Hole   **73**
Nicklin, Chuck   **53**
Nicolini, Rick   **6, 173**
nitrous oxide   **265**
NITROX   **20, 57, 99, 129, 134, 153, 157,
203, 206, 209, 210, 211, 213, 214, 215, 216,
220, 223, 224, 225, 226, 228, 231, 234, 238,
240, 258, 279, 292, 295, 313, 314, 340**
NITROX MANUAL   **206**
NOAA   **9, 30, 64, 128, 157, 164, 203, 204,
205, 206, 210, 216, 218, 224, 225, 230, 238,
239, 278, 302, 316, 340**
NOAA Continuous Mixing System   **223**
NOAA Nitrox I   **204, 205, 207, 208, 216,
217**
NOAA Nitrox II   **205**
Norfleet, Dr. William   **209**
normoxic   **57, 122, 124, 131, 134**

O

Ocean Management Systems   **159, 164**
OTU   **130, 132, 133, 134, 135.,
2099, 219**
Oxygen Enriched Air   **203, 205**
oxygen seizure   **117**
Oxygen Tolerance Unit (OTU)   **130, 132,
133, 134, 135, 209, 219**
oxygen toxicity   **26, 31, 34, 43, 107, 121,
123, 124, 126, 127, 130, 135**

P

Palermo, Rock   **6**
Palmer, Rob   **6, 79, 204**
Panic   **104**
panic-prone   **92**
Parry, Zale   **80**
Paul Bert Effect   **123**
Pelizarri, Umberto   **69**
Pepper, Dr. Sharee   **75, 80**
Perceptual narrowing   **102, 116**
Petroglyph Cave   **39**
Phoenix computer   **186, 216**
physical properties of gas   **237**
Pilmanis, Dr. Andrew   **272**
Pitcairn, Clark   **81**
pony bottle   **143, 199, 202**
Power, George   **226**
Poza Asufrosa   **37**
Poza Caracol   **37**
Poza La Pilita   **37**
Poza Verde   **37, 39**
progressive penetration   **193**
Prosser, Joe   **73**

R

Raimo, Bob   **226**
rapture of the deep   **109**
Rebikoff, Demitri   **53**
recompression chambers   **293**
Redundancy   **142**
Redundant Air Supply   **171**
redundant second stage   **200**
REPEX method   **130**
REPEX paper, Hamilton   **130, 133**
Response narrowing   **104**
Riffe, Jay   **68**
Rio Choy   **47**

Rio Frio   **47**
Rio Sabinos   **47**
RMV (respiratory minute volume)   **140, 141,
142**
Roberts, John David   **16**
Rodocker, Don   **53**
Roessler, Carl   **281**
Root, Hope   **25, 26**
Russell, Ron   **166**
Rutkowski, Dick   **6, , 128, 130, 206, 230**

S

SafeAir   **207, 220**
Salesman, Gary   **84**
Salt, Frank   **84**
Samazen, Jean Clarke   **26, 84**
Sayers, R. R.   **259**
Scuba Diving Resources Group   **209**
Scubapro AIR II   **200**
Sea Hunt   **80**
Sea Quest Source   **200**
Sea-Link   **66**
Seapro Tech BC   **176**
Sharkey, Phil   **207**
Sherwood   **164, 165**
Sherwood Genesis isolation manifold   **193**
Shreeves, Karl   **225**
Siebe, August   **257**
Sierra Madre Oriental   **47**
Silver Springs   **70**
Sinoia Caves   **84**
Sipperly, David   **6**
Skaggs, Mitch   **6, 101, 117, 160, 207,**
Skiles, Wes   **6, 80, 107, 112**
Skin Diver Magazine   **26, 53, 281**
Small, Peter   **60, 62, 84**
Solo Diving   176
Somers, Lee Dr.   **71**
Soto, Angel   **45**
SpareAir   **198, 202**
Spencer, Dr. Merril   **272**
Sports Illustrated   **42**
Squalus   **259**
St. Hermann's Cave   **39**
Stage Bottles   **143**
staged decompression   **137, 138, 140, 171**
Stenuit, Robert   **64**
Stone, Dr. Bill   **80, 242**
Stone, Jamie   **71**

Titles by Watersport Books

TECHNICAL SERIES

COMPLETE WRECK DIVING
A Guide to Diving Wrecks
by Henry Keatts and Brian Skerry

DEEP DIVING – *Revised*
An Advanced Guide to Physiology Procedures and Systems
by Bret Gilliam with Robert von Maier

DRY SUIT DIVING – *Revised*
A Guide to Diving Dry
by Steve Barsky, Dick Long, and Bob Stinton

WHEN WOMEN DIVE
A Female's Guide to Both Diving and Snorkeling
by Erin O'Neill and Ella Jean Morgan

DIVE COMPUTERS
A Consumer's Guide to History, Theory, and Performance
by Ken Loyst

MIXED GAS DIVING
The Ultimate Challenge for Technical Diving
by Tom Mount and Bret Gilliam

SOLO DIVING – *Revised*
The Art of Underwater Self-Sufficiency
by Robert von Maier